Electronic Warfare and System Management

Electronic Warfare and System Management

Col. (Retd.) S.C. Narang

PRASHANT PUBLISHING HOUSE
DELHI-110094

Published by :
Prashant Publishing House
C-34, 28 Foota Road, Gali-3,
West Karwal Nagar, Delhi-110094
Phone : 011-22963970, Mob. : 9810396373
e-mail.: prashantpublishinghouse@gmail.com

Electronic Warfare and System Management

First Published 2016

ISBN 978-93-80565-73-6

PRINTED IN INDIA
Published by Mr. R.K. Jha M/s Prashant Publishing House and Published at H.S. Offset House Press, Delhi.

Contents

Preface

Electronic Warfare (EW) is termed as military action involving the use of electromagnetic and directed energy to attack the enemy. Electronic warfare operations are the integrated planning and employment of military capabilities to achieve desired effects across the electromagnetic battle space in support of operational objectives - electronic attack, electronic protection and EW support being its operational elements.

Thales EWS customers use its multispectral electronic warfare solutions to detect the enemy well before the enemy can detect them, to optimise tactical situation analysis and to gather critical intelligence. As for its entire range of solutions, Thales EWS leverages systems developed for the latest-generation platforms (in the case of EWS Type 45, Horizon, FREMM, etc.), with the capacity for upgrading solutions for warships already in service.

Modern day Electronic Warfare (EW) has been proven to be the key to success in many recent combat situations. Even in peacetime, many new threats are being developed and defences tested with the aid of the Electromagnetic Spectrum. There is a vital need to gather, validate and process EW data from many different sources. Being able to understand what such electronic emitters are up to – whether friendly, hostile or unidentified – is crucial for effective electronic warfare operations, and for the decisions that have to be made when the pressure is on. A comprehensive knowledge of the electronic battlespace is critical to mission success.

Electronic warfare uses focused energy, usually radio waves or laser light, to confuse or disable an enemy's electronics. It can also involve listening —collecting an enemy's radio signals or sensing the radar of an incoming missile. Raytheon has been a leader in electronic warfare since World War II, when it developed a magnetron, or radio wave generator, that became a key part of the Allies' radar systems. In recent years it has pioneered the use of gallium nitride, a substance that produces five times more radio energy than previous technologies.

Today the company is developing tactical lasers, the Next Generation Jammer and other weapons, along with electrical systems capable of powering whatever innovations the future holds. Electronic warfare (EW) is any action involving the use of the electromagnetic spectrum ordirected energy to control the spectrum, attack an enemy, or impede enemy assaults via the spectrum. The purpose of electronic warfare is to deny the opponent the advantage of, and ensure friendly unimpeded access to, the EM spectrum. EW can be applied from air, sea, land, and space by manned and unmanned systems, and can target humans, communications, radar, or other assets.

This manual provides guidance to the army commanders on how the electromagnetic spectrum, can impact their operations and how friendly EW operations can be used to gain an advantage. This manual describes the application of EW in support of full spectrum operations and provides a baseline for ensuring a common understanding and operational consistency. Although new equipment, tactics, techniques and procedures continue to be developed, the physics of electromagnetic energy remains constant.

This updated doctrine and other modifications to the army's operational strategies are testimony to the innovation and vision on which a nation can rely in this era of cyber revolution.

—*Editor*

1

Introduction

WHAT IS ELECTRONIC WARFARE?

Electronic warfare uses focused energy, usually radio waves or laser light, to confuse or disable an enemy's electronics. It can also involve listening —collecting an enemy's radio signals or sensing the radar of an incoming missile. Raytheon has been a leader in electronic warfare since World War II, when it developed a magnetron, or radio wave generator, that became a key part of the Allies' radar systems. In recent years it has pioneered the use of gallium nitride, a substance that produces five times more radio energy than previous technologies.

Today the company is developing tactical lasers, the Next Generation Jammer and other weapons, along with electrical systems capable of powering whatever innovations the future holds. Electronic warfare (EW) is any action involving the use of the electromagnetic spectrum ordirected energy to control the spectrum, attack an enemy, or impede enemy assaults via the spectrum. The purpose of electronic warfare is to deny the opponent the advantage of, and ensure friendly unimpeded access to, the EM spectrum. EW can be applied from air, sea, land, and space by manned and unmanned systems, and can target humans, communications, radar, or other assets.

The Electromagnetic Environment

Military operations are executed in an information environment increasingly complicated by the electromagnetic (EM) spectrum.

The electromagnetic spectrum portion of the information environment is referred to as the electromagnetic environment (EME). The recognized need for military forces to have unimpeded access to and use of the electromagnetic environment creates vulnerabilities and opportunities for electronic warfare (EW) in support of military operations.

Within the information operations construct, EW is an element of information warfare; more specifically, it is an element of offensive and defensive counter information.

NATO has a different and arguably more encompassing and comprehensive approach to EW. A Military Committee conceptual document from 2007 recognised the EME as an operational manoeuvre space and warfighting environment/domain. In NATO, EW is considered to be warfare in the EME. NATO has adopted simplified language which parallel those used in the other warfighting environments like maritime, land and air/space. For example, Electronic Attack is offensive use of EM energy. ED is electronic defence and ES electronic surveillance. The use of the traditional NATO EW measures (ECM, EPM and ESM) has been retained as they contribute to and support EA, ED and ES. Besides EW, other EM operations include ISTAR and SIGINT. Subsequently NATO has issued EW Policy and Doctrine and is addressing the other NATO defence lines of development.

Electronic Warfare Applications

Electronic warfare is any military action involving the use of the EM spectrum to include directed energy (DE) to control the EM spectrum or to attack an enemy. This is not limited to radio or radar frequencies but includes IR, visible, ultraviolet, and other less used portions of the EM spectrum. This includes self-protection, standoff, and escort jamming, and antiradiation attacks. EW is a specialized tool that enhances many air and space functions at multiple levels of conflict.

The purpose of EW is to deny the opponent an advantage in the EM spectrum and ensure friendly unimpeded access to the EM spectrum portion of the information environment. EW can be applied from air, sea, land, and space by manned and unmanned systems. EW is employed to support military operations involving various levels of detection, denial, deception, disruption, degradation, protection, and destruction.

EW contributes to the success of information operations (IO) by using offensive and defensive tactics and techniques in a variety of combinations to shape, disrupt, and exploit adversarial use of the EM spectrum while protecting friendly freedom of action in that spectrum. Expanding reliance on the EM spectrum increases both the potential and the challenges of EW in information operations. All of the core, supporting, and related information operations capabilities either directly use EW or indirectly benefit from EW.

The principal EW activities have been developed over time to exploit the opportunities and vulnerabilities that are inherent in the physics of EM energy. Activities used in EW include: electro-optical, infrared and radio frequency countermeasures; EM compatibility and deception; communications jamming, radar jamming and anti-jamming; electronic masking, probing, reconnaissance, and intelligence; electronics security; EW reprogramming; emission control; spectrum management; and wartime reserve modes.

SUBDIVISIONS

Electronic warfare includes three major subdivisions: electronic attack (EA), electronic protection (EP), and electronic warfare support (ES).

Electronic Attack (EA)

Electronic attack (EA) (previously known as Electronic Counter Measures (ECM)) involves the use of EM energy, directed energy, or anti-radiation weapons to attack personnel, facilities, or equipment with the intent of degrading, neutralizing, or destroying enemy combat capability. In the case of EM energy, this action is referred to as jamming and can be performed on communications systems or radar systems.

Electronic Protection (EP)

Electronic Protection (EP) (previously known as electronic protective measures (EPM) or electronic counter countermeasures

(ECCM)) involves actions taken to protect personnel, facilities, and equipment from any effects of friendly or enemy use of the electromagnetic spectrum that degrade, neutralize, or destroy friendly combat capability. Jamming is not part of EP, it is an EA measure.

The use of flare rejection logic on an Infrared homing missile to counter an adversary's use of flares is EP. While defensive EA actions and EP both protect personnel, facilities, capabilities, and equipment, EP protects from the *effects* of EA (friendly and/or adversary). Other examples of EP include spread spectrum technologies, use of Joint Restricted Frequency List (JRFL), emissions control (EMCON), and low observability or "stealth".

An Electronic Warfare Self Protection (EWSP) is a suite of countermeasure systems fitted primarily to aircraft for the purpose of protecting the aircraft from weapons fire and can include among others:DIRCM (protects against IR missiles), Infrared countermeasures (protects against IR missiles), Chaff(protects against RADAR guided missiles), DRFM Decoys (Protects against Radar guided missiles), Flare (protects against IR missiles).

An Electronic Warfare Tactics Range (EWTR) is a practice range which provides for the training of aircrew in electronic warfare. There are two such ranges in Europe; one at RAF Spadeadam in the United Kingdom and the POLYGON range in Germany and France. EWTRs are equipped with ground-based equipment to simulate electronic warfare threats that aircrew might encounter on missions.

Antifragile EW is a step beyond standard EP, occurring when a communications link being jammed actually increases in capability as a result of a jamming attack, although this is only possible under certain circumstances such as reactive forms of jamming.

Electronic Warfare Support (ES)

Electronic Warfare Support (ES), is the subdivision of EW involving actions tasked by, or under direct control of, an operational commander to search for, intercept, identify, and locate or localize sources of intentional and unintentional radiated electromagnetic (EM) energy for the purpose of immediate threat recognition, targeting, planning, and conduct of future operations. These measures begin with systems designed and operators trained to make Electronic Intercepts (ELINT) and then classification and analysis broadly known as Signals intelligence from such detection to return information and perhaps actionable intelligence (e.g. a ship's identification from unique characteristics of a specific radar) to the commander.

The overlapping discipline, signals intelligence (SIGINT) is the related process of analyzing and identifying the intercepted frequencies (e.g. as a mobile phone or radar). SIGINT is broken into three categories: ELINT, COMINT, and FISINT. the parameters of intercepted txn are-: communication equipment-: freq, bandwidth, modulation, polarisation etc. The distinction between intelligence and electronic warfare support (ES) is determined by who tasks or controls the collection assets, what they are tasked to provide, and for what purpose they are tasked. Electronic warfare support is achieved by assets tasked or controlled by an operational commander. The purpose of ES tasking is immediate threat recognition, targeting, planning and conduct of future operations, and other tactical actions such as threat avoidance and homing. However, the same assets and resources that are tasked with ES can simultaneously collect intelligence that meets other collection requirements.

Where these activities are under the control of an operational commander and being applied for the purpose of situational awareness, threat recognition, or EM targeting, they also serve the purpose of Electronic Warfare surveillance (ES).

Multifunctional EW System

In February 2015 the Russian army received their first set of the multifunctional electronic warfare system, known as Borisoglebsk 2. After some months of testing, has it been used in Ukraine. According to Svenska Dagbladet, its initial usage caused concern within NATO.

Russia describes Borisoglebsk 2 as "*The 'Borisoglebsk-2' when compared to its predecessors has better technical characteristics: wider frequency bandwidth for conducting radar collection and jamming, faster scanning times of the frequency spectrum, and higher precision when identifying the location and source of radar emissions, and increased capacity for suppression."*

ELECTRONIC WARFARE SUPPORT MEASURES

In military telecommunications, the terms Electronic Support (ES) or Electronic Support Measures (ESM) describe the division of electronic warfare involving actions taken under direct control of an operational commander to detect, intercept, identify, locate, record, and/or analyze sources of radiated electromagnetic energy for the purposes of immediate threat recognition (such as warning that fire control RADAR has locked on a combat vehicle, ship, or aircraft) or longer-term operational planning. Thus, Electronic Support provides a source of information required for decisions involving Electronic Protection (EP), Electronic Attack (EA), avoidance, targeting, and other tactical employment of forces. Electronic Support data can be used to produce signals intelligence (SIGINT), communications intelligence (COMINT) and electronics intelligence (ELINT).

Electronic support measures gather intelligence through passive "listening" to electromagnetic radiations of military interest. Electronic support measures can provide (1) initial detection or knowledge of foreign systems, (2) a library of technical and operational data on foreign systems, and (3) tactical combat information utilizing that library. ESM collection platforms can remain electronically silent and detect and analyze RADAR transmissions beyond the RADAR detection range because of the greater power of the transmitted electromagnetic pulse with respect to a reflected echo of that pulse. United States airborne ESM receivers are designated in the AN/ALR series.

Desirable characteristics for electromagnetic surveillance and collection equipment include (1) wide-spectrum or bandwidth capability because foreign frequencies are initially unknown, (2) wide dynamic range because signal strength is initially unknown, (3) narrow bandpass to discriminate the signal of interest from other electromagnetic radiation on nearby frequencies, and (4) good angle-of arrival measurement for bearings to locate the transmitter. The frequency spectrum of interest ranges from 30 MHz to 50 GHz. Multiple receivers are typically required for surveillance of the entire spectrum, but tactical receivers may be functional within a specific signal strength threshold of a smaller frequency range.

ELECTROMAGNETIC INTERFERENCE

Electromagnetic interference (EMI), also called radio-frequency interference (RFI) when in the radio frequency spectrum, is a disturbance generated by an external source that affects an electrical circuit by electromagnetic induction, electrostatic coupling, or conduction. The disturbance may degrade the performance of the circuit or even stop it from functioning. In the case of a data path, these effects can range from an increase in error rate to a total loss of the data. Both man-made and natural sources generate changing electrical currents and voltages that can cause EMI: automobile ignition systems, cell phones, thunder storms, the Sun, and the Northern Lights. EMI frequently affects AM radios. It can also affect cell phones, FM radios, and televisions. EMI can be used intentionally for radio jamming, as in electronic warfare.

History

Since the earliest days of radio communications, the negative effects of interference from both intentional and unintentional transmissions have been felt and the need to manage the radio frequency spectrum became apparent.

In 1933, a meeting of the International Electrotechnical Commission (IEC) in Paris recommended the International Special Committee on Radio Interference (CISPR) be set up to deal with the emerging problem of EMI. CISPR subsequently produced technical publications covering measurement and test techniques and recommended emission and immunity limits. These have evolved over the decades and form the basis of much of the world's EMC regulations today.

In 1979, legal limits were imposed on electromagnetic emissions from all digital equipment by the FCC in the USA in response to the increased number of digital systems that were interfering with wired and radio communications. Test methods and limits were based on CISPR publications, although similar limits were already enforced in parts of Europe.

In the mid 1980s, the European Union member states adopted a number of "new approach" directives with the intention of standardizing technical requirements for products so that they do not become a barrier to trade within the EC. One of these was the EMC Directive (89/336/EC) and it applies to all equipment placed on the market or taken into service. Its scope covers all apparatus "liable to cause electromagnetic disturbance or the performance of which is liable to be affected by such disturbance".

This was the first time there was a legal requirement on immunity as well as emissions on apparatus intended for the general population. And although there may be additional costs involved for some products to give them a known level of immunity, it increases their perceived quality as they are able to co-exist with apparatus in the active EM environment of modern times and with fewer problems. Many countries now have similar requirements for products to meet some level of Electromagnetic Compatibility (EMC) regulation.

Types

Electromagnetic interference can be categorized as follows:

- Narrowband EMI or RFI interference typically emanates from intended transmissions, such as radio and TV stations or cell phones.
- Broadband EMI or RFI interference is unintentional radiation from sources such as electric power transmission lines.

Conducted electromagnetic interference is caused by the physical contact of the conductors as opposed to radiated EMI, which is caused by induction (without physical contact of the conductors). Electromagnetic disturbances in the EM field of a conductor will no longer be confined to the surface of the conductor and will radiate away from it. This persists in all conductors and mutual inductance between two radiated electromagnetic fields will result in EMI.

SUSCEPTIBILITIES OF DIFFERENT RADIO TECHNOLOGIES

Interference tends to be more troublesome with older radio technologies such as analogue amplitude modulation, which have no way of distinguishing unwanted in-band signals from the intended signal, and the omnidirectional antennas used with broadcast systems. Newer radio systems incorporate several improvements that enhance the selectivity. In digital radio systems, such as Wi-Fi, error-correctiontechniques can be used. Spread-spectrum and frequency-hopping techniques can be used with both analogue and digital signalling to improve resistance to interference. A highly directional receiver, such as a parabolic antenna or a diversity receiver, can be used to select one signal in space to the exclusion of others.

The most extreme example of digital spread-spectrum signalling to date is ultra-wideband (UWB), which proposes the use of large sections of the radio spectrum at low amplitudes to transmit high-bandwidth digital data. UWB, if used exclusively, would enable very efficient use of the spectrum, but users of non-UWB technology are not yet prepared to share the spectrum with the new system because of the interference it would cause to their receivers.

INTERFERENCE TO CONSUMER DEVICES

In the United States, the 1982 Public Law 97-259 allowed the Federal Communications Commission (FCC) to regulate the susceptibility of consumer electronic equipment.

Potential sources of RFI and EMI include: various types of transmitters, doorbell transformers, toaster ovens, electric blankets, ultrasonic pest control devices, electric bug zappers, heating pads, and touch controlled lamps. Multiple CRT computer monitors or televisions sitting too close to one another can sometimes cause a "shimmy" effect in each other, due to the electromagnetic nature of their picture tubes, especially when one of their de-gaussing coils is activated. Electromagnetic interference at 2.4 GHz can be caused by 802.11b and 802.11g wireless devices, Bluetooth devices, baby monitors andcordless telephones, video senders, and microwave ovens. Switching loads (inductive, capacitive, and resistive), such as electric motors, transformers, heaters, lamps, ballast, power supplies, etc., all cause electromagnetic interference especially at currents above 2 A. The usual method used for suppressing EMI is by connecting asnubber network, a resistor in series with a capacitor, across a pair of contacts. While this may offer modest EMI reduction at very low currents, snubbers do not work at currents over 2 A with electromechanical contacts.

Switched-mode power supplies can be a source of EMI, but have become less of a problem as design techniques have improved, such as integrated power factor correction.

Most countries have legal requirements that mandate electromagnetic compatibility: electronic and electrical hardware must still work correctly when subjected to certain amounts of EMI, and should not emit EMI, which could interfere with other equipment (such as radios).

Radio frequency signal quality has declined throughout the 21st century by roughly one decibel per year as the spectrum becomes increasingly crowded.

This has inflicted a Red Queen's race on the mobile phone industry as companies have been forced to put up more cellular towers (at new frequencies) that then cause more interference thereby requiring more investment by the providers and frequent upgrades of mobile phones to match.

Standards

The International Special Committee for Radio Interference or CISPR (French acronym for "Comité International Spécial des Perturbations Radioélectriques"), which is a committee of the International Electrotechnical Commission (IEC) sets international standards for radiated and conducted electromagnetic interference. These are civilian standards for domestic, commercial, industrial and automotive sectors.

These standards form the basis of other national or regional standards, most notably the European Norms (EN) written by CENELEC (European committee for electrotechnical standardisation).

EMI IN INTEGRATED CIRCUITS

Integrated circuits are often a source of EMI, but they must usually couple their energy to larger objects such as heatsinks, circuit board planes and cables to radiate significantly.

On integrated circuits, important means of reducing EMI are: the use of bypass or decoupling capacitors on each active device (connected across the power supply, as close to the device as possible), rise time control of high-speed signals using series resistors, and IC power supply pin filtering. Shielding is usually a last resort after other techniques have failed, because of the added expense of shielding components such as conductive gaskets.

The efficiency of the radiation depends on the height above the ground plane or power plane (at RF, one is as good as the other) and the length of the conductor in relation to the wavelength of the signal component (fundamental frequency, harmonic or transient such as overshoot, undershoot or ringing). At lower frequencies, such as 133 MHz, radiation is almost exclusively via I/O cables; RF noise gets onto the power planes and is coupled to the line drivers via the VCC and GND pins. The RF is then coupled to the cable through the line driver ascommon-mode noise. Since the noise is common-mode, shielding has very little effect, even with differential pairs. The RF energy iscapacitively coupled from the signal pair to the shield and the shield itself does the radiating. One cure for this is to use a braid-breaker orchoke to reduce the common-mode signal.

At higher frequencies, usually above 500 MHz, traces get electrically longer and higher above the plane. Two techniques are used at these frequencies: wave shaping with series resistors and embedding the traces between the two planes. If all these measures still leave too much EMI, shielding such as RF gaskets and copper tape can be used. Most digital equipment is designed with metal or conductive-coated plastic cases.

RF immunity and Testing

Any unshielded semiconductor (e.g. an integrated circuit) will tend to act as a detector for those radio signals commonly found in the domestic environment (e.g. cell phones). Such a detector can demodulate the high frequency cell phone carrier (e.g., GSM850 and GSM1900, GSM900 and GSM1800) and produce low-frequency (e.g., 217 Hz) demodulated signals. This demodulation manifests itself as unwanted audible buzz in audio appliances such as microphone amplifier, speaker amplifier, car radio, telephones etc. Adding onboard EMI filters or special layout techniques can help in bypassing EMI or improving RF immunity. Some ICs are designed (e.g., LMV831-LMV834, MAX9724) to have integrated RF filters or a special design that helps reduce any demodulation of high-frequency carrier.

Designers often need to carry out special tests for RF immunity of parts to be used in a system. These tests are often done in an anechoic chamber with a controlled RF environment where the test vectors produce a RF field similar to that produced in an actual environment.

RFI in Radio Astronomy

Interference in radio astronomy, where it is commonly referred to as radio-frequency interference (RFI), is any source of transmission that is within the observed frequency band other than the celestial sources themselves. Because transmitters on and around the Earth can be many times stronger than the astronomical signal of interest, RFI is a major concern for performing radio astronomy. Natural sources of interference, such as lightning and the Sun, are also often referred to as RFI.

Some of the frequency bands that are very important for radio astronomy, such as the 21-cm HI line at 1420 MHz, are protected by regulation. This is called spectrum management. However, modern radio-astronomical observatories such as VLA, LOFAR and ALMA have a very large bandwidth over which they can observe. Because of the limited spectral space at radio frequencies, these frequency bands can not be completely allocated to radio astronomy. Therefore, observatories need to deal with RFI in their observations.

Techniques to deal with RFI range from filters in hardware to advanced algorithms in software. One way to deal with strong transmitters is to filter out the frequency of the source completely. This is for example the case for the LOFAR observatory, which filters out the FM radio stations between 90-110 MHz. It is important to remove such strong sources of interference as soon as possible, because they might "saturate" the highly sensitive receivers (amplifiers and analog-to-digital converters), which means that the received signal is stronger than the receiver can handle. However, filtering out a frequency band implies that these frequencies can never be observed with the instrument.

A common technique to deal with RFI within the observed frequency bandwidth, is to employ RFI detection in software. Such software can find samples in time, frequency or time-frequence space that are contaminated by an interfering source. These samples are subsequently ignored in further analysis of the observed data. This process is often referred to as *data flagging*. Because most transmitters have a small bandwidth and are not continuously present such as lightning or citizens' band (CB) radio devices, most of the data remains available for the astronomical analysis. However, data flagging can not solve issues with continuous broad-band transmitters, such as windmills, digital video or digital audio transmitters.

2

Intelligence and Electronic Warfare Operations

INFORMATION OPERATIONS

The effectiveness of information operations is predicated on a thorough understanding of the enemy, his C^2 system, and his decision making process. At all levels of war, the Intelligence BOS is an operational tool that assesses and exploits the vulnerabilities of the enemy's information and C^2 systems. IEW is an integral player in C^2 W and information operations. Its lead role in building information system IPB, developing C^2W COASs and assessing the effectiveness of information operations has taken Ml from a support to an operational role in military operations. IEW operations set the conditions for decisive

Information Age and IEW

Operation Desert Storm and other recent operations have shown that the nature of warfare has changed dramatically with the arrival of the information age. The information age is characterized by the proliferation of information systems and the increasing ability to rapidly collect, assimilate, and disseminate information. In the information age, those with access to, or control of, these systems can immediately influence public opinion, world commerce, political dialogue, and other issues affecting the security of nations. The impact of the information age on military operations has caused a revolutionary change in the way US Forces conduct operations and the nature of warfare itself. The key to this modern form of warfare is knowledge-based operations. The key to successful knowledge-based operations is exploiting and controlling information.

The information age has changed the conduct of IEW operations. Though MI can extend current IEW support to information operations, there are several aspects of information warfare that will generate new or more detailed IEW requirements. MI must –

- Learn and refine the capability to find and identify the vulnerabilities in the critical nodes of an adversary's decision making system.
- Monitor the information warfare capabilities of potential adversaries and assess this capability as a threat to friendly battle command systems.
- Develop the analytical skills necessary to identify, depict, and exploit the information base of the opposing commander's decision making process and the global information environment.
- Ensure IEW operations effectively support the development and maintenance of the commander's common picture of the battlefield.
- Refine the methods to synchronize IEW operations of fully-modernized, digitized forces with other forces—our own, other services, and allies.

MI must have a thorough understanding of the enemy C^2 structure and his decision making process to effectively support the development and maintenance of the commander's common picture of the battlefield. Information operations will require new analytic and synthesis techniques that describe the enemy C^2 information infrastructure in terms of the enemy commander's decisión making process, and the critical nodes that allow him to exercise effective C^2 of his combat forces. Inherent is the requirement to understand how the enemy commander will be affected by specific C^2W actions and predict his response.

Another impact on the intelligence system is the need to assess the effectiveness of the information operations effort. This "electronic" BDA will allow commanders to adjust their efforts to maximize the effects on the enemy. An important aspect of this "electronic". BDA will be real-time analysis and synthesis to determine when information operations have created a vulnerability in the enemy C^2 structure that can be exploited by fire and maneuver. Information operations pose a unique challenge to BDA because the effects of C^2W on the enemy C^2 may not be in the form of physical damage.

INFORMATION WARFARE

The concept of information warfare states that knowledge is becoming the Army's center of gravity. Technology now allows us to improve our commander's knowledge base while we diminish and degrade the quantity and quality of the enemy commander's knowledge base. A primary measure of effectiveness in this type warfare is the commander's decision making cycle. The intelligence system plays a vital role on both sides of this equation. On the friendly side, the ability to produce a common, coherent, real-time picture of the battlefield helps to reduce uncertainty and shorten the decision making process, while effective C^2W operations significantly increase and distort the enemy's decision making cycle.

PREPARE OF INFORMATION OPERATIONS

Information operations are the way the Army will prepare and execute knowledge-based warfare across the full range of military operations. Information operations are essential to winning the information war on the future battlefield, and IEW is the key to successful information operations. information operations enable, enhance, and protect the commander's decision making cycle while influencing an opponents. This is accomplished through effective intelligence, battle command, and C^2W operations as an integral part of joint, combined, or interagency operations. Battle command is about imposing control on the compressed dimensions of battle space by achieving and sustaining a high tempo of operations, overwhelming lethality, and superior survivability. Supporting battle command, information operations are conducted across the full range of military operations. In peacetime, information operations are conducted at various levels of intensity against assorted adversaries. In OOTW situations where restraint is often required, nonlethal C^2W is used to bring about a desired response from threat forces. In cases where the use of force is unavoidable, all elements of information operations are employed in concert to best achieve the objective. The effective pairing of the attack means with the information operation's targets is largely dependent on understanding and predicting the impact of the targeting effort on the adversary's decision making process.

The IEW battle space is frequently global as was demonstrated in Operation Desert Storm. The vast array of systems and sources available to the intelligence community will require a universal vision. This vision is crucial in providing the analytical perspective required to give commanders a common picture of the battlefield. The commander's ability to increase the quality of his decisions and compress his decision making process is directly related to his ability to visualize current and future situations. This common picture binds the intelligence and battle command functions together.

COMMAND AND CONTROL WARFARE

C^2W is knowledge-based and decision oriented. It is characterized by fast-paced moves and countermoves by opposing commanders. The HVTS in C^2W are the commander's decision making processes. The objectives in C^2W are to allow friendly commanders to make better decisions rapidly (inside the threat commander's decision making cycle), while causing the enemy to make bad decisions. C^2W integrates OPSEC, military deception, PSYOP, EW, and physical destruction with mutually supported intelligence to deny information, and to influence, degrade, or destroy adversary C^2 capabilities while protecting friendly C^2 capabilities. The C^2W part of information operations is not a system. It is a strategy that applies the primary C^2W components to reduce the adversary's C^2 capabilities (counter-C^2) while protecting friendly C^2 capabilities (C^2-protect). It applies across the full range of military operations and at all levels of war.

C²W is supported by an information system IPB. This form of IPB is the basis for developing C²W COAS and targeting. The process builds upon the standard IPB but requires-

- Understanding the "art" of decision making and leadership.
- Knowledge of the technical requirements of a wide array of information systems.
- Ability to conduct highly technical processing to produce C²W COA templates.

The effectiveness of C²W operations is predicated on a thorough understanding and assessment of the enemy's capabilities from equipment through his decision making process.

The Intelligence BOS is an operational tool that creates and exploits vulnerabilities in the enemy battle command. IEW is an operator in C²W and information operations. From conventional and information system IPB, developing C²W COAs, supporting information operations, and assessing the effectiveness of C²W operations, IEW has taken on an operational role in military operations.

The more capable Army of the future will still be based on a hierarchical force level command but will be empowered by fully digitized information management systems. The commander will drive information operations just as he drives the intelligence effort. He will use information operations to focus and leverage information to better command his force and apply the elements of combat power.

INTELLIGENCE AND ELECTRONIC WARFARE SUPPORT TO MILITARY OPERATIONS

Operational Continuum

The operational continuum is a dynamic spectrum consisting of three environments: peacetime competition, conflict, and war. Within this continuum, the US can find itself in peacetime competition with one nation and at war with another nation, while in conflict with still another nation — all at the same time. Moreover, as recent peacetime contingency missions (such as URGENT FURY, JUST CAUSE, OPERATION DESERT SHIELD, and OPERATION

DESERT STORM) reveal, the operational continuum is not a one-way street but rather a multi-path avenue which permits operations to flow in all directions.

The US was hoping to gain some influence over Baghdad and pull them out of the Soviet sphere. But in July 1990, Iraq massed troops on the Kuwait border and threatened to invade if Kuwait, among other things, did not cut its oil production. The US response was mostly in the diplomatic arena; however, we held some joint air defense exercises with our Persian Gulf allies which placed us on the verge of a conflict environment on the operational continuum.

When Iraq appeared to back off, the situation appeared to remain in a peacetime competition environment. However, after Iraq's invasion of Kuwait and the subsequent execution of OPERATION DESERT SHIELD, the US and Iraq entered the environment of conflict.

Had OPERATION DESERT SHIELD succeeded in convincing Iraq to withdraw from Kuwait, then it would not have been necessary to move into the next environment of the continuum — war. However, when months of diplomatic and military maneuvering failed, the US and its allies initiated OPERATION DESERT STORM. At this point, we crossed over into the war environment.

Initially, the allies limited their actions to aerial bombing, hoping to persuade Iraq to withdraw. However, Iraq's failure to withdraw forced the allied move deeper into the war environment. After the NM-hour ground war, the allies called a halt to offensive operations but maintained forces inside Iraq — thus moving into the conflict phase of the continuum.

Still within the conflict environment of the continuum, the situation with the Kurdish refugees in northern Iraq caused the US to initiate OPERATION PROVIDE COMFORT. This was a disaster (manmade) relief effort under the heading of a Peacetime Contingency Operation.

Although the final chapter in the war with Iraq remains uncompleted, the allied goal is to work through the operational continuum while rebuilding Kuwait and Iraq and to reestablish a peacetime competition environment. However, it is up to Iraq whether that happens. The potential exists for the US to shift backwards through conflict and war again before achieving peace.

The ARSOF SI0 must be prepared to meet the commander's intelligence requirements for any mission and be able to anticipate what new requirements might arise as the operation flows along the continuum.

HISTORICAL PERSPECTIVE

Timely and accurate intelligence and unprocessed combat information can be a significant factor in operational success. Historically, the commander who has superior knowledge of mission, enemy, terrain, troops, and time available (METT-T) factors has a critical edge in combat.

As the following examples show, the more information and intelligence commanders have, the greater their chances for success.

- In January 1945, timely and accurate intelligence enabled the 6th Ranger Battalion to rescue 511 American and Allied prisoners from a Japanese prisoner of war (PW) compound near Cabanatuan in the Philippines.
- During the Korean War the intelligence community identified enemy vulnerabilities for exploitation by psychological warfare teams. These efforts were very successful in lowering the morale, reducing combat effectiveness, and encouraging desertion and defection of communist troops. In summary, it is estimated that 65 percent of more than 150,000 communist PWs said US psychological warfare had some influence on their decision to surrender.
- In South Vietnam, the combined intelligence center's imagery interpretation (II) photographic study program provided valuable intelligence that helped SF units set up camp and hamlet security. Often these camps became isolated strongpoints astride communist infiltration routes and were a constant thorn in the side of the North Vietnamese.

- In Panama, timely and accurate intelligence enabled US forces to achieve all mission objectives within a short time. While this intelligence resulted in a quick end to the fighting, gaps in the intelligence support to post-hostilities operations (population resource control, military government) slowed the transition from combat to nation building.
- In Iraq, superb intelligence support resulted in an overwhelming victory over the Iraqi armed forces. Intelligence also played a key role in dealing with the Shiite Muslims in occupied southern Iraq. However, in northern Iraq, the US had to play catch-up to determine the direction the Kurdish rebellion was taking and was reconnoitering for suitable sites for refugee camps. This occurred only days before the camps were to be established.

What history tells us is that the intelligence community does an excellent job of supporting combat operations. However, it is incumbent upon both the IEW system and ARSOF to identify intelligence requirements for operations across the operational continuum to include pre- and post-hostilities phases.

COMBAT INFORMATION

Combat information is unevaluated data. It is gathered by ARSOF elements during any combat operation or wartime environment. This information is provided directly to the ARSOF commander which, due to its highly perishable nature or the criticality of the situation, cannot be processed into intelligence in time to satisfy the user's intelligence requirements.

Information becomes intelligence once it is collected, evaluated, analyzed, integrated, and interpreted. In other words, the distinction between combat and intelligence is in how the information is processed and used.

When information must be processed and analyzed, or if it needs to be integrated with other data and then analyzed and interpreted, it is intelligence and not combat information. Information may be both combat information and intelligence, but in sequence.

Unevaluated information collected by ARSOF units during target specific operations is considered combat information. It can be combined later with other intelligence or information as part of the all-source intelligence product. Only after the data is validated, analyzed, and processed does it become intelligence. There are two types of intelligence products: single-source and all-source.

Single-source Intelligence

If the sources of an intelligence product are from only one intelligence discipline, the final product is called a single-source intelligence product. The following are SOF-related examples of each intelligence discipline:

- Human intelligence (HUMINT) is intelligence derived from information collected and provided by human sources. ARSOF units provide the IEW system with HUMINT through SR and debriefings of units after operations. SR is explained in detail inChapter 4. MI units support ARSOF with HUMINT through controlled collection and tactical interrogation operations.
- Signals intelligence (SIGINT) is intelligence that includes all communications intelligence (COMINT), electronics intelligence (ELINT), and foreign instrumentation signals intelligence (FISINT). ARSOF units use SIGINT to prepare for and conduct infiltration and exfiltration; to locate actual or potential threat positions; and to analyze possible courses of action (COAs). ARSOF units can collect limited COMINT with organic assets.
- Imagery intelligence (IMINT) is intelligence derived from the exploitation of products from visual photography, infrared sensors, lasers, electro-optics, and radar sensors. ARSOF units use IMINT for targeting, infiltration and exfiltration, and general reconnaissance or area orientation.
- Technical intelligence (TECHINT) is intelligence concerning foreign technological developments, and the performance and operational capabilities of foreign materiel, which have or may eventually have a practical application for military

use. ARSOF use TECHINT products to exploit foreign weapons. Since ARSOF units operate deep in hostile or denied territory, they are often first to discover, identify, and provide information concerning new or previously unidentified material.

- Measurement and signature intelligence (MASINT) is a highly sophisticated application of state-of-the-art technology and processing techniques to detect and identify specific foreign weapon systems based on inadvertent signatures. This identification aids in determining capabilities and intentions. ARSOF units use MASINT for developing target data.

All-source Intelligence

All-source intelligence can be a combination of combat information, intelligence from more than one intelligence discipline, or even data from previously completed all-source intelligence products. To be called all-source intelligence, it must contain information from at least two of the intelligence disciplines.

THE NEED FOR INTELLIGENCE AND ELECTRONIC WARFARE SUPPORT

Today, ARSOF commanders depend even more on timely, accurate intelligence and combat information than did their historical counterparts. ARSOF commanders must be able to exploit METT-T factors to their advantage and to capture and keep the vital element of surprise throughout the operational continuum.

ARSOF commanders need IEW support because it is crucial in assisting the commander to make informed decisions during the decision-making process. All IEW disciplines are ARSOF operational multipliers. Each discipline provides the accurate, sensitive, and timely intelligence and combat information commanders need to complete their missions successfully. IEW supports ARSOF commanders as they plan and execute effective maneuver, firepower, force protection, and leadership.

SIGINT and EW are operational multipliers because these assets provide ARSOF commanders with passive and active means to protect C^3 systems. SIGINT and EW are employed by combining both offensive and defensive operations, as well as tactics, techniques, and procedures (TTP). Assets and products from disciplines like HUMINT and IMINT are also valuable combat multipliers because they provide information or intelligence that cannot be obtained otherwise.

Each intelligence discipline supports the final product by confirming or denying the validity of information collected by the other disciplines. IEW products are gathered and integrated into all-source intelligence products to support the commander's concept of operations.

ARSOF commanders and their staffs must understand how the IEW system works and how to integrate IEW assets and products, along with the principles of integration, synchronization, and interoperability, to support their concept of the mission. The environments and types of operations will, of course, vary. The key to effective ARSOF intelligence support is for ARSOF to fully use the intelligence system. To do this, ARSOF operators must work with supporting intelligence agencies to sensitize the intelligence community to ARSOF requirements.

INTELLIGENCE BATTLEFIELD OPERATING SYSTEM

Intelligence supports the Army as a whole through the Intelligence BOS. The Intelligence BOS is a flexible and tailorable architecture of procedures, personnel, organizations, and equipment that responds to the intelligence needs of commanders at all echelons. The Intelligence BOS architecture provides specific intelligence and communications structures at each echelon from the national level through the tactical level. These structures include intelligence organizations, systems, and procedures for collecting, processing, analyzing, and delivering intelligence to decision makers who need it. Effective communications connectivity and automation are essential components of this architecture.

Since no echelon has all the organic intelligence capabilities it needs to fully support the commander, IEW assets must be employed to support the needs of all echelons. This support is comprehensive and reaches across the range of military operations and levels of intelligence. It is the collective entity the force commander uses to produce the intelligence he needs to win on the battlefield. The Intelligence BOS is built upon the premise that the whole is greater than the sum of its parts. It is a combination of space, airborne, and ground-based systems providing the most comprehensive intelligence possible. The Intelligence BOS is always engaged in supporting the commander in war and OOTW.

During force projection operations, MI uses Intelligence BOS procedures and architecture, established during peacetime, to ensure that the force commander is supported with accurate and responsive intelligence from predeployment through redeployment.

PRIMARY FEATURES OF THE INTELLIGENCE BOS

There are seven primary features of the Intelligence BOS. Each is described below.

Always Engaged

The Intelligence BOS is always engaged. Through continuous peacetime intelligence operations, commanders ensure collection, processing, analysis, and dissemination infrastructure is in place and prepared to provide intelligence support throughout the range of military operations. Early intelligence preparation is critical to the commander's decision making and planning process for force projection operations. The commander and G2 (S2) must assess each contingency to determine intelligence requirements and develop a plan for filling intelligence voids. This primary feature is tempered, however, by the imperative to prioritize efforts and prepare thoroughly for top priority contingency areas.

Downwardly Focused

Commanders and MI organizations must focus intelligence downwardly to the commander on the ground. Intelligence should get to the subordinate commander, when requested, in a usable format, and focused on his echelon and battle space. Commanders and MI leaders at higher echelons should anticipate the intelligence needs of lower echelons, and "push" tailored intelligence support down to them. Staffs at each echelon should produce intelligence reports (INTREPs) and other products tailored to the needs of their subordinate units. To the extent possible, INTREPs and intelligence summaries (INTSUMs) should be in graphic format with enough text to reduce confusion. Higher echelons must also facilitate the "push"of intelligence from their data bases for both bulk-data requests and specific queries. The lowest echelons should be able to "push" echelons to access the data bases they require to support the commander.

Simultaneously Supported

Advances in dissemination capabilities allow the Intelligence BOS to provide commanders at multiple echelons with a common picture of the battlefield derived from national, joint, and Army collection assets. In addition, the connectivity available through the Intelligence BOS architecture enables commanders to directly access and "pull" critical intelligence products from different echelons. Thus, while the IEW assets of a corps are focused on the corps commander's PIR, the corps' collection assets and intelligence products are also available and simultaneously supporting the needs of higher and lower echelon commanders.

Coverage Enhanced

The capabilities and technologies embedded in MI systems enhance the commander's ability to see the width and depth of the battlefield at a higher, more consistent degree of resolution than ever. As a result, commanders have at their disposal more near-real time (NRT) and real-time information with targeting accuracy. This enables G2s (S2s) to quickly gather and synthesize information. They can then present the intelligence so that the commander and his staff can quickly assimilate it. Intelligence organizations at each echelon facilitate the synthesis of information through complementing collection, processing, and balanced all-source reporting.

Skip Echelon Flexibility

The flexibility of the Intelligence BOS supports skip echelon "push" of critical perishable intelligence from national, joint, and theatre organizations to the tactical commander. At the same time, a tactical unit is capable of conducting skip echelon "pull" of information from theatre, joint, and national data bases to answer the commander's intelligence requirements. The extent of skip echelon support is determined by the commanders and the intelligence organizations at each echelon. It is the responsibility of organizations conducting skip echelon Activities to provide intermediate echelons with the same information. The utility of skip echelon intelligence support is most evident when preparing for and during force projection operations.

Organizations Redesigned

MI organizations are, or will be redesigned to take advantage of technology and incorporate lessons learned in order to better serve the needs of commanders. From theatre MI brigade to direct support MI company, commanders are provided with a balanced, scalable, and flexible force which can be tailored to meet any contingency. In cases such as the ACE, assets have been consolidated to permit more effective control and efficient use of limited resources. Organizations like the CMISE, ACE, and DISE were developed to facilitate the "pull" of intelligence for all commanders. Underpinning these structural changes is the manning of MI organizations from battalion to national level with soldiers trained to deal effectively with new technology and concepts.

Disciplined Operations

The following laws, regulations, and policies ensure disciplined operations support commanders:

- AR 381-10 ensures that intelligence activities will not violate the right to privacy of US citizens.
- United States Signal Intelligence Directives (USSIDs) are the policies and procedures that provide the authority for production and dissemination of SIGINT. USSIDs establish uniform techniques, standards, and support mechanisms for collecting, processing, and reporting SIGINT-derived information.
- Status of Forces Agreements (SOFAs), Rules of Engagement (ROE), international laws, and other documents ensure

that intelligence activities do not exacerbate the political situation which the intelligence operation supports.

- Doctrinal principles and TTPs ensure that intelligence activities maximize support to the commander and eliminate nonessential operations.

LIMITATIONS OF THE INTELLIGENCE BOS

The Intelligence BOS is a seamless, unified system that anticipates and satisfies intelligence needs. Commanders ensure its proper employment by clearly articulating intent, decisively designating PIR, and boldly prioritizing the types of targets they want engaged to the entire Intelligence BOS. Commanders must, however, understand the limitations of the Intelligence BOS and not place unrealistic expectations on the system. Major limitations are discussed below.

- Intelligence reduces uncertainty on the battlefield, but it cannot eliminate it entirely. The commander will always have to accept some risk.
- The Intelligence BOS is comprised of finite resources and capabilities. he density of MI soldiers and IEW systems with in a unit is limited. Once lost to action or accident, these soldiers and systems cannot easily be replaced. The loss of qualified language-trained soldiers, and in particular soldiers trained in low-density languages, could adversely affect the ability of a MI unit to accomplish its mission. In addition, IEW systems operate within limited technical parameters and are designed to exploit a specific threat system or type of system.
- The Intelligence BOS cannot effectively and efficiently provide IEW support without adequate communications equipment, capacity, and connectivity. Commanders and G2s (S2s) must ensure communications support to intelligence is given appropriate priority during planning and execution of operations.
- Commanders and G2s (S2s) cannot expect everything needed will be automatically to them from higher levels. The "push" of products from higher echelons does not

relieve subordinate staffs from conducting detailed analysis and focusing the efforts of higher headquarters (HQ). Nor can they expect products "push"to them will always be at the level of detail they require. Commanders and G2s (S2s) must focus higher echelons by clearly articulating and actively pursuing intelligence requirements.

TRAINING THE INTELLIGENCE BOS

Training the Intelligence BOS means training commanders, MI leaders, MI soldiers, and organizations. Commanders must understand the capabilities of the Intelligence BOS and be trained to drive and integrate the system with their operations. MI leaders must understand the tactics of their supported command and learn to synchronize IEW operations with the commander's concept of operation.

MI soldiers must master the technical, tactical, and leadership skills required to employ and maintain sophisticated intelligence systems on the battlefield. Organizations and crew-served systems must be trained to function as a team and integrate their efforts within the Intelligence BOS and with other BOSs.

The responsibility for training the Intelligence BOS rests with commanders and intelligence leaders. Commanders are ultimately responsible for the overall training proficiency of their units; however, the G2 (S2) and other intelligence leaders share in that responsibility. The G2 (S2) must assist the commander in developing and integrating realistic intelligence activity into The training of combat, combat support (CS), and combat service support (CSS) units. Realistic training fosters awareness of the capabilities and limitations of the Intelligence BOS in non-MI units while honing the skills of MI soldiers and organizations.

Intelligence training should be derived from the organization's Mission Essential Task List (METL), battle tasks, and operation plan (OPLAN) requirements. To the extent possible, intelligence training should be used to enhance and refine real-world intelligence operations of the organization. Force projection operations, in particular, require realistic and battle focused training of MI personnel and organizations to ensure intelligence readiness.

Training the Total Force in the Intelligence BOS requires embedding realistic intelligence activities into unit training and that conducted in the Combat Training Center programs. Whenever possible, commanders should expand the scope of training at these centers or homestations by linking field training exercises with computer simulations play at other locations. Combat information and intelligence should be incorporated into programs of system trainers and computerized battle simulations to provide realism to crew and staff training.

Intelligence Training Principles

The following intelligence training principles assist the commander in training his unit:

Execute Real-World Operations. Real-world intelligence operations use all aspects of the Intelligence BOS from the commander developing his PIR to disseminating graphic intelligence products to subordinate commanders. Using the intelligence system in peacetime trains personnel to plan, collect, process, analyze, synthesize, report, and evaluate intelligence. It supports contingency planning and ensures the procedures and connectivity required for force projection operations are valid and available to the commander.

Integrate Intelligence. Integrate intelligence into training and exercises. Use the intelligence cycle and decision making process to train commanders and G2s (S2s) how to interact and develop plans that synchronize IEW support with the commander's operation. The G2 (S2) should always support this effort with appropriate intelligence products and integrate the Intelligence BOS with other battlefield systems.

Understand the Battlefield. Teach the G2 (S2) and MI unit personnel about friendly tactics and operations. Have the G2 (S2) staff participate in or observe training events of combat, CS, and CSS units. The performance of intelligence analysts and collectors at all levels is directly proportional to their understanding of battlefield dynamics.

Apply Standards. Apply standards to IEW training. Standards provide commanders a means of measuring intelligence readiness and equipping subordinates with clearly defined training objectives. TCS 34-10-20, 34-10-20-1, and 34-10 -20-2contain standards which commanders can use to develop METL, plan and execute training, and assess performance. By applying these standards with established doctrine and TTP, commanders can ensure commonality of operations between their units and contribute to the effectiveness of the Intelligence BOS.

Maintain Proficiency. Establish consistent approaches to collective and individual training. Collective training should be conducted at a baseline proficiency level consistent with unit readiness standards. Individual training, particularly language training, should be creative and challenge soldiers to go beyond Army standards. The Readiness Training (REDTRAIN) program is one means of maintaining both individual and unit proficiency. Through live environment training, REDTRAIN allows units to employ their soldiers and equipment against potential wartime or OOTW targets. Other REDTRAIN opportunities allow soldiers to improve their military occupational specialty (MOS) skills and language proficiency through attendance at specialized technical and language courses.

MISSION OF ARMY INTELLIGENCE

The mission of Army intelligence is to provide timely, relevant, accurate, and synchronized IEW support to tactical, operational, and strategic commanders across the range of military operations. In war, IEW operations support the winning of battles and campaigns. In OOTW, IEW operations support the promotion of peace, the resolution of conflict, and the deterrence of war. These operations reduce uncertainty and risk to US Forces and permit the effective application of force.

IEW in the Force Projection Army

The post-Cold War Army is a force projection Army. Continental United States (CONUS)-based with a limited forward presence, the Army must be capable of rapidly deploying anywhere in the world, operating in a joint or combined environment, and defeating regional threats on the battlefield or conducting 00TW.

IEW is fundamental to effective planning, security, and execution of force projection operations.

IEW operations have changed fundamentally from those of the Cold War model. The environment in which the Army now operates requires IEW support based on the mission rather than on a monolithic threat. During the Cold War era, intelligence developed into a threat-based system upon which the Army based its doctrine, training, and modernization. For over four decades, the"threat" was the Soviet Union. The Army developed organizations, systems, tactics, and procedures needed to conduct defensive operations against Soviet and Warsaw Pact forces attacking through central Europe. Our defense was built upon the movement of heavy corps from in-theatre garrisons to general defense positions with follow-on forces arriving later from the CONUS, Movement and support of the corps would occur within a robust communication zone containing extensive communications and logistics infrastructures, From alert through the termination of hostilities, tactical IEW units were to be the principal sources of tactical intelligence flowing up to divisions, corps, and theatre. Intelligence, in general, would flow from the ground up to higher echelons. And, because the US focused the national intelligence effort on our nation's most likely threat, we possessed in-depth, continuous, and nearly automatic intelligence on the forces of the Soviet Union. From the two premises of tactical intelligence coming from the ground up and in-depth knowledge on the threat, we built our entire vision for IEW support.

In the force projection Army, mission-based intelligence focuses on developing broad baseline knowledge of potential threats and operational environments supporting numerous plans and likely contingency missions. From this broad baseline, commanders possess the capability to prioritize, focus, and surge the intelligence system supporting force projection operations. The commander plays a key role in mission-based intelligence and intelligence readiness. Since there is no longer one threat facing the US, command involvement is essential in ensuring that the intelligence system is focused on the commander's top contingencies. Force projection operations build force levels from the bottom up vice top down as during the Cold War. IEW assets are tailored to meet the requirements of the mission and deployment sequence. In force projection operations, commanders depend on small, deployable teams with access to national and joint intelligence. Intelligence in the initial stages of the operation will flow from higher to lower. The size and capabilities of follow-on lEW assets will be dictated by the situation and the commander's concept of operation.

The nature of force projection operations and mission-based intelligence requires commanders to redefine intelligence readiness. Intelligence readiness means that Ml must develop broad knowledge on priority contingency areas, update those data bases daily, and be prepared to surge in support of emerging missions. Commanders and G2s (S2s) must direct the intelligence effort daily to ensure the data bases will be there upon alert to support contingency planning and execution. If our divisions, corps, and theatre forces stand ready to project force anywhere in several potential contingencies, then it is essential that their intelligence support be at the same or higher level of readiness. To maintain that level of readiness, Ml must provide commanders with routine, direct, and habitual links into the intelligence system to provide and, perhaps more important, to focus intelligence on their tactical and operational needs early.

Principles Of Force Projection IEW

Successful force projection IEW support is based on understanding five key principles: the commander drives intelligence; intelligence synchronization; split-based operations; tactical tailoring; and broadcast dissemination.

The Commander Drives Intelligence

The commander's role in IEW, not just when the crisis begins, but well before and throughout the operation, is central to the success or failure of IEW support in force projection operations. The commander must take an active role in focusing, integrating, and training the intelligence system. He must focus the effort and ensure it is responsive to his information requirements (IR) and those of his subordinates. The commander must —

- Identify, clearly articulate, and prioritize intelligence and targeting requirements.
- Understand the capabilities and limitations of the Intelligence BOS.
- Know how to leverage and employ the intelligence system to its full potential.
- Broker subordinates' information and resource requirements.
- Meld the Intelligence BOS into the total combined arms effort.

Intelligence Synchronization

Intelligence synchronization ensures IEW operations are linked to the commander's requirements and respond in time to influence decisions and operations. In the synchronization process, the G2 (S2) takes the commander's priority intelligence requirements (PIR) and backward plans to ensure that collection and production efforts are orchestrated with the operation, and deliver intelligence when required. The collection manager ensures specific orders and requests (SORs) fully support all PIR and IR. The collection manager also synchronizes collection and reporting to deliver relevant information, on time, to support operational decisions. Intelligence synchronization ensures the MI unit commander has the time, guidance, and resources to execute IEW operations. Intelligence synchronization is a continuous process which keeps the intelligence cycle and IEW operations tied to the commander's critical decisions and concept of operations.

Split-based Operations

Split-based operations are an integral part of IEW support to force projection operations. in split-based operations, the commander deploys small, flexible, tailored IEW organizations with access to intelligence data bases and systems outside the area of operations (AO), particularly national systems. Split-basing takes advantage of direct broadcast technology from collection platforms and assured intelligence communications to provide commanders with continuous, relevant, and timely IEW support during all stages of force projection operations.

Organizations like the Deployable Intelligence Support Element (DISE) support split-based operations by bringing together communications capability, automated intelligence fusion systems, and broadcast downlink in a scalable package able to deploy with the entry force. It is not a specific piece of equipment or a particular configuration of equipment. It is a flexible organization able to support any type of ground force commander whether from Army, joint, or combined forces. The DISE provides the commander with a link from his forward deployed force to an intelligence support base located in CONUS or other locations outside the AO.

Split-based operations allow uncommitted IEW assets, including MDCI assets, to support the deployed force through remote collection, processing and analysis, and TENCAP operations in garrison, or from secure locations outside the AO. This includes intelligence of units as they deploy from garrison to port of debarkation (POD) and onward to the AO. The support relationship established between deployment and uncommitted assets in turn facilitates the smooth integration of follow-on assets once they deploy to theatre. The deployment of these follow on assets allows the commander to transition from IEW support provided primarily by national assets, the commander can focus the intelligence effort to the resolution required for tactical operations while receiving the unique support available only from national means.

Tactical Tailoring

In force projection operations, the commander tactically tailors IEW support for each contingency. Commanders should attempt to maintain unit integrity and established command relationships to the extent possible; however, deployment of a more traditional unit such as a divisional MI battalion in full may not be the best organization for the mission. Tailoring allows the commander to build a more efficient, mission specific force by —

- Assessing IEW mission requirements. This includes determining the capabilities of remotely based and joint intelligence collection assets to support the mission; identifying the compositionof the IEW force based on mission, enemy, troops, terrain and weather, and time available (METT-T); determining communications and processing requirements; and planning the deployment sequence of IEW assets based on mission, strategic lift resources, and host nation support.

- Developing scalable IEW support packages like the DISE with communications, processing, and downlink assets for top priority contingency missions. Employment of these packages should be practiced often to refine force researching and tailoring procedures, load plans, communications connectivity, and support relationships.
- Tailoring the Intelligence BOS to ensure it provides the commander with accurate and responsive intelligence. The intelligence system should cover the entire width and depth of the battle space and area of interest (AI) throughout the duration of the operation, at the resolution required by commanders at each echelon.
- Deploying early, an IEW package that is portable, logistically sustainable, and sufficient to conduct operations for the short-term. Sufficiency in the short-term includes being prepared to provide immediate IEW support for combat operations and force protection.
- Integrating IEW assets into the deployment flow early. Depending on the availability of information and threat capabilities, commanders must phase in intelligence personnel and, equipment that offer redundancy and that serve as the cornerstone for assets that arrive in the theatre later. These initial "building blocks" are critical to early success and follow-on capabilities. Follow-on IEW forces should enhance the capabilities of in-theatre assets and satisfy the commander's long-term concerns.
- Maintaining habitual peacetime IEW support relationships and accesses between the forward deployed intelligence element and its higher echelon intelligence organization. This allows forward deployed assets to pull from their"pull"normal intelligence sources between the predeployment and operations stages of force projection. This reduces the possibility of intelligence shortfalls which could arise from reliance on evolving intelligence

organizations. For example, a CONUS-based corps may commit a maneuver brigade as part of a forward deployed joint task force (JTF). The deployed brigade could continue to receive support through a DISE from the CON US-based analysis and control element (ACE) of its parent division in addition to support from the JTF Joint Intelligence Center (JIC).

- Maximizing intelligence support from the host nation by establishing, if possible, liaison with host nation intelligence organizations in peacetime.

Broadcast Dissemination

Broadcast dissemination of intelligence and targeting information is an important element in providing commanders at multiple echelons with a common intelligence picture of the battlefield. Broadcasting facilitates the direct or skip echelon of information down to commanders in the field. Use of broadcast technology also reduces the number of collection sensors, processors, and personnel needed to support these operations. More importantly, broadcasting intelligence and targeting information directly to multiple terminals, eliminates bottlenecks inherent in point-to-point communications and provides all echelons common sources from which to "pull" information. Some of the products available through broadcast systems are TENCAP imagery and targeting information, Joint STARS radar imagery, UAV video, and Air Force RC135 (Rivet Joint) and Army GUARDRAIL SIGINT reports. Host terminals, when tied to broadcast terminals, are capable of providing filtered, processed, and tailored intelligence to satisfy specific intelligence and targeting requirements.

The ACE is the commander's primary organization for pulling information from broadcast systems and fusing it into tailored intelligence and targeting information. Through its capability to rapidly pull, process, and disseminate intelligence, the ACE provides the commander with the means to focus and synchronize the intelligence system with his intent and concept of operation. In addition, the ACEs at brigade, division, corps, and theatre form a seamless bridge linking the tactical commander with higher echelon organizations where intelligence data bases and knowledge reside.

ELECTRONIC WARFARE AND MILITARY OPERATIONS

Electronic Warfare (EW) became an integral support component to more traditional warfare-offensive and defensive-in the late 20th Century. In 1973, having watched Israel jam Syrian guided missiles during the Yom Kippur War, a Soviet admiral summed it up succinctly: "The next war will be won by the side that best exploits the electromagnetic spectrum."

EW took on new dimensions and importance in post-9/11 Southwest Asia, where the enemy used electronic means to detonate their weapon of choice-improvised explosive devices (IEDs). The U.S. and its allies sought to combat those low-tech, but deadly, attacks with the components and capabilities arising from a technology boom that changed all aspects of warfare.

With the drawdown in Southwest Asia and the planned Pacific Pivot, EW now is entering yet another new stage of development, requirements and importance. Andrew Dunn, vice president of business development for Integrated and electronic warfare for Exelis Electronic Systems Division, calls it a "whole new mindset" for the U.S. military as the U.S. Department of Defense (DOD) shifts its focus to an area where uncontested access to the electromagnetic spectrum and physical battlespace may no longer exist. Instead, U.S. and allied forces must be ready to deal with near-peer anti-access/area denial (A2/AD) environments and a greater emphasis on the air-sea battle.

The fight against IEDs

In Southwest Asia, the Army and Marine Corps bore the brunt of low-tech attacks on the fringe of EW. That was especially true with the Army, as the internal EW capabilities they had developed during the Cold War were determined no longer necessary. It would prove to be a costly mistake the Army does not want to repeat-but fears it may. "When the USSR fell and the Cold War ended, all the organization in the U.S. Army dedicated to tactical jamming in combat EW intel battalions went away, leaving ourselves pretty vulnerable on the EW front," says Col. Rob Murray, outgoing branch chief for cyber electromagnetic activities (CEMA) at the Army Cyber Center of Excellence at Fort Gordon, Ga. "With the new challenges brought on by 9/11, going into Afghanistan and then Iraq, we found ourselves with no one responsible for EW in the Army.

The enemy quickly found that seam and ways to exploit it. IEDs at first were pretty easy to spot, then they started burying the explosives and lines to them-command-detonated by hidden observers. Every time we developed a counter to what they were doing, they kept moving to new approaches."

CEMA Deputy Branch chief Matt Cullen said the insurgents' move to radio-controlled IEDs escalated the U.S. and allied death toll: "Our challenge was to 'reinvigorate' EW as the means to counter, combat and defeat RC IEDs." The Army turned for help to the U.S. Navy, which had become DOD's lead agent for EW, but it was far from a perfect solution because the EW requirements of a ground force differ from those of the Air Force and Navy.

"The Navy has a lot of its EW capability on airplanes flying off carriers and they don't turn that capability on until they are a couple of hundred miles away, so the possibility of those systems causing problems on the ship are minimal. Ships have their own EW defenses against missiles, of course, but when a missile is coming, they don't care what disruptions there may be," Cullen explains.

"But the Army has jammers in the middle of convoys in the middle of bad-guy territory-and when those jammers are turned on, they also disrupt our communications on the ground," Cullen continues. "Early in the war, the Army was buying jammers from the Air Force and Navy and support from those service's EW officers, but what they didn't understand was the jammers also disrupted our soldiers' communications."

CEMA's three pillars of EW are:

1. electronic attack;
2. electronic support-what frequencies and technologies do friendly forces use to defeat the enemy; and

3. electronic protection-keeping U.S. and friendly forces safe from fratricide and enemy EW

"The artillery guys-such as Col. Murray-take that very seriously regarding mortars. They figure out problems during planning. The same has to be done with jammers," Cullen explains. Military forces have important RF frequencies that are restricted from U.S. and allied electronic countermeasures called the Joint Restricted Frequency List (JFRL). Despite the best intention, the JFRL does not protect against accidental disruptions-especially if using a frequency that is not on the JFRL. "In a modern Army, where we have portable computing and internet capabilities that can move information around the battlefield, we should be using radio frequency engineering during the planning process, to predict the effect of jammers on our own radios."

It was not until 2008 to 2010 that the Army was able to begin restoring an organic EW capability, says Lt. Col. Keith Cantrell, CEMA's incoming branch chief. That included standing up the Cyber Center of Excellence (COE), incorporating the work of the Signals COE it replaced, and slowly incorporating EW.

Shipboard and airborne EW

Despite the Navy's role as DOD's executive agency for EW, its leaders are being forced to redesign the Navy's own capabilities-air- and ship-borne. That includes the Surface Electronic Warfare Improvement Program (SEWIP) to upgrade existing shipboard signals technologies used to identify, assess and analyze EM signals and EW threats. A major problem, especially with aircraft carriers, is the massive number of radars, antennas, and other electronic systems operating simultaneously in a highly complex shipboard electromagnetic spectrum.

With the prospect of near-peer EW threats in the future, carriers and other combat and support vessels will need even greater capabilities to conduct offensive and defensive EW. That includes the NGJ, designed to give the EA-18G Growler advanced technologies for offensive EW missions when the jammer goes operational by 2020.

"The vision for the future is to take what our collection, exploitation, and early warning capabilities [find] and turn them into offensive ways to use electronic attack," says Christine Fox, who recently retired from the Pentagon after serving as acting deputy secretary of defense. "If we can go after the C2 or ISR pieces of a threat instead of putting a missile against a missile, I can potentially disrupt that missile's ability to find its target."

In addition, the Office of Naval Research (ONR) in Arlington, Va., is developing a prototype technology called Integrated Topside (InTop) to extend the range and flexibility of shipboard EW. For example, InTop would integrate the current forest of antennas on a ship's deck into a shared multi-function, multi-beam aperture array that could collect signals across a wide range of frequencies, then use a central resource allocation manager to share that information with several EW processes.

Perhaps equally important is the 21st Century version of "quiet running." The Chief of Naval Operations is pushing for greater education of officers and enlisted personnel on electronic spectrum awareness and understanding all aspects of a ship's electromagnetic signature. "We have to be more mindful of how we operate in the electromagnetic domain and in cyberspace and how those capabilities come together," wrote Margaret Palmieri, director of the Navy's Integrated Fires Division, in the July 2014 issue of U.S. Naval Institute Proceedings. "We are working on better understanding how networks and signals and networks and information come together. What do we really look like to the enemy?

"Integrated-fires capabilities are a central part of the asymmetric advantage our Navy, joint and coalition forces bring to a fight. They include capabilities that disrupt adversary C4ISR systems, deliver electronic payloads that limit an enemy's freedom of maneuver and action and enhance the ability of our own forces to place ordnance on target," Palmieri wrote. "It integrates lethal and non-lethal fires, underpinned by superior battlespace awareness and assured C2, to provide commanders an expanded set of warfighting tools especially important in A2/AD environments, like Air-Sea Battle."

In that same issue, Vice Adm. Ted N. Branch, deputy chief of naval operations (CNO) for information dominance, discussed the

Navy's need to dominate all segments of future battlespaces-on, above, and below the sea, as well as outer space-to sustain America's "global primacy'.

"However, commanding, controlling and fighting our forces in these areas requires dominance in the information domain, to include the electromagnetic spectrum and cyberspace," he wrote. "The name we've given to this concept-information dominance-is still new and unfamiliar to some, but it's indispensable to Fleet operations, so much so that we've adopted it as a distinct warfare discipline.

"Formerly perceived by many as a collection of support activities performed by specialized restricted line officers, information dominance is increasingly recognized by Fleet operators as a critical force multiplier. It's no longer just an adjunct to warfighting. It is warfighting," Branch wrote.

Navy information dominance focuses on three goals: robust and agile C2 in all operating environments; superior knowledge of the battlespace, the physical environment as well as threat capability, disposition and intent; and projecting power through the integration of kinetic and non-kinetic effects.

"We refer to these three elements, or pillars, as assured C2, battlespace awareness and integrated fires. Through them, information dominance creates decision superiority, provides asymmetric advantage and enhances the lethality of our deployed forces with non-kinetic options," Branch added. Those pillars, in turn, are designed to correspond to the CNO's three tenets: warfighting first; operate forward; and be ready.

"The critical element of the information dominance definition is integration, Branch wrote. "Blending the attributes of ISR, oceanography, meteorology, networks, cyber, and EW allows for better planning, smarter decisions and earlier results.

Aligning the related restricted-line communities of naval oceanography, information warfare, information professional, intelligence and the space cadre into the information dominance corps has likewise advanced our concept and capability development and improved data and system interoperability."

U.S. Marine Corps

While the Army and Marine Corps both are viewed as ground forces, the Marine Corps' EW requirements differ significantly from those of the Army, especially in meeting future anticipated threats. In recognition of that, the Corps has created a Marine Air/Ground Task Force (MAGTF) EW concept to develop an integrated system of distributed, platform-agnostic EW systems, including the progressive inclusion of technologies and capabilities from other services and commercial vendors.

MAGTF EW elements have several programs in development. Among them are Intrepid Tiger II (IT-2): An EW pod for communications-based targets, expandable to radar-based targets, currently deployed to CENTCOM and with Marine expeditionary units in three different versions for fixed-wing aircraft, unmanned aerial vehicles (UAVs), and helicopters.

Another program is the Electronic Warfare Service Architecture (EWSA)-an extended data exchange and hardware protocol to connect EW/SIGINT airborne nodes, via an adaptive multi-waveform network, to ground operators, Cyber/EW Coordination Cells (C/EWCCs) and other air EW nodes. The Corps also has stood up several new or redefined units, including the Cyber and Electronic Warfare Integration Division (CEWID), the Capabilities Development Directorate's integration and execution authority for all Marine Corps warfighting development activities associated with Cyberspace and EW.

CEWID coordinates with operating forces, supporting establishment and mission partners in order to identify, prioritize and integrate capability solutions across DOD's Doctrine, Organization, Training, Materiel, Leadership and Education, Personnel and Facilities (DOTMLPF) protocols. CEWID, in turn, comprises three branches: computer network attack, computer network defense, and MAGTF EW.

The General Atomics Aeronautical Systems Predator B/MQ-9 Reaper's new electronic attack capability, using the Northrop Grumman Pandora EW system, is a major part of the Marine Corps future EW effort. The system could advance the Reaper from its existing role as a counter-insurgency ISR/hunter-killer aircraft to a broader spectrum of EW missions, says GA-ASI President Frank W. Pace.

Pandora is a pod-based, multi-function, wideband system providing electronic attack, such as jamming, support and protection. Demonstrations at Yuma Marine Corps Air Station, Ariz., were designed to evaluate the ability of Pandora-equipped aircraft to conduct coordinated EW missions in a multi-node approach against a more capable integrated air defense system.

"Pandora brings optimal size, weight and power to current and future high-endurance platforms, opening up a new world of electronic attack capabilities," says Janine Nyre, vice president of radio frequency combat information systems at Northrop Grumman.

"We demonstrated operational concepts using a layered approach to electronic warfare with Reaper, EA-6B Prowlers, and other Group 3 UAVs," adds Brig. Gen. Matthew G. Glavy, assistant deputy commandant for Marine aviation. "By conducting multiple events, we were able to evaluate the viability of UAVs to conduct EW missions against enemy air defenses in support of tactical strike aircraft."

The 2013 Marine Corps Operating Concept for Information Operations termed information operations (IO) as a complex box of tools the Corps must incorporate and exploit within the context of its overall maneuver warfare philosophy and expeditionary culture to operate "effectively against a myriad of potential adversaries and perform multiple, diverse and simultaneous tasks across the ROMO [range of military operations]".

"In the Marine Corps, IO is not a warfighting function in its own right; it is an integrating function which facilitates the six warfighting functions of C2, fires, maneuver, logistics, intelligence and force protection. This distinction between warfighting and integrating function is key to the Marine Corps' belief IO does not-and will not-replace any of the time-tested warfighting functions. It will enable each of them," says the OCIC.

"IO is not a discrete, stand-alone capability, but is the integrated, coordinated and synchronized operational application of all information-related capabilities (IRCs), organic and non-organic, to affect decision-making by adversaries and potential adversaries, thereby creating an operational advantage. Integration is accomplished under the purview of the operations section, based upon commander's guidance, and supports achievement of the commander's end state. "IO is not synonymous with individual discrete capabilities or activities, much like fire support is not synonymous with artillery or aviation. More art than science, IO is focused on the human mind and seeks to influence behaviors to produce operational advantages."

EW in the air

While emphasizing they "do not generally comment on EW requirements, specific technologies or capabilities of our or others' systems", the Acquisition, Science, Technology and Engineering Directorate within the office of the Secretary of the Air Force (SAF/AQRM) did provide the following statement: "The Air Force recognizes that increased budgetary constraints, coupled with widespread availability of modern electronics, requires new technology and acquisition approaches for EW. The Air Force is tackling the problem along five fronts: 1) enabling fundamental components, 2) new techniques, 3) new adaptive modular approaches, 4) early prototyping and rapid reaction developments and 5) early in-the-loop testing.

"Today's EW, Communications, Navigation, Sensing and Cyber technologies require a more integrated use of the electromagnetic spectrum than ever before. The Air Force Research Laboratory (AFRL) is working on full spectrum science and technology, which includes: radio frequency EW; avionics protection; position, navigation and timing [PNT] in contested/denied environments; electro-optical/infrared threat warning and countermeasures; protected communications and robust cyber."

In its "Strategy for Spectrum Warfare", SAF/AQRM noted it is pursuing those goals through a comprehensive Advanced Components for EW (ACE) program and developing cognitive and distributed techniques, adaptive modular approaches and rapid prototyping.

AFRL issued a broad agency announcement (BAA) last fall for the Advanced Novel Spectrum Warfare Environment Research

(ANSWER) program to develop adaptive spectrum warfare technologies to maintain warfighting capabilities in contested and denied environments consistent with A2/AD scenarios. AFRL encouraged industry to employ unconventional thinking on the use of advanced computing power, signals processing, modeling and simulation, anti-tamper and software protection technologies, GPS alternatives with comparable accuracies for warfighters in A2/AD environments, vision and laser-based navigation and electro-optics countermeasures.

"With an ever-changing environment between red and blue forces, the ability to control the electromagnetic spectrum is a key requirement to achieving success in warfighter operations. This is a daunting task under benign conditions and becomes even more of a challenge as adversaries are able to employ various denial capabilities," the BAA noted. "If one can conduct electromagnetic spectrum operations under A2/AD conditions, then successful operations in other less challenging environments should be achievable as well. To accomplish this, the warfighter needs to be able to control adversary use of electromagnetic spectrum, ensure friendly access to/use of electromagnetic spectrum, protect sensor/avionics end nodes, establish/maintain secure communications/data links in dense electromagnetic spectrum environments and assure the availability of accurate PNT information. The ANSWER program is designed to address these challenges."

The Post-OEF/OIF EW Environment

"When it comes to EW, it doesn't have to be a near-peer or even a known rival. Electronics that can be made to be a problem are ubiquitous throughout the world," says the Army Cyber Center's Murray. "You can find a thousand types of cell phones in Afghanistan, which I certainly wouldn't call the modern world. So a lot of technology is out there, worldwide, that, in the wrong hands, can be a very severe problem, no matter what kind of advanced weapons or armor we have.

"Technology changes so fast that what is considered SOTA today may not be in another year," Murray says. "And that's one of the challenges on things we would like to have now and in the future. But the processes we must go through to acquire the equipment we would like to have and need to have are not as agile as we need them to be. They're OK now, but if we get into a new fight, you can't wait for what you need."

The possibility of near-peer conflict is growing as the U.S. puts a greater focus on the Asia/Pacific region and Eastern Europe once again feels threatened by Russia, even as the Middle East continues increasingly tech-based rounds of ancient conflicts. In addition, the vast distances involved and the lack of U.S. land bases in the Asia/Pacific-outside of South Korea and Okinawa in the north-will mean a greater focus on the Navy and Marine Corps, especially with respect to EW.

There was a sharp reduction in the Pentagon's EW research and development budget from 2013 to 2015-a cut from $3.5 billion to $2.1 billion-more than half from the Navy and Marine Corps. Of course, an unknown-but suspected substantial-part of EW research falls under classified "black" budgets.

"Although EW is declining through 2015, we expect to start seeing a resumption of spending from 2016 on," says John Hernandez, a senior aerospace and defense industry analyst at market researcher Frost and Sullivan. "That is an area that is being underdeveloped right now, but with the potential new adversaries in the coming years, it will need to be reinvigorated. Some analysts are predicting an increase in small, even hand-held jammers, but our analysts expect to see more modularity, especially for shipboard systems.

"There was a move for a while to make the F-35 the new EW platform, but I don't think the expense was worth it, given the fine job the Growler is doing. But in the future, I can see unmanned systems doing more EW, whether that is a single platform or a flock of UAVs doing jamming or AD missions. Personally, I suspect protecting our own systems is and will continue to be a priority over offensive technologies."

Defense industry adapts

The new environment and focus on naval assets also has been reflected in industry. In February 2014, for example, Raytheon Space and Airborne Systems combined several EW efforts into a new mission area called Electronic Warfare Systems, based at the company's El Segundo, CA, campus. The new unit will focus on the Navy's Next-Generation Jammer (NGJ);; EW self-protection systems; EW communications systems; advanced EW programs; and airborne information operations.

At the Northrop Grumman Integrated Systems sector, meanwhile, airborne early warning and electronic warfare systems have seen a similar growth in importance, including the June 2014 award of a joint service (Army/Navy) contract for 18 APR-39D(V)2 radar warning receiver (RWR)/EW management system (EWMS) pre-production units.

"Our APR-39D(V)2 merges the baseline capability of previous systems with the Northrop Grumman digital receiver technology to provide advanced capability for today's and tomorrow's threat environment," says Northrop Grumman's Nyre. "This lightweight system maintains interfaces with legacy systems and includes flexibility for future growth enhancements."

The company is to deliver the systems in late 2014 preparatory to hardware-software and platform integration testing in 2015.

Also next year, Northrop Grumman is scheduled to complete equipping the Navy's MQ-8C Fire Scout rotary UAV with a new external Multi-Capability Pod, providing it with "multiple EW sensors for employment in the littorals", says a DOD announcement in May 2014.

BAE Systems is leveraging advances in signals processing and machine learning under a DARPA-funded program called Adaptive Radar Countermeasures (ARC). The goal is a next-generation EW algorithm suite as a software upgrade existing EW hardware to can use to operate against emerging radar threats and help achieve and maintain U.S. air dominance in future battlespaces. Special emphasis will be on countering never-before-seen threats with unknown waveform characteristics and behaviors.

"This technology will provide a revolutionary capability to EW systems on U.S. military airborne platforms to counter adaptive radar threats and significantly improve survivability," says Joshua Niedzwiecki, BAE's director of strategic development. ARC is projected to be ready for live demonstration flight tests by 2018.

Mercury Systems in Chelmsford, Mass., has been predominantly involved with air-to-air/surface-to-air systems, but Chief Technology Officer Chris Lewis says the current SOTA for them "has been the transition from classic denial-jamming-to more deceiving your adversary".

"The world today is less bifurcated between EW and Cyber, which I consider part of the same continuum," he says. "The kinds of things we're seeing starting to come on line are systems that are much tighter in their response. Where conventional systems saw a new waveform that then was captured and technology to deal with it developed in the lab, today's system is tighter, with techniques being developed in days rather than months. And the goal is be instantaneous.

"Enabling technologies for future EW include continuing improvement in the performance of FPGAs and microprocessors, the continued drive in communications and great improvement in solid state amplifiers due to gallium nitride. Further down the line is photonics for very wide bandwidth and high dynamic range. Another, not a technology so much as capability, is the adaptive learning system. Some of the SOTA things being done today are just scratching that surface and I see more of that coming online in the next few years."

Lewis sees the largest EW market for the foreseeable future being retrofits for legacy platforms DOD cannot afford to replace: "As the U.S. goes forward, there will be more and more demand to do things with less and less. And the leverage of doing that in terms of retrofits will have a lot of benefits for the country as a whole."

Spectrum warfare

Rapid advances in technology have complicated the definition of EW. The Air Force uses spectrum warfare to bring together all elements of EW with cyber warfare, information operations and essential capabilities to enable a full range of electromagnetic operations-offensive and defensive-in A2/AD environments against all levels of adversaries.

The Army prefers cyber electromagnetic activities. According to recently revised Army Doctrine for Unified Land Operations,

CEMA involves "activities leveraged to seize, retain and exploit an advantage over adversaries and enemies in cyberspace and the electromagnetic spectrum, while simultaneously denying and degrading adversary and enemy use of the same and protecting the mission command system". Implementation is achieved through synchronization and integration of cyberspace operations, EW and electromagnetic spectrum operations (electromagnetic spectrum).

Terminology aside, nearly every aspect of command, control, communications, computers, intelligence, surveillance and reconnaissance (C4ISR) has (or is) a component of or dependent on 21st century EW.

Frequency-hopping radios and radar soon may be replaced by "cognitive" systems that don't rely on a set list of frequencies, but look for available "holes" throughout the full spectrum, jumping from one to the next on the fly. A primitive version of that is a smartphone that uses the best available way to connect, from nearby WiFi to 4G.

But control and unchallenged access to battlespace spectrum also is critical for navigation-from precision-guided munitions to logistics-semi-autonomous combat robots, field and battlespace medicine and more. And as spectrum becomes ever-more crucial to military and commercial communications and data transfer, two long-standing "laws" of technology continue to converge.

The more widely known Moore's Law, named for Intel co-founder Gordon Moore, states that CPU speeds double every two years (although purists note it is more accurate to say the number of transistors on an affordable CPU is what doubles).

The lesser known Cooper's Law, formulated by the inventor of the cell phone Martin Cooper, notes the number of conversations, whether voice or data, that theoretically can be conducted using a specific piece of useful radio spectrum has doubled every 30 months for more than a century. As a result, total spectrum allocation for personal communications alone has increased more than one trillion-fold in the last 90 years.

Increasingly competitive, congested and contested cyberspace and electromagnetic spectrum will be even more important as the

U.S. faces potential conflict with a near-peer adversary for the first time since World War II-and as CEMA capabilities spread and grow down to the level of individual terrorist cells, criminal organizations and Third World nations, none of whom could ever hope to survive a traditional engagement with the U.S.

The services' differing views of the involved technologies are more than semantic, they also are operational. The Navy sees EW as modern warfighting, the Air Force considers it an essential and integrated component to the success of A2/AD and air dominance, but the Army continues to view it as a support component, not warfighting.

"When you talk about maneuver commanders, the objective is to seize and secure terrain. The EW mission is to support that, but EW and cyber have separate roles to play. Cyber can and is moving into a major combat role; the EW role is to control the spectrum to allow the maneuver commander to achieve his goals," says the Army Cyber Center's Cantrell.

CEMA's Cullen agrees, adding those in combat are only interested in what works: "From a maneuver commander's perspective-infantry or armor-they don't care if it is EW or cyber or whatever. There are advantages and disadvantages to both EW effects, cyber effects and kinetic effects. The requirement is to figure out which is best in a given situation."

In April 2014, the Naval Air Warfare Center Weapons Division and the Association of Old Crows held the 43rd Electronic Warfare Symposium at Point Mugu, Calif., with the theme "Enabling Collaborative EW Through Innovation and Invention."

"Staying up-to-date in EW technology is essential to supporting the warfighter, said Dr. Ron Smiley, director of the EW/Combat Systems and Avionics departments at the Naval Air Systems Command at Patuxent River Naval Air Station, Md., told the conference. "Electronic warfare is changing, becoming more challenging and has continued to become a lot more esoteric, particularly with the convergence of EW and Cyber Warfare."

Rear Adm. Mark Darrah, commander of the Naval Air Warfare Center Aircraft Division, summarized the conference discussions with a view to potential enemy developments and the changing nature of U.S. technology development. "Unlike 20 years ago, our advisories are developing similar technologies that we are-and are doing it right now," he says. "The only way we will stay ahead of the threat of our enemies is to take paper ideas and give it to our people for trial-and-error until we succeed."

CONVERGENCE OF CYBERSPACE OPERATIONS AND ELECTRONIC WARFARE EFFECTS

Convergence is the foundry for new possibilities. Convergence of Cyberspace Operations (CO) and Electronic Warfare (EW) effects creates combined effects to achieve both offensive and defensive overmatch. Recently the US Air Force revealed the use of a modified EC-130 Compass Call aircraft to remotely attack enemy networks.The 24th Air Force commander, Major General Burke "Ed" Wilson, spoke of this capability enabling the ability to "touch a network that in most cases might be closed." While the need for convergence of cyberspace operations and electronic warfare is recognized within the Department of Defense (DoD), differences between how these two capabilities are trained, resourced, organized and employed combined with the significant functional level differences between the two have hindered efforts to converge their capabilities. A concerted effort must be undertaken at the both the Joint and Service levels to closely integrate CO with EW effects to achieve combined effects, enabling comprehensive shaping of the operational environment. The first step in this effort is for CO and EW professionals to commit themselves to professional self-development in their counterparts' field.

Description of Issue / Problem Statement

Describing the challenge of converging CO and EW effects requires first to define each and their interaction within the Open Systems Interconnection (OSI) model. The OSI model is a standard model to describe a seven-layer network protocol stack starting at the physical layer and ending at the application layer. Joint Publication 1-02, *Department of Defense Dictionary of Military and Associated Terms* defines cyberspace operations as "the employment of cyberspace capabilities where the primary purpose is to achieve objectives in or through cyberspace". JP 1-02 defines electronic warfare as "military action involving the use of electromagnetic and directed energy to control the electromagnetic spectrum or to attack the enemy". While the definitions have little in common, CO and EW are both based on three roughly similar pillars: attack, defense, and support/operations. For cyberspace operations, the pillars are defined as Offensive Cyber Operations (OCO), Defensive Cyber Operations (DCO) and DoD Information Network (DODIN) Operations. These mission categories align well with the electronic warfare missions of Electronic Attack (EA), Electronic Protection (EP) and Electronic Warfare Support (ES). OCO projects power "by the application of force in and through cyberspace", while EA involves the use of "EM energy, DE, or antiradiation weapons to attack personnel, facilities, or equipment with the intent of degrading, neutralizing, or destroying enemy combat capability."

DCO uses passive and active cyberspace capabilities to "protect data, networks, net-centric capabilities, and other designated systems," with EP being "actions taken to protect personnel, facilities, and equipment from any effects of friendly or enemy use of the electromagnetic spectrum that degrade, neutralize, or destroy friendly combat capability." DODIN Operations are actions taken to "design, build, configure, secure, operate, maintain, and sustain DoD communications systems and networks in a way that creates and preserves data availability, integrity, confidentiality, as well as user/entity authentication and non-repudiation", whereas ES is "actions tasked by, or under direct control of, an operational commander to search for, intercept, identify, and locate or localize sources of intentional and unintentional radiated electromagnetic energy for the purpose of immediate threat recognition, targeting, planning, and conduct of future operations."

CO and EW effects are likewise overlapped within the OSI model. Both CO and EW begin at Layer 1, the physical layer. A common misconception is that EW stops at Layer 1, but the integration of Internet Protocol (IP) into a wide range of communications systems enables intelligent jamming. In intelligent jamming, knowledge of the protocol is incorporated into the jamming technique.Solid understanding each of these specific areas and their overlap is critical to achieving capability convergence and the resulting combined CO and EW effects.

In *Convergence of Electronic Warfare and Computer Network Exploitation/Attacks Within the Radio Frequency Spectrum,* David Rohret and Abiud Jimenez, members of the Joint Information Operations Warfare Center (JIOWC) / Vulnerability Assessment Team (VAT), describe how the integration of IP capabilities in systems using Radio Frequency (RF) for communication provides attackers the ability to exploit systems on isolated networks. Unlike current cyber and EW protection teams, which are focused on vulnerabilities within their respective areas, adversaries are focused on achieving desired effects and end state goals.

This threat is heightened by oversights in software and communications system developers in recognizing vulnerabilities introduced during the integration of hardware and software. This paper covers three case studies based on actual vulnerability assessments highlighting these issues.

In the first case study, an IP over radio system developed to provide high bandwidth connections from an aerial platform to users on the ground was effectively disabled through the use of intelligent jamming. The IP over radio system was protected from traditional networks attacks through the use of a proprietary secure wireless protocol, but it proved highly vulnerable to center band frequency jamming at power levels so low, the denial of service was attributed to a system error instead of jamming. In the second case, OCO and EW capabilities were synchronized in a simulated attack against a satellite communication (SATCOM) network. OCO was used to gain access and enumerate the SATCOM network to identify the ground station, which was them jammed forcing the target to use alternate communications methods, thus providing potential new avenues of attack with their own vulnerabilities. In the third case study, a coordinated CO and EW attack on a sensor network enabled the mesh network to be severely degraded, preventing data from the sensors from being received without triggering an alert from a denial of service or jamming attack. These examples demonstrate the power of synergistic effects created through the convergence of CO and EW. Combined effects dramatically increase the difficulty for an enemy to mount an effective response as they struggle to identify the source of the attack.

Our adversaries will use every tool and combination thereof to achieve decisive effects on the battlefield. Prospective near-peer adversaries, Russia and China, understand the capability of converged CO and EW effects and have long standing doctrine integrating CO and EW under the umbrella of Information Warfare (IW). Although the definition of IW and the elements of IW differ between Russia and China, both are focused on achieving combined effects. While Russian definition of IW varies depending on the agency involved, it is roughly defined as an integrated system of system for "establishing control over other states' information resources ... disrupting ... information networks and communications systems, and developing information weapons." Russian IW includes elements of "intelligence and counterintelligence gathering, disinformation, use of EW systems, debilitation of communications and scrambling of enemy data, use of psychological pressure on the enemy, and destruction of enemy computer nets and software programs." The Chinese definition of IW is more vague, but generally emphasizes three pillars, psychological operations, denial and deception.Chinese IW includes elements of precision strike warfare to destroy enemy command and control facilities, EW to "dominate the spectrum while denying the enemy's effective use of electronic equipment", computer network warfare, which covers a wide spectrum of capabilities and psychological warfare and deception to influence behavior of targeted elements. The key takeaway is that both of these potential near-peer adversaries have integrated CO and EW capabilities to achieve combined IW effects. Given their interest and investment in asymmetric capabilities to overcome US military superiority and the DoD's reliance on the availability of the electromagnetic spectrum for command and control, the threat of combined CO and EW operations poses a significant threat.

While the Air Force, Marine Corps and Navy has well established EW career fields, organizations and training programs, the Army's Electronic Warfare branch, Career Management Field (CMF) 29 was established in 2012. The Army maintained communications electronic warfare battalions during the Cold War, but were disbanded in the 1990s, causing significant deficiencies in electronic warfare capabilities, which were grimly recognized during combat operations in Iraq and Afghanistan. With less than 1,000 officers, warrant officers and enlisted personnel, the EW career field has struggled with finding its role as combat deployments have significantly decreased. As a result, when not deployed, EW personnel are often assigned to other duties, resulting in EW is often derided as standing for "extra worker".Exacerbating this problem, the Army will not field a standard electronic warfare capability, with the Multifunctional Electronic Warfare (MFEW) program not slated to reach initial operating capability until 2023. Currently the Army electronic warfare capabilities are focused on countering remote controlled improvised explosive devices, but programs are in place to develop an integrated EW Planning and Management Tool (EWPMT) to provide commanders spectrum situational awareness and enable enhanced synchronization of EW capabilities.The Army's Cyber branch, CMF 17 is now responsible for the management of the Army's Electronic Warfare branch, CMF 29. The organization construct has the potential to spearhead CO and EW effects convergence within the DoD.

Recommendations

The Army should serve as a proving ground for CO and EW effects convergence due to several factors that minimize the friction to achieve effects convergence. These advantages include established doctrine converging CO and EW, unity of command at the force proponent level for CO and EW career fields and combined research and development efforts in these fields. In February 2014, the Army published FM 3-38 *Cyber Electromagnetic Activities*. This document provides doctrinal guidance and conducting cyber electromagnetic activities (CEMA) and the procedures and tactics for commanders and their staffs for planning, synchronizing and integrating CEMA. Due to the Army's recent creation of both the Electronic Warfare Branch (29) and Cyber Branch (17), it is in a unique position to develop the force structures, capabilities and tools for converged CO and EW operations and effects. Both branches also currently fall under the Cyber Center of Excellence, the force modernization proponent (FMP) for cyberspace operations, signal/communications networks and information services, and Electronic Warfare. Furthermore, a single organization, the Army's Intelligence and Information Warfare Directorate (I2WD) of the Communications-Electronic Research, Development and Engineering Center (CERDEC) is responsible for research and development of both offensive cyber operations and electronic warfare. While the Army has several advantages in being a proving ground for CO and EW effects convergence, it must leverage the knowledge and capabilities of the Air Force and Navy EW communities to tap into their wealth of experience. Lessons learned and successful pilot programs from the Army's efforts on CO and EW effects convergence can then be introduced to Air Force and Navy CO and EW communities to accelerate the introduction of new techniques and operating concepts.

Additionally each Service should embrace the Marine Corps approach towards integrating CO and EW effects. The Marine Corps approach for integrating CO and EW effects focuses on the creation of a Cyber Electronic Warfare Coordination Center (CEWCC). The CEWCC is placed within a Marine Air-Ground Task Force (MAGTF) to synchronize Spectrum Warfare (SW) with a "combined arms concept for the integration of cyberspace operations, electronic warfare (EW), signals intelligence (SIGINT), spectrum management operations, and technical Information operations with conventional fires and maneuver". The CEWCC is a distributed organization, which will include members and liaisons from the fields of information operations, electronic warfare, cyberspace operations and spectrum management. While still in development, the Marine Corps is aggressively developing the CEWCC concept with an interim publication and ongoing proof of concept within the 13th Marine Expeditionary Unit. The concept of SW, which focuses on the relationships within cyberspace and the electromagnetic spectrum, provides a good framework for the integration of cyberspace operations and electronic warfare.

Counterargument

Convergence of CO and EW effects will reduce the ability of commanders to employ offensive EW capabilities given national level approval is required to conduct OCO. In contrast, employment of offensive EW, or EA capabilities typically requires approval only at the operational or tactical level. Commanders with EA assets are able to rapidly impact an adversary's radio communications network through jamming of the links or use of directed energy weapons to destroy the transmitters. The use of OCO to produce the same effect of denying the enemy use of the radio communications network would require "careful planning, in-depth intelligence support, and interagency coordination" in addition to national level approval. Convergence of OCO and EA has the potential of denying commanders the use of an effective, rapidly employable capability by tying a capability that requires only tactical or operational level approval to one that requires national level approval.

Convergence of CO and EW effects will further limit the resources available for EW given the near insatiable demand for resources to develop OCO capabilities, conduct DCO and operate the DODIN. EW capabilities are employed primarily during Phase 2: Seize the Initiative of the continuum of military operations. Conversely CO are employed during all phases of the continuum of military operations, which helps account for the high level of resourcing invested in CO capabilities.

Given the Army's nascent CO and EW capabilities and experience, it is a poor choice to serve as a proving ground for CO and EW effects convergence. Even successful CO and EW effects convergence pilot programs in the Army will be difficult to transition to the Air Force and Navy with fundamentally different requirements for the employment of employment and desired effects of CO and EW effects. Additionally, given the current budget constrained environment and heightened threat level, resources should be focused on enhancing current capabilities instead of investing in unproven concepts.

3

Joint Information Warfare and the Information Age

INTRODUCTION

The passage of the Goldwater-Nichols Act in 1986 generated a new emphasis on "jointness". Current concepts of jointness and joint operations are defined as "activities, operations, organizations, etc., in which elements of more than one Service [emphasis added] of the same nation participate." The blending of the operations and capabilities of the military Services, however, is no longer sufficient for information warfare/information operations (IW/IO) and the needs of national security in the information age. The impacts and implications of the information revolution are so widespread that they necessitate a broader, more inclusive concept incorporating all of the various elements of national information power.

INNATE FEATURES OF INFORMATION WARFARE

While information warfare in the true sense has not yet arrived in the battlefield arena, the repeated live-troop maneuvers and simulated drills of the armies of Western nations such as the United States, as well as the Gulf War, have enabled us to determine certain innate features of information warfare:

- Battlefield transparency. While "battlefield fog" used to be a major problem troubling battlefield commanders, with digitized units, the battlefield is transparent. All belligerent troops will have the battlefield situation at their fingertips both day and night, and be able to see clearly on computer terminal display screens both their own and the enemy's positions, postures, concentrations, and movements. Sullivan says that the transparency of coming wars will be "a quantitative step higher than in the Gulf War."

- Battlefield transparency will be the result of digitized technology. Digitized technology can transmit battlefield intelligence to commanders quickly and accurately in a noiseless and graphics-plus-words form. Digitized cameras on reconnaissance planes can send, in 30 seconds, a 24-power photo that was shot in the morning to an operational command center as far as 315 km away. Frontline troops using digitized infrared sights can detect maneuvers by over 100 enemy tanks, immediately reporting them to their superiors with digitized information equipment. Digital compression technology can determine enemy detection distance, raising information processing capability, and transmitting intelligence in real time to all units (subunits), even to individual soldiers, for joint information sharing.
- Overall coordination. Overall coordination is another feature of information warfare. The building of the battlefield information superhighway will mean that all operational systems such as combat forces, combat support units, and combat logistics support units, as well as all operational functions such as battlefield intelligence, command, control, communications, and assaults, will be linked into an organic whole. Coordinated actions by all units of this whole can raise combat effectiveness. For instance, coordinated firepower can raise fire assault effectiveness. Air and land sensors detect enemy target activity, which is immediately displayed on screens at the support arm operational center, with the target positioning system accurately converting enemy target coordinates; the target assignment system then assigns suitable targets to the weapons-launching platforms (such as cannons, helicopters, and tanks) that are most suited to attack.

- Operations in real time. Real time is defined as the time of dealing with a certain event being almost the same as the real time of the occurrence of the event. Real-time operations mean immediate responses to all events that occur on the battlefield between ourselves and the enemy and involves the taking of countermeasures such as timely target detection, timely command, timely mobility, real-time strikes, and real-time support. The advantage of this is that missions that used to be hours or even longer can now be completed in minutes or even seconds, making decisionmaking and the course of battle nearly simultaneous.
- Precision strike. Long-range precision strikes without collateral damage will become the essential fire-assault form of future information warfare, making carpet bombing and area fire part of history. Future warfare will be as accurate, clean, and neat as a scalpel cutting out a brain tumor, because future wars will use smart weapons on a large scale. Such weapons include guided bombs, guided shells, guided shrapnel, cruise missiles, no-tip guided missiles, and antiradiation missiles. Their sensors will be capable of capturing all useable direct or indirect target information, such as sound waves, electric waves, visible light, infrared waves, lasers, and even odors and gasses, which information computers will be able to differentiate and analyze. Such smart ammunition not only can hit targets 100 percent of the time, but can also hit predetermined target positions. To conduct and win information warfare, two major supports will be needed.

A Digitized Battlefield

A digitized battlefield is a composite network system covering the whole operational space. It is made up of a communications system, a command and control system, an intelligence transmission system, a computerized battlefield database, and user terminals, all of which can provide users with large amounts of operation-related information in real time or nearly real time. This network system's function is to use information technology to acquire, exchange, and use digitized information in real time, promptly meeting the information demand of commanders, combat personnel, and combat support personnel, so that they can clearly and accurately grasp all battlefield conditions needed to draw up and apply operational plans. This system can transmit information such as voice, graphics, text, and data, and can also provide users with a battlefield image portrayed by a common database and the supreme battlefield command knowledge-base (including substance such as one's own posture, the enemy's posture, combat readiness, logistics conditions, and operating environment).

This picture is dynamic, changing with the movements of both combatants and changes in terrain and weather. A digitized battlefield is a prerequisite for information warfare. The establishment of a digitized battlefield has many advantages. For instance, information sharing clarifies the position of the enemy and one's own units, sharply lowering accidental injuries; it enables battlefield commanders to amass key units at crucial sites at critical times; it can effectively coordinate short-distance, in-depth, and rear operations, providing intelligence support for all-out, in-depth, simultaneous offensive operations. As all come to know the battlefield conditions, subordinate commanders can bring their initiative into play, acting promptly at their own discretion in line with their superiors' intentions; it makes logistics support "very accurate," for such activities as material provision variety and quantity "accuracy," logistics support provision-time "accuracy," and wounded treatment "timely accuracy."

The establishment of a digitized battlefield is a sort of systems engineering. Many U.S. military specialists claim that this project is more challenging than the Manhattan Project. To carry out this project, the United States is taking many steps.

In line with Clinton's Presidential Order #29 issued in September 1994, the U.S. Defense Department has set up the National Security Policy Commission and the National Information System Security Commission. The former is charged with formulating military security policy and digitized battlefield establishment principles, while the latter is responsible for controlling the security and secrecy of classified and sensitive information on the military information superhighway and the digitized battlefield. The U.S. Army set up in January 1994 the Army Digitized Special Taskforce under the direct leadership of the Army's first deputy chief of staff. In June 1994, that taskforce was expanded into the Army Digitized Office, and charged with the design and establishment of the digitized army battlefield. In July 1994, the U.S. Navy set up the Theatre of Operations Information Warfare Center; in January 1995, it established the Fleet Information Warfare Center. Their joint responsibilities are to study and design the technology and software needed for the digitized naval battlefield. The U.S. Air Force Information Warfare Center was set up in October 1993, and charged with establishing a digitized air battlefield.

To build a digitized land, sea, and air battlefield, the computer system structures, operating programs, program design languages, software applications, database languages, and communications rules of all information systems must be standardized and interchangeable throughout all branches of the military. Thus the U.S. military is now pursuing two information resource standardization plans: 1) the all-service command, control, communications, computer, and intelligence system standardization plan, which will set up a global military information database and a global joint network system, thus deploying throughout the world global information sharing for the U.S. military; and 2) the defense information control standardization plan, which is aimed at upgrading the interchangeable software technology of all Defense Department information systems, to eventually make information control and usage standardized and interchangeable.

To achieve battlefield digitization for all arms of the service, the U.S. military is now pursuing a diversified C&C digitized joint-network plan. For instance, the U.S. Army has seven plans:

- The "composite unit C&C, a high-tech demonstration" plan aimed at improving and developing the computer assisted C&C system
- The "joint ground station" plan to provide rapid operational intelligence information to brigade commanders

- The "global network grid" plan to bring many combat units into a single working network
- The "survival adaptation system demonstration" plan that uses multi-media technology to transmit information such as voice, graphics, and data to combat troops
- The "21st century ground warrior" plan to achieve a free battlefield dialogue between man and machine
- The "brigade and below unit (subunit) C&C plan" to provide battlefield information to units (subunits) at the brigade level and below
- The "battlefield combat friend and foe recognition demonstration" plan.

An Informationized Military

The second major support for information warfare [IW] is an informationized military. While many developed Western nations are now considering the establishment of technology-intensive informationized armies, the United States is the only one that has drawn up and started to implement plans for an informationized military establishment.

An informationized army is a brand-new "information-based" military category, with its combat theory, system establishment, personnel quality, and weaponry being completely suited to IW needs. The U.S. informationized military establishment plans are in two stages, which are estimated to be completed by the mid-21st century.

In the first stage, the U.S. Army will first be digitized. While digitized units will be essentially the same in authorized strength and structure as units with ordinary equipment, they will be units with digitized communications technology; integrated command, control, communications, and intelligence; smart weaponry; and networking of all operating systems. The major signs that a unit is digitized will be that its main outfits will be equipped with digitized communications equipment, second-generation forward-looking radar, identification friend-and-foe [IFF] equipment, and the global positioning system [GPS]. Such equipment will include M1A2 tanks, M2A2 fire support vehicles, M2A3 fighting vehicles,

Black Eagle command helicopters, Apache attack choppers, Kiowa Brave reconnaissance choppers, M109A6 Warrior self-propelled guns, and M106A2 mortars. The U.S. Army now has a digitized battalion and will have established a digitized army by 1999, with all Army units digitized by 2010.

To test the combat capability of digitized units, the U.S. Army has conducted repeated simulated tests and live-troop confrontation exercises between digitized task forces and nondigitized units. The simulated tests show that digitized technology can shorten the time of choppers going into action from 26 minutes to 18 minutes, while raising the hit rate of antitank missiles from 55 percent to 90 percent. The live-troop exercises show that using conventional communications means to send on-site reports to battalion headquarters takes 9 minutes, while digitized communications means takes only 5 minutes; that the repetition rate is 30 percent for (telegram) text sent by conventional means, but only 4 percent for that sent by digitized means; and that the completion rate of on-site reports is only 22 percent by phone, but as high as 98 percent by digitized means. Through repeated demonstrations the U.S. Army has reached the initial conclusion that "digitized units have enormous combat potential," with their combat effectiveness being "about three times that of ordinary units."

In the second stage, the U.S. Army will grow more informationized on that digitized foundation, as well as build the entire U.S. military, including the Navy and Air Force, into a fully informationized force. After 2010, the U.S. Army will probably be the first to draw up "IW theory," as well as act in line with that theory to reform its system establishment, carry out military training, and develop weaponry, to informationize its units. For two reasons this will probably take about three decades, with completion by 2040:

- The shortage of money for military expenditures dictates that, only once its key combat equipment is digitized, can its related combat support and combat logistics support equipment be gradually digitized. Also, it will have to develop a batch of new smart weapons. So projected from an arms development cycle of about 15 years, it is estimated that its equipment will be completely informationized by 2030.

- The conversion of a military establishment from one structure to another that can operate effectively will take roughly two decades. The U.S. military that can begin to adjust its troop structure after 2010 will still need around two decades to establish the mechanisms suited to fight an information war. Also, as weaponry informationization and military establishment reform cannot be completely synchronous, with an approximate time lag of at least a decade, it is projected that the U.S. Army will be fully informationized only by 2040. The U.S. Navy and Air Force are now also informationizing. By about 2040, once all services are informationized, it will still take more than a decade to get the entire military into a digitized joint network. So it is obvious that by mid-century, the United States probably will have built the world's first completely smart military.

While IW has not yet occurred or at most has only started to show up, as it is an exceptional and new form of warfare with milestone significance, it will have an enormous impact on all aspects of the military arena.

The IW Impact on Combat Concepts

The IW proposition will have an impact on many aspects of combat concepts:

- It will make the rivalry over "information dominance" particularly intense. Certain experts note, "information dominance can be defined most easily and accurately as knowing all enemy information, while keeping the enemy from learning one's own." In future wars, most participating troops in most situations will be dealing not with material, but rather with information. The formation and development of troop combat effectiveness will rely mainly on information collection, processing, transmission, control, and usage. A superior force that loses "information dominance" will be passive, beaten, and in trouble, while an inferior one that seizes the information advantage will be able to win the battlefield initiative. As future combat actions will all be dependent and focused on information, the struggle to wrest information dominance will permeate everything and will be exceptionally fierce and intense.

- It will expand the implications of warfare. This will be manifested mainly in two areas. 1) It will make it harder to win wars. In the agricultural age, it was necessary only to exterminate the enemy's armed forces to win the war. In the industrial age, in addition to wiping out the enemy country's military, it has also been necessary to destroy its military-industrial base. However, in the information age, it will be necessary not only to eliminate the enemy country's war making "material base," but also to control and destroy the enemy's information systems, which will be the primary assault targets. 2) It will expand the limits of war into outer space. That is because the key IW systems space monitoring, positioning, guidance, and communications systems will all be deployed there.
- It will shorten the time of battle. The institution of IW will shorten future wars for two reasons: 1) On one hand, attack means will be highly precise, with the strike targets also being key enemy military positions such as "brain centers," which can be forced to submit very quickly. 2) On the other, in the information age as compared to the industrial age, the combat objectives pursued by both belligerents will be more limited, not total surrender or extermination of the other side, but rather limited political objectives.
- It will make combat more integrated. As information will flow more quickly and not be subject to service branch or time-space limitations, future wars are going to be unprecedentedly integrated.

-Land, sea, air, and space warfare will be highly integrated, which will be the case not only in large-scale wars, but also in small-scale armed conflicts. - The combat lines among service arms will be hard to distinguish. For instance, the weapons that destroy enemy tanks may not be one's own [friendly] tanks, but rather smart missiles fired from friendly naval submarines. -War zone combat operations will be integrated. As information-age units will have real-time information for rapid mobility both day and night, "the decentralized campaigns developed in the industrial age will no longer exist, being replaced by integrated combat operations in the entire theatre of operations." -The lines among the strategic, campaign, and tactical levels will be blurred. As smart weapons will provide effective means of meeting combat objectives, it will be possible at times to meet strategic and campaign objectives without losing large units.

- It will change the substance of force concentrations. As the use of precision-strike and stealth weapons will make it possible for force concentrations to meet campaign and even strategic objectives, the force-concentration priority will change from the tactical to the campaign and strategic level. A concentration of mostly personnel will change to a concentration of mainly firepower and information, and a concentration of mostly troop and weapons quantity will change to mainly quality. Force concentrations will occur faster, more precisely, and more often during operations.

THE IW IMPACT ON MILITARY ORGANIZATIONAL STRUCTURE

Wars during the industrial age have had military structures determined by the "firepower casualty system" base, but wars in the information age will require an "information-based" troop organization. With a changed base, the military system establishment will also be bound to change significantly.

Alvin Toffler noted recently that in the information age, "as the winning of wars will rely on military quality, not quantity, the military will shrink in size." Therefore IW in a certain sense is "precision warfare," with objectives achievable without using large amounts of troops or arms.

The military makeup will change. To adapt to IW needs, changes in military makeup will experience the following trends:

In the balance of army, naval and air force might, the ratio of army troops will decline, while that of naval and air force troops will grow; in support units, technical support will grow, while logistics support will decline; in the officer-to-men ration, there will be more officers and less men; in the officer makeup, there will be more technical officers and less commanding and ordinary staff officers. Also, there are likely to be new service arms such as a space force and computer soldiers.

The unit establishment will tend to be smaller, more integrated, and more multifunctional. While Western nations have not yet determined the IW unit establishment, they hold that these units will have the following features: "The best combination of men and machines," with quality personnel and high-tech arms both being as efficient as possible; flexible mobility suited to command, control, and information flow; light equipment that is easy to deploy; high combat effectiveness, fewer command levels, multifunctional commanders, and crack commanding organs.

There are two implications for smaller units. 1) Unit might at all levels will be smaller. For instance, U.S. Army divisions will be cut from 18,000 to 12,000 troops each, with British and French Army divisions likely to be reduced from 12,000 to under 10,000 troops each; 2) The status and role of units at all levels will be obviously higher. For instance, the U.S. military plans to raise the role of the army in campaign planning to the group army level, replacing the division with the brigade as the basic tactical operations unit equipped with all sorts of combat and support platoons. The Russian military is also planning to institute an "army brigade system." The factors in the appearance of such a situation include higher-quality officers and men, weaponry advances, and robot-equipped units.

Unit integration means that composite units will reach new heights, with a transition from composite service arms to composite armed forces. For instance, the U.S. military is considering the establishment of two units, one being a composite army-air force unit the "flying tank" or "air mechanized unit," and the other a land, sea and air "joint task force." This latter unit will be made up of an army brigade task force, an air force fighter squadron, a naval fleet unit, and a marine expedition platoon, suited to countering low-force conflicts and breakouts overseas.

Multifunctional units will mean that units at all levels will have to fulfill diverse combat missions in wars on all combat terms and all degrees of force, including "noncombat operations." Meanwhile, army, navy, and air force combat units are also likely to break the traditional service arm operating limits, and perform the combat operations of other service arms. For instance, land units will fight naval and air battles, with naval and air force units fighting land battles. Therefore, some Western military experts predict that as units diversify, unit establishment categories will decrease.

The IW Impact on Organizational Structure

Because of the "effects" of IW and military spending shortages, developed nations are adopting an equipment establishment policy of "more research and new technology, and less production and arms purchases." To implement this policy, they are taking three steps:

- Terminating and adjusting preset unit development projects and purchase plans. For instance, the United States has eliminated over 150 arms production plans, and delayed over 20 equipment purchase plans; Germany has eliminated and postponed over 40 arms purchase plans.
- Increasing their research input. In the past decade, the defense research outlays of Japan, the United States, France, and Germany have increased, respectively, by 120 percent, 67 percent, 66 percent, and 56 percent. Most of this outlay is going to develop the "crucial technologies" of smart ammunition, smart weapons platforms, and the C3I system.
- Upgrading their existing weapons. While the Western nations are slowing their rate of production of new weapons, they are paying more attention to the use of electronic information technology to modernize and upgrade their existing equipment. For instance, the U.S. Air force is planning to upgrade its B-52 bombers by outfitting them with high-tech systems such as new radar,

global positioning systems, and cruise missile launching units, to keep them in service until the year 2000.

To be able to fight IW in the next century, developed nations such as the United States will place priority on the development of equipment such as the C4I system (command, control, communications, computers, and intelligence system), personal digitized equipment, and stealth weapons.

THE SERVICES AND INFORMATION WARFARE

All of the Services are responding in some manner to the challenges of the information age and the imperatives of information warfare. The Marines, while uncertain about the broader theories of IW, are deeply involved in exploring the means by which they can attain "command dominance" over their adversaries. While acknowledging and leveraging the recent dramatic technological advances in information and communication systems, the Marines' focus is clearly on the human dimension of conflict, with the objective of maximizing human and operational flexibility instead of relying on technology to minimize friction.

The Army, also cautious about the broader theories of IO, has no such qualms about the technological opportunities of the future, and the Army's vision for the next century, incorporated in "Force XXI" and based on digitization of the battlefield, is heavily, perhaps critically, dependent on the technologies of the information age. The Army is investigating the means and implications of these concepts and capabilities, and its Land Information Warfare Activity (LIWA), located at Fort Belvoir and associated with its Intelligence and Security Command (INSCOM), is one of the Army's focal points for this effort.

Another is its Training and Doctrine Command (TRADOC) at Fort Monroe, which recently issued the Army's first doctrinal manual in this area, Field Manual (FM) 100-6, "Information Operations." (The exact meaning of "information operations" varies according to the user, and while the term is used by DOD, the Army, and the Air Force, it means something different to all three.) The Navy has possibly more personnel engaged in "nuts and bolts" IW/IO than any other Service and has (perhaps more than any other Service) for decades practiced some of the elements of Command and Control Warfare (C2W), defined as "the military strategy that implements information warfare on the battlefield." While still exploring the broader ramifications of IO, the Navy is exercising and practicing IW/C2W increasingly in its daily operations. While the Naval Information Warfare Activity (NIWA) at Fort Meade is a geographical reflection of the Navy's long history of cryptology, the Fleet Information Warfare Center (FIWC) at Little Creek Amphibious Base near Norfolk and Atlantic Fleet HQ, and its several branches around the country, are heavily involved in developing and refining concepts for fleet IW/C2W operations.

The Air Force has taken dramatic steps, both organizationally and doctrinally, to move into information age warfare. In 1993 the Air Force established its Information Warfare Center around what had been its Electronic Warfare Center, and the newly-activated 609th IW Squadron is the first unit dedicated to an operational IW mission. The Air Force's white paper "Cornerstones of IW", published over the signatures of Dr. Sheila Widnall, Secretary of the Air Force, and General Ron Fogleman, Chief of Staff, expresses the broadest view of IW of any of the Services, stating information is a "realm" to be dominated in a manner alike to air or space. Evolving doctrinal concepts speak to the need to integrate Air Force operations across three realms-air, space and information-in order to attain superiority and freedom of action in each. Joint information warfare involves integrating and coordinating IW across the doctrinal, organizational, and conceptual differences of the four Services.

IW in the Department of Defense

Any discussion of IW that does not take into account the capabilities, responsibilities, and operations of a myriad of DOD organizations and agencies apart and aside from the four Services, however, is incomplete. The most immediately apparent are those that respond directly to the Chairman of the Joint Chiefs of Staff or through the Joint Staff, or are in the direct chain of operational command through the Unified Commands ("theatre CINCs").

The CINCs are the most obvious players, because they are charged with the responsibility of planning for and conducting IW, and the Chairman issued detailed guidance in the early 1996 issue of CJCS Instruction 3210.1, "Joint IW Policy."

The Unified Commands are exploring means to integrate information warfare into their plans and operations; indeed, some see it as a centerpiece of their future mission. The Unified Commands are jointness personified, as is the organization charged with supporting their IW/C2W efforts, the Joint C2W Center (JC2WC, or "jake-wick"), collocated with the Air Force Information Warfare Center at Kelly AFB. Information warfare in the real world simply is not possible without these elements of the joint force. Other members of the joint community also contribute to our IW capability. The Joint Warfighting Analysis Center, Joint Doctrine Center, and Joint Warfighting Center, for example, all have a role in shaping our IW capability, as do the elements of the Joint Staff such as J-6 or J-3, which serves as the OPR for joint IW/IO matters.

However, several DOD organizations outside of the JCS structure are also critical to our national IW/IO capability. The Defense Information Services Agency(DISA) manages DOD communications systems and is critical in the effort to provide information assurance and security to DOD communications. DISA, through the National Communications System (NCS), provides the DOD's interface with the National Strategic Telecommunications Advisory Council (NSTAC), which is comprised of the chief executives of the nation's largest telecommunications firms who provide the President with strategic advice on matters relating to telematics (the marriage of telecommunications and computer networks) and information policy. The Defense Intelligence Agency is the internal DOD focal point for intelligence matters relating to IW, while the National Security Agency is a key player in the effort to analyze the threat and provide information security and defensive IW/IO. Any discussion of national information power and security must take into account the responsibilities and capabilities of these DOD agencies. No discussion of "joint IW" would be complete without them. A comprehensive approach to joint IW, therefore, requires coordinating the activities and policies of several Joint and DOD elements as well as the Services.

IW in the Federal Government

But, the new paradigm of information warfare is unsettling for traditional DOD warriors, because from a national security perspective several other elements of the federal government are crucially important to the use of information for national security, the development of national information power, and the conduct of IW in its broadest sense. The Central Intelligence Agency is the focal point for national security intelligence. This not only includes potential IW/IO threats to national capabilities, systems and infrastructures but also the explosively expanding world of "open source intelligence", and the CIA is wisely and aggressively looking at ways to incorporate this new and technologically-driven source of information into its processes and databases. Another key provider of American information power is the United States Information Agency (USIA), and although its staffers would bristle if told they were involved in IW, the use of information as a weapon in the "contest of ideas" and the worldwide nurturing of democracy clearly fits into a larger and more inclusive view of IW.

One might wonder what role the Justice Department has in IW, but Justice is one of the core members of the President's Commission on Critical Infrastructure Protection, established in mid-1996 with President Clinton's Executive Order 13010, and the FBI is conducting an ever-increasing number of investigations into computer crime and cybernetic espionage. The Bureau has an active program underway in computer and telecommunications security. If a DOD or other federal computer system suffers a break-in or intrusion, the FBI will almost certainly be one of the first agencies called. Another organization that at first glance might seem miscast in the IW arena is the Secret Service, but one of their critical responsibilities is security of the currency, which tasks them with protecting the electronic funds transfer systems upon which our national economy is becoming increasingly dependent. The Commerce Department's *Office of Export Control and National Institute for Standards and Technology (NIST),* and the President's Office of Scientific and Technology Policy (an autonomous element not associated with a Cabinet office), and the Office of Management and Budget are involved with issues such as electronic data encryption or national information infrastructure policy. These might not seem like national security issues to a traditional warrior, but similar issues are becoming increasingly important to areas such as technology exports, terrorism, and the war on drugs, all of which have some degree of current military interest or involvement. Most other federal agencies-*Energy, FEMA, Transportation,* and more-also increasingly rely on the smooth and uninterrupted flow of electronic digital information to carry out their functions and thus have interest and involvement in national information power. Thus, the paradigm of joint IW/IO must incorporate not only the Services but the Joint, DOD, and Federal communities as well.

National Information Power

The paradigm of joint information power has a broad and troubling perspective for the traditional concept of "jointness". The "defense" of cyberspace (that place where computers and electronic telecommunications systems connect and interact, a field of study known as "telematics") is being waged in part by entities such as the computer emergency response teams (CERTs) at universities such as Purdue or Carnegie Mellon. Information age "warriors" are trained not by military drill instructors but by computer science departments around the country. Educational organizations such as the *National Computer Security Association and the Infosec Institute* also play a role. Myriad public interest groups represent all points of the political and social compass, from the National Military Intelligence Association and the Armed Forces Communications & Electronics Association, to the Center for Democracy and Technology, and the Electronic Frontier Foundation. They all help shape and set the political terrain and social context for the ongoing evolution of information age security issues.

Finally, and certainly not least, there is the commercial sector, because the issues involved in information age security would be meaningless without the activities, advances, and involvement of Microsoft, AT&T, NASDAQ, Citibank, etc. The information revolution is, at heart, not a military revolution but a commercial, cultural and technological one, albeit with extremely important impact on and implications for the uniformed military. Neither the Services nor DOD are leading this revolution; rather they are running fast to merely stay abreast of the changes in technology and society.

Summary

National security in the information age and the development and exercise of the information component of national power requires a new paradigm of jointness that incorporates and synchronizes the policies and activities of all the players in the information realm. The development and exercise of national information power spans the organizational spectrum from the members in a military IW unit to the leadership of the largest information-related corporations and commercial entities. Although the DOD cannot direct these widespread activities, the paradigm of Joint IW/IO must of necessity encompass military, governmental, and private sector organizations and actions. This will require changes, both organizational and cultural, that will allow discussion and coordination of activities, even if the coordination is informal and non-directive. Perhaps the recent formation of the President's *Commission on Critical Infrastructure Protection* presents a baseline model for the integration of federal and private sector concepts and activities. Within the military Services, doctrines for IW/IO must take into account the dual nature of information power and help to set a mindset that sees the civil sector as a partner in the new paradigm of information age jointness. Without such a paradigm, information age national security increasingly will become a chimera towards which we will strive but find unattainable.

JOINT INFORMATION OPERATIONS WARFARE CENTER

The Joint Information Operations Warfare Center (JIOWC) supports the Joint Staff in improving DOD ability to meet combatant command information-related requirements, improve development of information-related capabilities, and ensure operational integration and coherence across combatant commands and other DOD activities.

IO involves The integrated employment, during military operations, of information-related capabilities in concert with other lines of operation to influence, disrupt, corrupt, or usurp the decision-making of adversaries and potential adversaries while protecting our own.

They apply across all phases of an operation, the range of military operations, and at every level of war. They are a critical factor in the joint force commander's capability to achieve and sustain the level of information superiority required for decisive joint operations.

Located at Lackland AFB, Texas, the JIOWC's mission is to assist in planning, coordinating and executing information operations. The center deploys information operations planning teams worldwide at a moment's notice to deliver tailored, highly skilled support and sophisticated models and simulations to joint commanders, joint task forces and the Joint Staff.

Direct support is provided to unified commands, joint task forces, functional and service components, and subordinate combat commanders. Support is also provided to the Office of the Secretary of Defense, the Joint Staff, the services and other government agencies. The JIOWC has a balanced mixture of personnel from all four military services, the civil service and three allied nations.

History

The Joint Electronic Warfare Center (JEWC) was established by the Secretary of Defense in October 1980 and reported to the Joint Staff. In September 1994, the JEWC'S mission was expanded and the organization was renamed the Joint Command and Control Warfare Center (JC2WC). In 1998, as a result of the Defense Reform Initiative (DRI), the JC2WC was realigned from the Joint Staff to US Atlantic Command. Further expansion of the JC2WC mission resulted in redesignation as the Joint Information Operations Center (JIOC). In October 1999, the JIOC was realigned as a subordinate command of USSPACECOM. In conjunction with the 1 October 2002 transition of USSPACECOM to USSTRATCOM, the JIOC was realigned as a subordinate command to USSTRATCOM. In 2006 the JIOC was redesignated the Joint Information Operations Warfare Command with a mission focused on operational IO planning and operations.

From the establishment of the JEWC, the Commander of AFISRA also held the position of JIOWC director. In 2008, the AFISRA commander,Maj Gen Koziol realized that the AFISRA commander could not give the attention the JIOWC needed while also commanding AFISRA.

As such, he proposed that the positions be severed and the JIOWC be led by a Senior Executive Service civilian. This occurred when Gen Koziol departed in February 2009 and the JIOWC changed from a command to a center. On 1 October 2011, the JIOWC was chartered as a Chairman's Controlled Activity aligned under the Joint Staff. The JIOWC Director reports to Joint Staff J3, through the Deputy Director Global Operations, J39 (DDGO).

JIOWC support to the warfighter: JIOWC has provided direct support to CCMDs and Joint Force Commands and involvement in numerous operations since the early 80s: Operation URGENT FURY - Grenada (1983), Operation ELDORADO CANYON - Libya (1986), Operation JUST CAUSE - Panama (1989), Operations DESERT SHIELD and DESERT STORM, Balkans (1992), Kosovo (1998), Operations NOBLE ANVIL - Yugoslavia (1999) and VALIANT RETURN - EP-3 (2001), ENDURING FREEDOM and NOBLE EAGLE, Operation ENDURING FREEDOM - Afghanistan (2001–Present), Operation ENDURING FREEDOM - Philippines (2002), Multi-Force Iraq (2003-2011), Indonesia Tsunami (2004), and Hurricane Katrina relief (2005), Haiti Humanitarian Assistance and Disaster Relief (2010). JIOWC led the creation of the Joint Publication 3-13 series (Information Operations Doctrine), provided IO exercise development and support evaluation, maintenance of OPSEC programs with assistance in programmatic setup, evaluation and training of forces.

Additionally, JIOWC provides IO professionals with initial training by conducting the Joint Information Operations Orientation Course. Finally, JIOWC provides trans-regional, cross-AOR, SME support and Information Operations Intelligence Integration.

IMPACTS OF INFORMATION AGE TECHNOLOGIES

To understand the future one needs to develop at least a broad conceptual understanding of the nature of the impacts that these technologies are likely to have. The impacts that these technologies are projected to have can be grouped into the following six areas.

First, the speed at which information can be transmitted, managed, manipulated, and interpreted will increase significantly. Information flows within and between organizations and among organizations and international actors will also accelerate, although at differing rates depending upon a host of factors. Increased speed will matter more for some uses than for others, and some international actors will benefit more from more rapid information flows than will others. But in general, the increased speed of information flow will increase the tempo of interactions within and between international actors.

Second, the capacity to transmit information will also increase significantly. Again, increased capacity will become available at different rates to different international actors. As with increased speed, greater information and communication capacity will benefit some organizations and international actors more than others. Here, however, the point to stress is that for many international actors, the ability to transmit and interpret greater amounts of information will mean that decision makers could have a greatly enhanced picture of the world, themselves, and others upon which to base their decisions.

Third, Information Age technologies will enhance the flexibility of information flows. Those needing information will be able to reach out and get it from more sources. Those needing to communicate with someone will find it ever more easy to do so quickly and directly. Put differently, these technologies will decrease the location-dependence of information and communication transactions. This greater flexibility will be available to some more quickly than to others, will matter more for some than for others, and will be embraced more quickly by some than by others.

Fourth, these technologies will provide more and more individuals greater access to more and more people, organizations, and information than ever before. This, some observers have argued, will lead to the democratization of information and communication flows throughout the world, that is, a decreased ability of a few (e.g. governments, businesses, and the other "haves") to dominate information and communication channels. This will free information from the hierarchy, or in the case of the military, from the chain of command. Although this may be true, improved access will not occur—or in some cases, be permitted—at the organizations, societies, and international actors.

None of these anticipated impacts means that time, distance, or location no longer matter—they still do. Indeed, as pointed out several times above, Information Age technologies will be absorbed, diffused, and operationalized by different international actors in different ways and at different speeds. This will lead to different types and rates of change in different international actors. Factors that will influence the way and rate in which advanced technologies will be absorbed, diffused, and operationalized include but are not limited to:

1. purchase and upkeep cost;
2. age and utility of in-place technology;
3. an actor's social and cultural receptivity to new technology;
4. degree of insularity within an actor;
5. level and reliability of an actor's human, technical, and economic support infrastructures;
6. level and strength of traditional values and outlooks within an actor;
7. levels of concern over sovereignty on the part of states, and over control of decision-making processes on the part of the actors; and
8. many political, social, and economic factors idiosyncratic to each actor and therefore impossible to detail.

Despite these constraints on adoption, Information Age technologies are indeed lessening the role that time, distance, and location play in human interactions. It is also noteworthy—and fraught with implications for national security—that this process is uneven and will create new "gaps" and a new power relationship among players on the world stage.

INFORMATION AGE

The Information Age (also known as the Computer Age, Digital Age, or New Media Age) is a period in human history characterized by the shift from traditional industry that theIndustrial Revolution brought through industrialization, to an economy based on information computerization. The onset of the Information Age is associated with the Digital Revolution, just as the Industrial Revolution marked the onset of the Industrial Age.

During the information age, the phenomenon is that the digital industry creates a knowledge-based society surrounded by a high-tech global economy that spans over its influence on how the manufacturing throughput and the service sector operate in an efficient and convenient way. In a commercialized society, the information industry is able to allow individuals to explore their personalized needs, therefore simplifying the procedure of making decisions for transactions and significantly lowering costs for both the producers and buyers. This is accepted overwhelmingly by participants throughout the entire economic activities for efficacypurposes, and new economic incentives would then be indigenously encouraged, such as theknowledge economy.

The Information Age formed by capitalizing on computer microminiaturization advances.This evolution of technology in daily life and social organization has led to the fact that the modernization of information and communication processes has become the driving force of social evolution.

Internet

The Internet was conceived as a fail-proof network that could connect computers together and be resistant to any single point of failure. It is said that the Internet cannot be totally destroyed in one event, and if large areas are disabled, the information is easily rerouted. It was created mainly by DARPA on work carried out by British scientists like Donald Davies; its initial software applications were e-mail and computer file transfer.

Though the Internet itself has existed since 1969, it was with the invention of the World Wide Web in 1989 by British scientist Tim Berners-Lee and its introduction in 1991 that the Internet became an easily accessible network. The Internet is now a global platform for accelerating the flow of information and is pushing many, if not most, older forms of media into obsolescence.

PROGRESSION

Library Expansion

Library expansion was calculated in 1945 by Fremont Rider to double in capacity every 16 years, if sufficient space were made available.He advocated replacing bulky, decaying printed works with miniaturized microform analog photographs, which could be duplicated on-demand for library patrons or other institutions. He did not foresee the digital technology that would follow decades later to replace analog microform with digital imaging, storage, and transmission mediums. Automated, potentially lossless digital technologies allowed vast increases in the rapidity of information growth. Moore's law, which was formulated around 1965, calculated that the number of transistors in a dense integrated circuit doubles approximately every two years.

The proliferation of the smaller and less expensive personal computers and improvements in computing power by the early 1980s resulted in a sudden access to and ability to share and store information for increasing numbers of workers. Connectivity between computers within companies led to the ability of workers at different levels to access greater amounts of information.

Information Storage

The world's technological capacity to store information grew from 2.6 (optimally compressed) exabytes in 1986 to 15.8 in 1993, over 54.5 in 2000, and to 295 (optimally compressed) exabytes in 2007. This is the informational equivalent to less than one 730-MB CD-ROM per person in 1986 (539 MB per person), roughly 4 CD-

ROM per person of 1993, 12 CD-ROM per person in the year 2000, and almost 61 CD-ROM per person in 2007.

Information Transmission

The world's technological capacity to receive information through one-way broadcast networks was 432 exabytes of (optimally compressed) information in 1986, 715 (optimally compressed) exabytes in 1993, 1.2 (optimally compressed) zettabytes in 2000, and 1.9 zettabytes in 2007 (this is the information equivalent of 174 newspapers per person per day). The world's effective capacity to exchange information through two-way telecommunication networks was 281 petabytes of (optimally compressed) information in 1986, 471 petabytes in 1993, 2.2 (optimally compressed) exabytes in 2000, and 65 (optimally compressed) exabytes in 2007 (this is the information equivalent of 6 newspapers per person per day). In the 1990s, the spread of the Internet caused a sudden leap in access to and ability to share information in businesses and homes globally. Technology was developing so quickly that a computer costing $3000 in 1997 would cost $2000 two years later and $1000 the following year.

Computation

The world's technological capacity to compute information with humanly guided general-purpose computers grew from 3.0×10^8 MIPS in 1986, to 4.4×10^9 MIPS in 1993, 2.9×10^{11} MIPS in 2000 to 6.4×10^{12} MIPS in 2007.

RELATION TO ECONOMICS

Eventually, Information and Communication Technology—computers, computerized machinery, fiber optics, communication satellites, Internet, and other ICT tools—became a significant part of the economy. Microcomputers were developed and many businesses and industries were greatly changed by ICT.

Nicholas Negroponte captured the essence of these changes in his 1995 book, *Being Digital.* His book discusses similarities and differences between products made of atoms and products made of bits. In essence, a copy of a product made of bits can be made cheaply and quickly, and shipped across the country or internationally quickly and at very low cost.

Impact on Jobs and Income Distribution

The Information Age has affected the workforce in several ways. It has created a situation in which workers who perform tasks which are easily automated are being forced to find work which involves tasks that are not easily automated. Workers are also being forced to compete in a global job market. Lastly, workers are being replaced by computers that can do their jobs faster and more effectively. This poses problems for workers in industrial societies, which are still to be solved. However, solutions that involve lowering the working time are usually highly resisted.

Jobs traditionally associated with the middle class (assembly line workers, data processors, foremen and supervisors) are beginning to disappear, either through outsourcing or automation. Individuals who lose their jobs must either move up, joining a group of "mind workers" (engineers, doctors, attorneys, teachers, scientists, professors, executives, journalists, consultants), or settle for low-skill, low-wage service jobs.

The "mind workers" are able to compete successfully in the world market and receive high wages. Conversely, production workers and service workers in industrialized nations are unable to compete with workers in developing countries and either lose their jobs through outsourcing or are forced to accept wage cuts. In addition, the internet makes it possible for workers in developing countries to provide in-person services and compete directly with their counterparts in other nations.

This has had several major consequences, including increased opportunity in developing countries and the globalization of the workforce.

Workers in developing countries have a competitive advantage which translates into increased opportunities and higher wages. The full impact on the workforce in developing countries is complex and has downsides.

In the past, the economic fate of workers was tied to the fate of national economies. For example, workers in the United States were once well paid in comparison to the workers in other countries. With the advent of the Information Age and improvements in communication, this is no longer the case. Because workers are forced to compete in a global job market, wages are less dependent on the success or failure of individual economies.

Automation, Productivity, and Job Loss

The Information Age has affected the workforce in that automation and computerization have resulted in higher productivity coupled with net job loss. In the United States for example, from January 1972 to August 2010, the number of people employed in manufacturing jobs fell from 17,500,000 to 11,500,000 while manufacturing value rose 270%.

Although it initially appeared that job loss in the industrial sector might be partially offset by the rapid growth of jobs in the IT sector, the recession of March 2001 foreshadowed a sharp drop in the number of jobs in the IT sector. This pattern of decrease in jobs continued until 2003.

Data has shown that overall, technology creates more jobs than it destroys even in the short run.

Rise of Information-intensive Industry

Industry is becoming more information-intensive and less labor and capital-intensive. This trend has important implications for the workforce; workers are becoming increasingly productive as the value of their labor decreases. However, there are also important implications for capitalism itself; not only is the value of labor decreased, the value of capital is also diminished. In the classical model, investments in human capital and financial capital are important predictors of the performance of a new venture. However, as demonstrated by Mark Zuckerberg and Facebook, it now seems possible for a group of relatively inexperienced people with limited capital to succeed on a large scale.

INNOVATIONS

The Information Age was enabled by technology developed in the Digital Revolution, which was itself enabled by building on the developments in the Technological Revolution.

Computers

Before the advent of electronics, mechanical computers, like the Analytical Engine in 1837, were designed to provide routine mathematical calculation and simple decision-making capabilities. Military needs during World War II drove development of the first electronic computers, based on vacuum tubes, including the Z3, the Atanasoff–Berry Computer, Colossus computer, and ENIAC.

The invention of the transistor in 1947 enabled the era of mainframe computers (1950s – 1970s), typified by the IBM 360. These large room-sized computers provided data calculation and manipulation that was much faster than humanly possible, but were expensive to buy and maintain, so were initially limited to a few scientific institutions, large corporations and government agencies. As transistor technologyrapidly improved, the ratio of computing power to size increased dramatically, giving direct access to computers to ever smaller groups of people.

Along with electronic arcade machines and home video game consoles in the 1980s, the development of the personal computers like theCommodore PET and Apple II (both in 1977) gave individuals access to the computer. But data sharing between individual computers was either non-existent or largely manual, at first using punched cards and magnetic tape, and later floppy disks.

Data

The first developments for storing data were initially based on photographs, starting with microphotography in 1851 and then microform in the 1920s, with the ability to store documents on film, making them much more compact. In the 1970s, electronic paper allowed digital information appear as paper documents.

Early information theory and Hamming codes were developed about 1950, but awaited technical innovations in data transmission and storage to be put to full use. While cables transmitting digital data connected computer terminals and peripherals to mainframes were common, and special message-sharing systems leading to email were first developed in the 1960s, independent computer-to-computer networking began with ARPANET in 1969. This expanded to become the Internet (coined in 1974), and then the World Wide Web in 1989.

Public digital data transmission first utilized existing phone lines using dial-up, starting in the 1950s, and this was the mainstay of the Internet until broadband in the 2000s. The introduction of wireless networking in the 1990s combined with the proliferation ofcommunications satellites in the 2000s allowed for public digital transmission without the need for cables. This technology led to digital television, GPS, and satellite radio through the 1990s and 2000s.

Computers continued to become smaller and more powerful, to the point where they could be carried. In the 1980s and 1990s, laptops first allowed computers to become portable, and PDAs allowed use while standing or walking. Pagers existing since the 1950s, were largely replaced by mobile phones beginning in the 1980s, giving mobile networking ability to a few at first. These have now become commonplace, and include digital cameras. Starting in the 1990s, tablets and then smartphones combined and extended these abilities of computing, mobility, and information sharing.

INFORMATION AGE STRATEGIC ENVIRONMENT

The Information Age, like the agricultural and industrial ages which preceded it, is a global phenomenon. Global communications are virtually instantaneous, computers and other Information Age technologies are found in even the most underdeveloped states, and almost every country has least one system connected to the Internet.

However, again like the preceding agricultural and industrial ages, changes being introduced by the Information Age are not equally pervasive everywhere. Change induced by Information Age technologies is taking place in different countries at different rates of speed, with different impacts, different organizational characteristics, and with different strategic implications. As pointed out earlier, different societies absorb, diffuse, and operationalize Information Age technologies at different rates because of cost and cultural considerations. These factors include the age and utility of in-place technology; a society's social and cultural receptivity to new technology; the degree of insularity of a society; the level and reliability of a society's human, technical, and economic support infrastructures; the level and strength of a society's traditional values and outlooks; the level of education within a society; the degree of technical sophistication of users and potential users of Information Age technology within a society; the level of concern over sovereignty on the part of states, and over control of decision-making processes on the part of a society's leadership elites; and many other political, social, and economic factors idiosyncratic to each society and therefore impossible to detail.

What, then, will the emerging strategic environment look like? Here, we will begin with the view of Alvin and Heidi Toffler as a point of departure. This view is criticized by some as being too simplistic and by others as overlooking important historical facts. However, it is a widely recognized view that provides a common reference point, one whose assumptions can be "tested" in a systematic way.

To the Tofflers, the world is moving toward a global socio-economic revolution that will lead to the development of a global "trisected power structure." This new strategic environment will entail a trisected global power structure that will supersede the Industrial Age's bisected structure in which states that developed industrial "smokestack" based economies enjoyed economic, social, and military superiority over more primitive agriculturally based societies.

In the Information Age, the Tofflers argue, those states that use and benefit most from Information Age technologies will be at the apex of a new three-tiered global power structure dominated by knowledge and knowledge-related "intangibles." They will be superior in capabilities to those states that remain dependent on either an industrial or agricultural economy.30 In an effort to gain the advantages afforded by Information Age technological capabilities, some states may even attempt to bypass the industrial stage of development, moving directly from an agricultural economy to an information economy. But all three types of societies, with many countries not fitting clearly into one or another of the three dominant types, will coexist even as they coexist in today's bisected power structure.

Countries at the apex of this trisected global power structure will be more dependent on the technologies of the Information Age than will those states that remain with an industrial or agricultural economy. Because of this greater dependency, they as societies will be more vulnerable than industrial or agricultural societies to any alteration, disruption, or destruction of the technologies upon which they rely (e.g., information or critical infrastructure warfare), much the same way as industrial societies are more vulnerable to the disruption or destruction of energy and fuel supplies than are agricultural societies. Despite the enhanced economic and military capabilities that flow from the technologies of the Information Age, the security equation for post-industrial states will be complicated because of this vulnerability, which we will discuss later.

At the same time, as the trisected global power structure emerges, the capabilities provided by the technologies of the Information Age are likely to further blur the boundaries between domestic and international affairs. In the emerging strategic environment, the combination of increased speed, capacity, and flexibility of information flow combined with greater access to, more types of, and heightened demand for information will make it increasingly difficult for states to control inward and outward information flows. Some states will try to control access to freely available information, as China has with access to Internet sites.31 However, few will succeed unless they are willing to impose truly draconian social or technological solutions to their perceived problem. Such solutions might include capital punishment or long-term imprisonment for accessing information sites deemed unacceptable, restricting Internet access via licenses to only a few loyal subjects, or otherwise restricting access to advanced information and communication technologies. States that apply such solutions, while perhaps maintaining control of information flows, will suffer other social and economic losses, including limiting their ability to move from agricultural or industrial level to an information based level of economic development.

Because of the capabilities that they provide, the technologies of the Information Age are also likely to increase the role that non-state actors play in the international system. Multinational corporations have long been major actors in the international scene, but they are likely to grow even more influential as businesses becomes increasingly regionalized and globalized. Already, taking advantage of opportunities afforded by advanced information and communication technologies to increase the speed, capacity, and flexibility of information flows, many businesses have made geography and national borders less relevant as they have created an international marketplace and increased profitability by moving their labor intensive back room operations to countries where labor costs are low. Similarly, nongovernmental organizations (NGOs) have proliferated, increasing in number from perhaps four thousand such organizations in the late

1970s to perhaps as many as thirty thousand in the late 1990s. A significant but uncertain percentage of

this growth is undoubtedly due to the ability that like- minded or like-interested people now have on a global base to share information and to collaborate. Thus, the emerging strategic environment will be more complex than the one that exists today.

If this analysis is substantially correct, more fissures of change and potential conflict will divide the global community than in the past. Inevitably, the technologies of the Information Age will continue to be absorbed, diffused, and operationalized at different speeds and with different results in different countries. Without denying that states will, for the foreseeable future, remain the dominant type of international actor, more types of actors, and more actors of each type, will gain importance on different issues. Given the potential provided by Information Age technologies for collections of individuals to articulate and perhaps act on their viewpoints, the strategic environment of the Information Age may well be far more complex than that which preceded it. This view is contrary to those who argue that the Information Age will drive us to global homogeneity.

There are at least four views about the speed with the Information Age will usher in changes to the strategic environment, and about how extensive those changes may be. A few voices urge caution about leaping to conclusions that the Information Age is truly upon us. These analysts do not deny that change is taking place nor that advanced technologies provide humankind with capabilities far beyond those previously available, but they are skeptical that, in the final analysis, much other than capabilities will change. This perspective is not widely shared, but it can not be overlooked.

One such skeptic is Frank Webster, who has observed that there are immense difficulties in measuring what is meant by an Information Age.32 He also warns that information by itself means nothing, and that humankind must take into consideration the meaning and quality of information, not just its quantity. Even with the proliferation of information-related technologies, Webster wonders whether society has or will change profoundly enough to warrant calling the near term future an Information Age. While Webster and others with similar perspectives fully admit that information technologies provide humankind with capabilities that were unimaginable a few short years ago, their premise is that little in human interrelationships or organizations has changed fundamentally or is likely to change fundamentally as a result of advanced information and communication technologies.

What does this imply for national security affairs? If Webster's view is accurate, this means that new and emerging technologies will continue to enhance military capabilities, but that the strategic environment will change little. Military systems, weapons platforms, and kill mechanisms may grow more capable, more lethal, more accurate, and obtain greater reach, but national security planners and strategists will be able to proceed with their planning as if little else other than capabilities have changed.

A second perspective sees strategic change taking place in an evolutionary rather than revolutionary way. Without denying that the cumulative impact of new technologies will be revolutionary, this school nonetheless sees change occurring in a paced and evolutionary manner. Advocates of this school of thought accept that future human and organizational relationships will be fundamentally different from past relationships, but that these changes will unfold over time, permitting individuals and organizations to adjust slowly or coevolve.

DIFFUSION OF INFORMATION AGE TECHNOLOGIES

It is widely recognized that advances in information and communication technologies are occurring incredibly rapidly. As important as the advances themselves are, however, three aspects of their diffusion require additional comment; diffusion is rapid, global, and uneven. There will be differences from society to society and from industry to industry and from organization to organization. It seems reasonable to assert that the future of organizations, industries, and even societies will depend in some significant measure upon their ability to harness information to create and maintain a competitive advantage in the domain in which they operate.

STRATEGIC IMPACT OF THE INFORMATION AGE

The arrival of the new millennium not only marks a milestone in the Christian calendar but also signals a technological watershed for mankind. This happens to be a coincidence, not planned by man or nature, yet it provides us with a rare occasion to pause and reflect.

The reason I say we are approaching a technological watershed is that many believe, and I agree, that we are passing from the industrial age to the information age, driven by rapid and remarkable advances in information and communication technologies. New products and services based on these advances are everywhere. Although they are not always visible to us as consumers, they have permeated our lives as if we were living in an infon-nation-communication ether.

Management of industrial R&D in the next 10- 15 years will be profoundly influenced by the all-connecting, all-pervading nature of this information-communication ether. The impact will be felt in many ways, some obvious, some not so obvious and some not yet foreseen. In my view, there are at least five significant impacts with strategic implications for R&D leaders in industry:

Shrinking Time and Distance

This is the most direct and obvious impact of the information-communication revolution. Members of an R&D project team can now be dispersed around the world yet work together around the clock as if they were next-door neighbors, thanks to innovations like videoconferencing and on-line meetings. Multi-site videoconferencing with high-fidelity document transfer is bringing together technology users and suppliers on short notice and overcoming the inconvenience of time zones. Real-time (or near real-time) on-line meetings involving many individuals from as many locations are becoming fairly routine.

Such cybermeetings are being organized and run just like traditional, face-to-face get-togethers. On-line brainstorming sessions are gaining particular popularity. In some companies, videoconferencing is being combined with simultaneous on-line meetings to provide a truly powerful tool. For example, British Petroleum technologists were reportedly able to see, analyze, diagnose, and solve equipment malfunction problems on off-shore oil-drilling equipment-from their comfortable offices and laboratories in England!

Lowering Cost and Increasing Output

In addition to saving travel expenses and time, R&D people everywhere are reducing activity cost and increasing work output through intelligent use of information and communication technologies. Computer-aided design tools, laboratory information management systems, molecular modeling techniques, process modeling and simulation exercises, and electronic submission of new drug applications (NDAs) to regulatory agencies are just a few examples. R&D and engineering managers are making use of computer-aided project management to reduce product development cycle time. And use of computers and robots in conjunction with statistical planning of experiments is reducing the amount of trial-and-error in R&D.

Enhancing Organizational Networking/Learning

Even five years ago, most individuals in an organization depended on face-to-face interactions to build linkages, share knowledge, and generate ideas. Telephone and paper exchange complemented these face-to-face interactions. Because of widespread availability and use of network-based tools and systems such as electronic mail, groupware, search engines, web crawlers, etc., organizational networking and knowledge-sharing have now become much easier and more widespread within (and outside) R&D. Thanks to Internet and e-mail, opportunities to access external information rapidly and communicate with individuals at distant places have multiplied by several orders of magnitude.

Secure Intranets (and Extranets) are not just opening doors to similarly rapid access and exchange internally (and externally with selected partners) but also creating computerized information archives as lasting knowledge legacies for R&D organizations. Push technologies are allowing individuals and groups to broadcast information to wide audiences yet reach targeted groups and individuals to meet their specified interests. Last but not least, distributed information systems are providing the opportunity for every user to become a provider as well. Thanks to such self-managed networks and systems, organizational knowledge is building up within companies at a rapid rate, without bureaucratic and costly involvement of librarians, screening agents ("gatekeepers"), or editors.

Bringing Technologies Together in Novel Ways

Because information and communication advances are able to find their ways into so many applications, they are proving to be catalysts for converging multiple technologies that create new products, new services, and even totally new markets and channels. Although early examples were seen in the 1970s (e.g., computerized axial tomography) and in the 1980s (e.g., video games, industrial robots, VCRs, etc.), the 1990s have witnessed a truly dramatic rise in the number of such innovations. Examples are all around us: video camera, ATM, PC-TV, digital phone, DVD, Internet and e-commerce, and the list goes on.

In BOC, for example, we have combined advanced telemetry systems (to remotely monitor levels of our liquified gas products in storage vessels at customer sites) and predictive modeling techniques (to forecast timing for fresh product supply) to schedule timely delivery and eliminate product "run out." Taking a cue from other industries, we have initiated use of "smart tags" to track movement of our gas cylinders within our operations and at our customers' sites. Our vacuum pumps and related products for the semiconductor industry have built-in networking and diagnostic/predictive capabilities—capabilities that were virtually unimaginable 10 years ago. Looking 10 years ahead, I can only see an explosive proliferation of intelligent devices and components ranging from smart refrigerators (e.g., recently announced by GE) to intelligent lawnmowers.

Blurring of Traditional Boundaries

Last but not least, the information—communication revolution is blurring, if not eliminating, many of the traditional boundaries to which we have grown accustomed. We are witnessing not only the shrinking of time and distance and the merging of multiple technology streams but also an increasing level of cross-functional and cross-organizational collaboration. While the harsh realities of globalization and competition may have driven most firms to promote internal and external collaboration, the widespread availability and use of information and communication tools and systems has clearly accelerated the phenomenon.

It is no longer rare for a salesperson to interact with his R&D counterpart on a real-time basis to clinch a deal, or for R&D in one division to directly access market research done in another, or for a general manager to hook up to the company's Intranet to review the latest status of a new product development effort. Finding an expert across the globe to answer someone's burning question, without many frustrating phone calls, is now relatively easy in many companies. Employees, whether they are in R&D or Planning or Finance, can now log-in their ideas, technical and non-technical, on their company-wide network, get feedback from familiar as well as unfamiliar individuals and may even be able to secure management approval for exploratory efforts. Ideas no longer carry national or ethnic tags of origin as they can move across geographic and other boundaries almost instantaneously.

Probably the strongest indication of the move away from traditional functional mindsets is found in the new enterprise resource-planning (ERP) systems being rapidly adopted by large corporations everywhere. The modules and elements within these systems are designed around work processes, not traditional functional responsibilities and requirements.

Silently, invisibly and usually without fanfare, information and communication networks and systems are bringing together people from different organizations, backgrounds and responsibilities. Thus, the traditional organizational silos are slowly but surely being eroded to create a more integrated and efficient work environment. At ABB, for example, Percy Bernavik and his senior management team were able to run over 1,000 companies in more than 100 countries with a headquarters staff of only about 100!

Advice to R&D Leaders

In view of these significant impacts, how should R&D leaders in industry adjust their management strategies and processes as they approach the new millennium? The exact answer, as always, will depend on individual circumstances. With that in mind, I offer a few suggestions:

There is no turning back for the forces unleashed by the information-communication revolution. We should, therefore, embrace and leverage them to the fullest for the benefit for our organizations. At the very least, we must take full advantage of the many time- and energy-saving features of information and communication advances to reduce cost of operation and increase output quality and quantity. However, we should not be satisfied with such a reactive and minimalist mindset. Instead, we must continually push toward a more proactive and expansive approach.

In almost every industrial firm, R&D was the first function to welcome and exploit "computing." Yet, with time, R&D seems to have fallen behind. The adoption of manufacturing and logistics planning systems (MRPs) and ERPs by other functions has positioned them as the more imaginative and influential proponents of information (and communication) technologies. R&D management should pursue aggressively every opportunity to utilize information and communication technologies to support and enhance all aspects of the innovation process.

One area in which R&D should be able to take a legitimate lead is "knowledge management" for the corporation. Knowledge management, of course, refers to an actively managed process of capturing, disseminating, leveraging, and enriching knowledge within an enterprise, both explicit knowledge that is documented and implicit knowledge that is embedded in the experience and expertise of its people in informal and unwritten forms. Technical know-how often forms the largest (and probably the most valuable) part of an organization's knowledge assets. For R&D to assume the leadership role in knowledge management would appear logical, provided R&D takes a broad-based, enterprise-wide approach and does not limit the scope to technical matters.

R&D leaders should not just recognize the phenomenon of multiple technology convergence but capitalize on it. They should proactively look for opportunities to marry information and/or communication technologies with advances in their own areas of interest and competence to create innovative products and services. If they do not, their competitors will do so and gain the advantage.

Blurring of traditional organizational boundaries gives R&D leaders the opportunity to establish truly close working relationships with Marketing, Manufacturing, Finance and the other key stakeholders in their companies. Additionally, R&D leaders should take advantage of this general trend and aggressively pursue and develop strategic collaborations with external sources of technology and innovation. In thus moving away from the traditional "make" model of R&D to the more balanced approach of "make or buy," R&D leaders will serve their organizations well in the future.

In conclusion, the new century will no doubt witness numerous innovations, and some will probably be more breathtaking than even the most spectacular innovations of the 20th century. R&D managers will certainly play critical roles in bringing about many of these innovations. Advances in information and communication technologies will provide invaluable support to future generations of R&D managers, especially those who aggressively institutionalize timely absorption and exploitation of such advances.

4

Electronic Information Systems

The importance of electronic information systems is obvious to all participants in the modern economy. When information fails to circulate, whole sectors of the economy are vulnerable. Finance, wholesale and retail trade, transportation, much of manufacturing, and many service industries would slow to a crawl without computers. Vital public services–utilities, national defence, and medicine–are equally dependent.

Information security–the safeguarding of computer systems and the integrity, confidentiality, and availability of the data they contain–has long been recognized as a critical national policy issue. Two current trends indicate that its importance is growing. First, the integration of computers into more and more aspects of modern life continues. Second, cyber-attacks, or breaches of information security, appear to be increasing in frequency, and few observers are willing to ignore the possibility that future attacks could have much more severe consequences than what has been observed to date.

The core issue, in both public and private sectors, is whether we are devoting enough resources to information security. Part of the answer must come from economic analysis. What are the costs, both historical and potential, of security breaches? How frequently can attacks be expected? Can these factors be quantified precisely, so that business firms and other organizations can determine the optimal amount to spend on information security and measure the effectiveness of that spending? This report surveys the state of knowledge on the cost of cyber-attacks and the economics of information security.

We summarize several studies that use stock market capitalization as a measure of the cost of cyber-attacks to victim firms. The studies find substantial short-term drops in the prices of shares of firms following the announcement of an information security breach: between 1% and 5% of market capitalization, with greater losses (up to 15%) recorded by some financial institutions where attackers had gained access to confidential customer records.

Present summaries of the existing empirical data on costs attributable to cyber-crime and computer worms and viruses. What is available is a limited amount of survey data, which is frankly described by its compilers as anecdotal, but is nonetheless widely reported in the press.

The reasons for the lack of statistical data: firms and organizations have strong incentives to conceal information about cyber-attacks, and there are significant uncertainties and measurement difficulties that limit our ability to specify the dollar amount at risk from information security breaches. Theoretical models that describe the returns to spending on information security shed some light on the size of potential losses, but–in the absence of better statistical data–assigning an overall figure to the cost of cyber-attacks remains highly speculative. Fourth, we examine the efforts of the insurance industry to develop policies that cover cyber-risk. These initiatives are in their infancy; the chief obstacle has been a lack of data with which to construct actuarial tables on the costs and frequency of attacks.

The cyber-attacks as macroeconomic events.

Appendices to this report include a summary of information risk assessment practices in a Fortune 500 manufacturing company and an overview of efforts by financial institutions and regulators to manage cyber-risk in that industry.

EFFECT OF CYBER-ATTACKS ON STOCK PRICES

Thus far, reported cyber-attacks have been relatively limited in scope, and have not yet been on a scale that would have significant macroeconomic consequences. Individual firms, however, may have suffered significant losses as a result of past attacks. An examination of the effects of those attacks might be illuminating. Most estimates of the cost to companies of cyber-attacks are based on surveys. Survey responses are often expressed in such a wide range as to indicate considerable subjectivity and thus they may be of limited use. There may, however, be a more objective measure of the effect of cyber-attacks on individual firms.

In theory, the price of a company's stock is primarily determined by the present discounted value of the cash flows expected to result from that firm's output. That cash flow is what contributes to the wealth of the stockholders, either in the form of dividends or in the expansion of the firm's stock of productive capital. Any event that changes investors' expectations about that future stream of income is likely to affect the price of the stock.

Four recent studies have examined a number of actual cyber-attacks in an effort to see if any of those attacks could be linked to a change in the stock prices of the affected companies. In some cases, the studies attempted to measure if any stock-price effect depended on the different characteristics of either the firm or the attacks.

It seems at least intuitively obvious that some firms are more exposed to cyber-attacks than are others. It is conceivable that firm size may affect vulnerability to attack, but more to the point some firms are more dependent on computer networks than others to conduct business.1 Conventional firms, which have been referred to in this context as "brick and mortar" firms, might be expected to be the least vulnerable to cyber-attacks as they are the least dependent on the Internet to conduct business. Some firms, characterized as "click and mortar," conduct business both off-line and over the Internet. These firms face an increased vulnerability because of the risk that the business they conduct via the Internet might be interrupted.

Finally, there are firms whose business is conducted almost exclusively over the Internet. These firms would seem to be most at risk. The extent to which a business is affected might reasonably be expected to depend on the type of attack. Most attacks have fallen into one of two categories. The first is a "denial-of-service" attack (DoS). A DoS attack renders a firm's Internet portal inaccessible and interferes with its ability to conduct on-line business. For the most part, this kind of attack causes no lasting harm. The more serious category of attacks are those that involve the theft or destruction of secure information. This kind of security breach is more likely to have lasting effects on the targeted firm.

Other things being equal, the more dependent a firm is on the Internet, and the more intrusive an attack is, the more likely it is that any attack will have significant consequences for the financial health of that firm.

In contrast, firms that provide computer security might be expected to benefit from cyber-attacks (unless their products were publicly blamed for an attack's success). An increase in the apparent vulnerability of computer networks could be expected to raise future earnings of those companies and thus boost their stock price.

Cavusoglu, et. al., examined five specified hypotheses regarding the consequences of cyber-attacks. To do so, they identified 66 distinct security breaches that occurred between 1996 and 2001. Of those 66 events, 34 were availability (DoS) attacks. Of the 66 events, 31 affected firms whose business was conducted almost entirely over the Internet.

The attacks were divided into four distinct types: simple web site defacing; DoS; theft of credit card information; and theft of other customer information. In the case of web site defacing, the average loss in stock value was 2% on the second day, which rebounded somewhat to a 1.1% loss on the third day. DoS attacks resulted in a 2.9% drop on the second day, and a 3.6% decline on the third day. For attacks that compromise non-financial information, there was an average drop in stock value of 0.5% on the day of the attack, and a total decline of 1.5% on the third day. Attacks which compromised financial information, chiefly credit card data, caused the largest declines. On the day of the attack, stock prices of affected firms fell a average of 9.3% and by the third day the decline reached 15%. The authors also found that there was a correlation between the number of credit cards that were compromised and the magnitude of the stock price hit. All the studies found that there was a significant decline in stock prices of affected firms in the days immediately following a cyber-attack. The time frame is necessarily restricted in an effort to isolate the effects of the attack. To extend the time horizon would increase the likelihood that any variation in stock prices was due to other events. Therefore, the studies do not attempt to determine if there is any persistent change in stock prices, or if the drop in stock prices is temporary.

Two of the studies determined that the drop in stock price was related to the type of attack, with DoS attacks generally having a smaller effect than attacks which compromised confidential information. One of the studies found that there was no significant correlation between the kind of attack and the magnitude of the effect on stock prices. The fourth study found that the magnitude of the drop in price of stock was correlated with managers' assessments of the firm's exposure to the risk of cyber-attacks.

Cyber-Attack Costs

In 2003, the Computer Security Institute (CSI) and the Federal Bureau of Investigation (FBI) published their eighth annual survey on computer crime and security. Computer security practitioners in 530 U.S. corporations, financial institutions, government agencies (federal, state, and local), medical institutions, and universities provided information about their organizations' experience with computer crime over the previous year.

In 2003, 56% of respondents reported some unauthorized use of computer systems within the last 12 months. No such unauthorized use was reported by 29%, and 15% did not know. The 2003 data on the percentage of respondents reporting various types of misuse and attacks, and the expected dollar value of losses by type attack.

The distribution of losses by type of attack has not been consistent over the years that the survey has been conducted. In the 2000 survey, for example, theft of proprietary information was the most expensive type of attack, as it was in 2003. However, financial fraud accounted for 21.1% of all losses reported in 2000, as opposed to only 5.0% in 2003.

There is no consistent trend in total reported financial losses to computer crime It is likely that the results are skewed from year to year by a small number of relatively large loss reports. In addition, the number of respondents varies from year to year.

The survey also presents data on the reported costs of individual attacks, with highest, lowest, and average values, by type of incident. For 2003, the lowest cost reports drop into the hundreds of dollars; the highest values range up to $35 million (theft of proprietary information) and $60 million (denial of service).

Besides the cost and frequency of attack data summarized here, the CSI/FBI surveys include information on incidents related to web sites, computer security practices, and the sources and methods of attacks.

What do the CSI/FBI survey results have to tell us about the overall costs of cyber-attacks in the United States? Unfortunately, not much. The survey's authors do not claim that their respondents are a representative sample of the businesses, organizations, and other entities that are exposed to cyber-risk. Survey recipients are not randomly chosen, but are self-selected from among security professionals. As a result, there is no rigorous, statistically sound method for extrapolating the loss reports of the 530 respondents to the national level.

Secondly, the cost data reported are incomplete even for the sample. As noted above, 15% of respondents to the 2003 survey did not know whether there had been unauthorized use of their systems. More significantly, while 75% of respondents reported financial losses, only 47% could quantify the losses. Thus, the figures in the charts above represent only measurable losses, and substantially understate total losses, though no one can specify the degree of understatement. Furthermore, if less than half of respondents reporting losses can put a dollar figure on those losses, the clear inference is that there is no standard technique for quantifying the amount of loss.

The survey does provide numerical support for a number of propositions that are generally accepted in the computer security literature: that insiders are the source of a substantial percentage of attacks; that many attacks are unreported; and that there is no simple, standardized method for quantifying the costs of cyber-attacks. Although limited as a statistical tool, the surveys usefully provide, in the authors' own words, "a series of snapshots of how the people in the trenches viewed their situation at a given time."

Measuring Costs

While organizations may have good reasons not to make public disclosures regarding security breaches, one would expect their incentives to measure the costs of such incidents internally to be strong. Without accurate cost data, how would organizations assess the cyber-risks they face, make rational decisions about how much to spend on information security, or evaluate the effectiveness of security efforts? In fact, there are no standard methods for measuring the costs of cyber-attacks. Attacks produce many kinds of costs, some of which cannot be quantified easily, if at all. As a result, there is a presumed gap in private, internal data that mirrors the absence of public data on cyber-attack costs.

The costs associated with cyber-attacks can be divided into direct and indirect costs. Direct costs include the expenses incurred in restoring a computer system to its original, pre-attack state. Recovery from an attack will typically require extra spending on labour and materials; these are the easiest costs to measure. But even at this basic level of cost accounting, complexities may arise. If an attack leads to increased spending on IT security, to what extent are those costs attributable to the attack? If a planned upgrade in hardware or software is accelerated after an attack, should the upgrade be classified as a security cost?

Measurement of productivity loss is not always straightforward or uniform. Generally, this is not an added dollar cost: the workers are paid what they would have been paid anyway. Assigning a value to lost time depends on each individual organization's estimates of its own costs related to business opportunities forgone (during the disruption) or diversion of resources (during the recovery effort).

Another direct cost may involve the loss of value in information assets that are stolen, compromised, or otherwise degraded during an attack. Hoo summarizes the difficulties in measurement that may arise here:

The value of an information asset is highly dependent upon who possesses the information. Sensitive commercial R&D information in the hands of a competitor is significantly more problematic than if it were in the hands of a Netherlands teenager. Time sensitivity can also complicate the valuation problem. For example, a password that expires in ten seconds is worthless after it has expired, but it is quite valuable during the ten seconds that it could be used to gain system access. Add to these difficulties the quantification challenges posed by intangible values, such as reputation, trust, embarrassment, etc., and the task of valuation quickly becomes a highly uncertain and potentially contentious enterprise.

Attacks also have indirect costs, which may continue to accrue after the immediate damage has been repaired. Many indirect costs flow from loss of reputation, or damage to a firm's brand. Customers may defect to competitors, financial markets may raise the firm's cost of capital, insurance costs may rise, and lawsuits may be filed. Some of these cost factors are readily quantifiable, but other aspects of loss of trust or confidence are intangible and difficult to measure.

Some analysts regard these indirect, intangible costs as more significant than direct costs. Cavusoglu, Cavusoglu, and Raghunathan conclude that the inability to measure intangible costs leads many firms to grossly underestimate the costs of security breaches, and that this explains why estimates of incident costs reported in the CSI/FBI survey are much lower than the price of an attack on a major company would be in terms of stock market capitalization.

Indirect costs of cyber-attacks may also include economic harm to individuals and institutions other than the immediate target of an attack. An attack on one firm's computer networks may affect other firms up and down the supply chain. When credit card data is hacked, or an internet service provider goes down, consumers suffer costs. From an accounting perspective, these do not count as costs to the target firm, but from a policy perspective they can be significant. The possibility of cascade effects–disruption spreading from computer to interlinked computer–is well-known, but we are far from being able to quantify the economic impact of an event of this type. To a profit-seeking business, measurement of costs already incurred is useful primarily to the extent that it facilitates prevention or mitigation of future losses. In the cyber-security field, as elsewhere, risk assessment is primarily a forward-looking activity. It is no less important or necessary because certain costs cannot be quantified.

IT SECURITY SPENDING

For businesses facing cyber-risk, the "bottom line" question is how much to spend on information security. The difficulties in measuring risk set forth above translate into similar uncertainties regarding security spending. Security budgets cannot be justified through the basic financial tests–return on investment (ROI) and cost/benefit analysis–that are applied to most other corporate investments. It is hard to overstate the starkness with which this inability to quantify appears in the information security literature. As one observer stated:

It's fairly easy to find out how many people die from smoking cigarettes in the United States each year. It's impossible to find out how many hours of computer downtime result from computer virus outbreaks in a year.

It's fairly easy to find out how much physical money is stolen from banks in the United States each year. It's impossible to find out how much money is stolen from banks through electronic attacks.

It's easy to find out how likely you are to be injured in a head-on accident in a particular kind of vehicle in the United States. It's impossible to find out how likely your server is to be taken offline by a virus attack.

It's easy to find out how long a gun safe will resist the attentions of a thief armed with an acetylene torch. It's impossible to find out how long your server will resist the attentions of a thief armed with hacking tools publicly available on the Internet.

A core problem of the information security industry is that, as an industry, we do not have a unit which measures product effectiveness. We are selling something which is intangible and unquantifiable; we are basically selling fashion rather than function.

Of 1,400 organizations surveyed by Ernst & Young in 2003, 59% reported that they rarely or never made an ROI calculation for information security spending. Nevertheless, all organizations must decide how much to spend.

Survey evidence shows that many organizations are spending increasing amounts on IT security. International Data Corp. (IDC) found that nearly 40% of organizations polled in 2003 reported that security spending was growing faster than general IT spending. For very large organizations, the proportion was 51%. Only about 10% reported that IT security spending was growing at a slower rate than IT spending.

Rising security spending suggests that organizations perceive either an increase in risk or that past expenditures were inadequate to manage current risk. Does the level of IT security spending provide clues to the dollar amounts at risk from cyber-attacks?

Given the uncertainties in measuring costs, risks, and the effectiveness of security efforts, we cannot make simple statements like the following: a company that expects to lose x dollars per year to cyber-attacks will generally spend—dollars to mitigate those losses. Until better empirical cost data become available, such calculations will remain speculative.

However, theoretical models have been developed that attempt to shed some light on the returns to security spending. These models are fairly rudimentary, but as they are refined, or even in their present state, they may help put security spending decisions on a more rational and rigorous basis.

The Smokestack Curve

The first observation from these theoretical models is that there are diminishing returns to security spending. A little spending can bring a substantial reduction in expected losses (ALE). At higher levels of spending, the reduction per dollar spent will be less. At very high levels, the extra amount of loss reduction purchased may be very low, or even approach zero. In graphic terms, this pattern is called a smokestack curve, resembling a plume of smoke rising vertically at first, then flattening out as it cools and drifts away on the wind.

Diminishing returns are observed in many business situations; Moitra and Konda provide evidence for them in security spending. They conduct a simulation of malicious attacks against network systems, and measure survivability–the degree to which a system is able to withstand attack and still function at a certain level– when different levels of defence mechanisms are deployed. Their results show survivability at various levels of security expenditure. They summarize their findings as follows:

As cost increases, survivability increases rapidly at first, and then more slowly. Such a plot can provide a systems manager with the ability to make an informed decision about the level of defence that is most appropriate for his or her organization since it shows the tradeoff involved between cost and expected survivability.

In Moitra and Konda's analysis, firms' security spending decisions will depend upon how risk averse they are. If a particular security breach will cause intolerable losses, firms may continue to spend on security even when the marginal return is low. Gordon and Loeb introduce the assumption of risk neutrality, which means that the firm is indifferent to investments that have the same expected return, even though the investments may have varying amounts of risk. Under risk neutrality, a profit-maximizing firm would increase spending on IT security as long as the return (in terms of reduction in ALE, or expected loss) exceeded the marginal expenditure. The firm would stop spending when one additional dollar spent on security reduced ALE by less than a dollar.

By assuming risk neutrality, Gordon and Loeb identify an optimum level of security spending, found at the point on the smokestack curve where marginal security spending equals marginal loss reduction. The horizontal axis represents IT security spending (S); the vertical axis shows the amount by which ALE is reduced (L). The dotted line from the origin is a 45 degree line, along which an increase in S produces an equal increase in L. Optimal security spending (S1) is determined by the point at which the slope of the flattening curve is 1 (where the change in L divided by the change in S equals one), or where the tangent of the curve is parallel to the 45-degree line. This point on the curve is also where the difference between benefits and costs is maximized.

Loeb and Gordon push this analysis further. By making several assumptions about the shape of the cost/loss reduction curve, they reach some numerical conclusions about the optimal level of security spending as a percentage of ALE: Our analysis shows that for two broad classes of security breach probability functions, the optimal amount to spend on information security never exceeds 37% of the expected loss resulting from a security breach (and is typically much less than that 37%).

Hence, the optimal amount to spend on information security would typically be far less than the expected loss from a security breach.

Since Loeb and Gordon's model is theoretical and not based on empirical data, the nature of their assumptions determines their results. Without evaluating the robustness of their assumptions (or the completeness of the mathematical proofs of the propositions that flow from the assumptions), it may be interesting to see what their estimate of optimal IT security spending suggests for the value of ALE.

We can roughly estimate the amount spent on IT security, even though there is no standard definition of what constitutes security spending (as opposed to, for example, normal upgrades of hardware and software), and even though statistics based on direct measurement or reporting are not available.

A common rule of thumb is that organizations devote roughly 5% of their total IT spending to IT security. Forrester Research, Inc. projects that total IT spending by business and governments in the United States in 2004 will be $743 billion.44 With these two assumptions, we can estimate that IT security spending by U.S. businesses and governments in 2004 will be about $37 billion.

Gordon and Loeb's model suggests that this figure does not exceed (and is probably considerably less than) 37% of ALE, or the amount organizations expect to lose as a result of cyber-attacks.

Thus, a figure of $100 billion represents a lower bound estimate for the annual expected loss in the United States. To the extent that firms spend less than 37% of their expected loss on security, the estimated figure for ALE rises.

CYBER-ATTACKS AND THE INSURANCE INDUSTRY

As an industry dedicated to accepting risks that people and businesses want or need to shed, the insurance industry is unsurprisingly interested in the increasing risk of cyber-attack. As these risks became larger and more evident with the growth of the Internet, the insurance industry's reaction was essentially twofold. The initial reaction was largely to make it clear that existing business insurance did not include coverage of cyber-risks. The premiums charged for existing types of business insurance essentially did not account for the risk from some form of cyber-attack and thus to cover these risks at the existing lower premium rate would have been economically damaging to the insurance company. In general, the reaction of excluding a new risk once it becomes known is quite common in the insurance industry. One can see it, for example, in the reaction to the 9/11 attacks and in the industry's reaction to the increase of homeowners' claims for mold damage, particularly in Texas. In both cases, these risks were presumed to be included in policies when they were low frequency and low cost risks. Once it became clear that they were not such low frequency and low cost risks, insurance contracts began to specifically exclude them.

The second reaction to this new cyber-risk was to introduce specific policies to cover those risks that had been excluded from traditional business insurance coverage. This largely began occurring in 1999 although some coverage was offered as far back as 1997. The market leader in cyber-risk policies, AIG, is estimated to have approximately 70% of the market for cyber-risk insurance with approximately 2,500 policies issued. Other companies writing policies include Chubb, St. Paul, Zurich American, Hartford, and Ace Ltd. The total premium for such policies has been estimated to be between $60 million and $120 million in 2002. These numbers are, however, quite different compared to those found in other types of commercial insurance. For example, general business liability insurance premiums totaled more than $30 billion in 2002, and AIG is able to lead the market for commercial lines with only 9% of the total commercial market in 2002.53 Estimates for growth in cyber-insurance coverage are substantial, with the Insurance Information Institute seeing $2 billion in premiums by 2007 or 2008,[54] while Conning and Co. projects a 100% annual growth rate and a total premium volume as high as $6 billion by 2006.

The policies offered by the companies in this area vary greatly as to the terms and coverages. There is no standard cyber-insurance policy. Policies can include both first party and third party risks with most companies apparently showing a preference for covering third party risks before covering first party risks. This seems to be due to a faith that the computer systems under a company's direct control are sufficiently secured to prevent direct loss of company data or the like. Risks that can be covered include: network security (damage due to direct attack on a network/ transmission of a virus/unauthorized access), web content (copyright infringement/libel or slander claims from material posted on a website), business interruption (lost income due to loss of computer function after an attack), cyber-extortion (settlement of an extortion attempt against a network), and public relations (cost of repairing a company's image after a cyber-attack).

The principal challenge facing the insurance industry in this realm is a lack of data. Insurance pricing rests critically on an understanding of the risks that are being transferred, particularly the frequency of the risk and the possible damages that could result. With enough experience and data, the insurance industry can be extremely accurate in its predictions and very efficient at dealing with risk, even with risks that might be very rare or very damaging. The risks to be covered by cyber-insurance, however, were not only unexpected, but also are to a large degree qualitatively different from what has been seen in the past. This leads to a situation where insurers are writing policies without the type of information that they prefer, particularly when compared to lines like fire or auto where insurers have long historical experience. AIG might estimate, as it has, that computer viruses caused $13 billion in damage in 2001. However, this would only be the beginning of the questions that might need to be answered. What is the likely frequency of such attacks? Is this number a high number or low number compared to what the costs might be in the future? What steps has a particular company taken to mitigate the damage from a future attack and will these steps be successful in doing so? Successfully pricing insurance in the long run demands answers to such questions. The experience that a few years have given the companies is important and the estimates now are more accurate than they were five years ago, but more experience is certainly needed before insurers will as comfortably write cyber-risk polices as they write other lines today.

Cyber-terror Threat

In order to assess the macroeconomic effects of a cyber-attack on computers it may first be useful to examine how computers contribute to economic activity. It is that contribution that is presumed to be at some risk.

Robert Solow, a major contributor to the theory of economic growth, is often quoted for his remark that the effect of computers can be seen everywhere but in the productivity statistics. Through the 1980s and early 1990s, there seemed to be no big payoff from the growing stock of computers. That presented a puzzle to those who expected significant returns. But it is now believed that computers have had much to do with an acceleration in productivity growth that began in the mid-1990s.

Consumers have come to expect a rapid rate of innovation in the manufacture of computers. It is also widely expected that the speed and memory capacity of those computers will continue to improve rapidly. Such a rapid rate of technological advance in the development and manufacture of computers was predicted in 1965 by Gordon E. Moore, one of the co-founders of Intel Corporation. Specifically "Moore's Law" predicted that the number of transistors that could be put on a computer chip would double every 18 months. Whether or not that prediction was a self-fulfilling prophecy may be open to question, but the fact is that the pace of technological advance in the manufacture of computers has vindicated Moore's Law over time.

Because of the rapid innovation in the production of computer chips, the prices of computers, as well as other goods related to information processing and communications, sometimes referred to collectively as information technology (IT), have been falling steadily for some time. Between 1959 and 1995, computer prices fell at an average annual rate of nearly 16.9%, and between 1995 and 2002 prices fell at an annual rate of 20.1%.

These price declines reflect substantial improvements in the quality of computers. The Bureau of Labor Statistics (BLS) has developed a procedure for estimating price indexes for goods whose characteristics are changing rapidly. These are referred to as "hedonic" price indexes. Hedonic price indexes attempt to estimate a statistical relationship between prices and a set of characteristics, such as memory and processor speed.

These price indexes are important to the measurement of productivity, because estimating price change is necessary to estimating change in real output and thus productivity. If the rate of price decline in computers is overestimated, then measures of productivity will be overstated. Most studies estimate that, in the late 1990s, prices for personal computers alone fell at an annual rate of somewhere between 30% and 40%.

Rapid declines in computer prices have, not surprisingly, stimulated a surge in investment. Although there are data back to 1959, production of computers was negligible until the 1980s. Thus, even though real output of IT equipment was increasing rapidly, it did not account for a very large share of total output until recently.

Computers have affected growth in productivity in at least two ways. First, there has been rapid productivity growth in the production of computers which, as computers accounted for an increasing share of total production, tended to raise the overall measure of productivity growth. Second, the sharp drop in computer prices has stimulated increased investment in computers, which has contributed to an increase in the overall amount of capital available to the workforce. This is often referred to as "capital deepening." Increases in the capital stock generally tend to raise worker productivity.

In part because of increased spending on IT equipment, the overall rate of investment spending rose significantly in the 1990s. Prior to the recent acceleration in productivity growth, most analyses found that computers yielded little benefit. One reason is that, until recently, computers accounted for a relatively small share of the total capital stock. But, that view has now changed. Economists are encouraged that the acceleration in productivity growth of the late 1990s may mean that the economy is on a higher growth path and many believe that computers have had a lot to do with it.

Two recent studies found considerable evidence that the computer, or more generally IT equipment, is behind most of the recent acceleration in productivity growth. There is also evidence of a modest "spillover" into other sectors of the economy. In other words, investment in computers can raise the productivity of the workers who use them, but it may also lead firms to change the way they operate leading to further productivity gains.

The first study, by Oliner and Sichel at the Federal Reserve Board, found that of a 0.9 percentage point increase in the growth rate of total factor productivity from the first half of the 1990s to the second half, all could be accounted for by advances in the production of computers themselves and the also by the use of those computers.

THE CURRENT CYBER SECURITY ENVIRONMENT IN THE BANKING AND FINANCE SECTOR

The Banking and Finance Sector provides critical deposit, consumer credit, and payment processing services that have become integral aspects of everyday life. As with other U.S. critical infrastructure sectors, financial institutions face a combination of known and unknown vulnerabilities, including the expansion of adversaries' capabilities and challenges to threat and vulnerability awareness. Because financial institutions are critical to the Nation's economic security and handle large sums of money, malicious actors find them to be especially attractive targets. There are also risk considerations associated with the Banking and Finance Sector's dependencies on other critical infrastructure sectors. In simple terms, financial transactions would be significantly impacted by massive power outages or failures of U.S. communications services. In addition to providing regular updates on the latest threat mitigation techniques, DHS released the *Banking and Finance Sector Specific Plan* in 2007, which characterizes vulnerabilities associated with links between financial institutions and other sectors while offering sector-specific risk considerations.

Though malicious cyber actors have varying levels of access and technical sophistication, all seek to inappropriately leverage the systems they target. Analysis of criminal activities shows increasing levels of sophistication in technical and targeting capabilities as well as a willingness to sell these capabilities on the black market. Some adversaries are capable of disrupting, destroying, or exploiting U.S. information systems including those that support the Banking and Finance Sector while others pursue intelligence collection, intellectual-property theft, monetary theft, and the disruption of commercial activities. In response to these growing and persistent threats, the Banking and Finance Sector has developed sophisticated tools and frameworks to defend against, detect, respond to, and mitigate cyber threats in collaboration with other stakeholders, including IT sector companies and experts who often provide these capabilities to the financial sector.

Additionally, the Federal government's unique expertise and ability to coordinate analytical and response activities among government, law enforcement, and the intelligence community complements the Banking and Finance Sector's efforts. Based on the framework established by the *National Infrastructure Protection Plan (NIPP)*, DHS collaborates with the U.S. Department of the Treasury (Treasury) as the Sector-Specific Agency for the Banking and Finance Sector, the Financial Services Sector Coordinating Council (FSSCC) for Critical Infrastructure Protection and Homeland Security, the Financial Services Information Sharing and Analysis Centre (FS-ISAC), and other industry and interagency partners to reduce the risks posed to the critical systems that support the Nation's financial institutions. DHS also offers direct assistance to individual companies by assisting in analysis and improving their cyber security posture in addition to responding to requests for assistance from companies who have been compromised.

Despite significant outreach and relationship building, DHS faces a number of constraints in coordinating with the private sector, which may impact work with financial institutions. Some institutions have concerns about the privacy implications of sharing information with the Government or about brand damage that may result from reporting an incident. Through trusted relationships with financial sector institutions, including the Protected Critical Infrastructure Information programme, DHS works to prevent inappropriate disclosure of proprietary information or other sensitive data. Furthermore, the Administration's cyber security legislative proposal offers a chance to provide clear statutory authority to facilitate greater information sharing between DHS and the private sector.

DHS Cyber Security Mission

No single technology or government entity can overcome the cyber security challenges the Nation faces on its own. The public and private sectors must work collaboratively to address the risks posed to our Nation's critical systems.

At DHS's National Protection and Programs Directorate (NPPD), in addition to leading the effort to secure Federal Executive Branch civilian agencies' unclassified networks, we are responsible for several other cyber security missions, including:

- Providing technical expertise to the private sector and to critical infrastructure owners and operators, including at the state and local levels, in order to enhance their cyber security preparedness and broaden their risk assessment, mitigation, and incident response capabilities;
- Raising public cyber security awareness; and
- Coordinating the national mitigation response to cyber incidents.

In 2009, President Obama determined that the Comprehensive National Cyber security Initiative (CNCI) and its associated cyber activities should remain a priority for the federal government. Consistent with the CNCI's priorities, the President's *Cyberspace Policy Review*established a strategic framework for advancing the Nation's cyber security policies. Following the May 2009 publication of this review, DHS designated safeguarding and securing cyberspace as a priority mission area in the Quadrennial Homeland Security Review (QHSR).

To execute on this mission area, DHS established the following two overarching goals:

- Creation of a safe, secure, and resilient cyber environment and
- Promotion of cyber security knowledge and innovation.

Within NPPD, the Office of Cyber security and Communications (CS&C) focuses on reducing the risks posed to communications and information technology infrastructures, and to the sectors that depend on those infrastructures. CS&C also seeks to enable timely response and recovery of these infrastructures in all circumstances while coordinating information sharing efforts among Federal law enforcement, intelligence, defence, and homeland security communities to ensure a common operating picture of the cyber security and communications environment. Three divisions make up CS&C: the National Cyber Security Division (NCSD), the Office of Emergency Communications, and the National Communications System. In addition, CS&C established the National Cyber security and Communications Integration Centre (NCCIC), which coordinates interagency mitigation response efforts in the event of a significant cyber security incident.

Consistent with its role in implementing the NIPP, NCSD collaborates with the Banking and Finance Sector to conduct risk assessments and mitigate vulnerabilities and threats capable of affecting the sector's information technology assets and critical infrastructure. NCSD's Cyber Security Evaluations Programme conducts Cyber Resilience Reviews to proactively determine how various organizations manage the cyber security of significant information services and assets while offering guidance to improve cyber security management and reduce operational risks related to cyber security. In doing so, NCSD carries out the majority of DHS's non-law enforcement cyber security responsibilities within the financial services sector.

One of NCSD's operational arms, the U.S. Computer Emergency Readiness Team (US-CERT), works closely with banking and finance sector partners to provide analytical expertise and to share threat and vulnerability information in collaboration with other critical infrastructure sectors, law enforcement, and the intelligence community. Through the FS-ISAC, the Banking and Finance Sector provides US-CERT with threat, incident, and vulnerability data, which is then integrated into US-CERT's analytical and information sharing processes.

NCSD's Critical Infrastructure Cyber Protection & Awareness (CICPA) branch builds on this effort by providing security clearances to key cyber security officials within the Banking and Finance Sector. For example, DHS has sponsored Top Secret/SCI clearances for select members of the financial services sector and numerous Secret-level clearances in partnership with Treasury to broaden the scope of information that US-CERT can share. US-CERT has also benefits from close operational collaboration with DHS's U.S. Secret Service Criminal Investigative Division (USSS-CID), which has concurrent jurisdiction with the FBI over the investigation of computer crime and protects the Nation's financial payment systems while combating transnational financial crimes committed by terrorists and other criminals.

Research and Innovation

In addition to NPPD's cyber security activities, the DHS Science & Technology (S&T) Directorate is closely engaged with the Financial Services Sector. One of the many innovations emerging from S&T's partnership with the Financial Service Sector is the Distributed Environment for Critical Infrastructure Decision-Making Exercises (DECIDE) software suite. DECIDE will enable enterprise decision makers to evaluate responses to operational disruptions of market-based transactions across networks. This allows stakeholders to pursue effective business continuity practices that address increasingly sophisticated cyber threats. DHS Science & Technology (S&T) Directorate is closely engaged with the FSSCC to develop capabilities to protect citizens by enhancing the resilience, security, integrity, and accessibility of information systems used by financial institutions and other critical infrastructures. In December 2010, S&T signed a memorandum of understanding with the FSSCC and the National Institute of Standards and Technology (NIST) to expedite the coordinated development and availability of collaborative research, development, and testing activities for cyber security technologies and processes.

Interagency and Sector Coordination

The success of our efforts to reduce cyber security risks posed to the Banking and Finance Sector depends on effective communication and critical partnerships. No single entity has sole responsibility for securing cyberspace. To that end DHS works with its Federal partners to host a number of initiatives focused on enhancing coordination and information sharing with the private sector.

Private Sector Security Clearance Programme

The NCCIC maintains a programme that hosts Top Secret/SCI-cleared private sector representatives on the NCCIC operations floor including representatives from the FS-ISAC. This programme was created to closely integrate the operational capabilities of the NCCIC, various critical infrastructure sectors, and individual companies. The FS-ISAC's presence on the NCCIC floor enhances the analysis, warning, and response capabilities associated with critical information systems and improves the overall cyber security of the Banking and Finance Sector and the Nation.

Cyber Security Information Sharing and Collaboration Programme

In February 2010, DHS, the Department of Defense, and the FS-ISAC launched a pilot designed to help protect key critical networks and infrastructure within the Banking and Finance Sector by sharing actionable information. Based on knowledge gained from the pilot, DHS is expanding its information sharing and incident response coordination processes with other critical infrastructure sectors and leveraging capabilities from within DHS and across the response community. Specifically, DHS plans to launch the critical infrastructure Cyber security Information Sharing and Collaboration Programme this year, which seeks to create a secure online collaboration portal where registered critical infrastructure sector entities can provide accurate, timely, and thorough information about current, emerging, and evolving threats posed to critical infrastructure networks. The portal will have the capability to process Protected Critical Infrastructure Information while offering timely and actionable analysis and mitigation products for critical infrastructure participants based on stakeholder contributions and unclassified government reporting.

Cyber Operations Resiliency Review Pilot Programme

In addition, NCSD, in partnership with Treasury and the BITS Financial Services Roundtable, is implementing a two-phase pilot programme to proactively assess the degree of cyber resilience and presence of malicious activity on up to five financial institutions' enterprise networks. In the first phase, analysts from CICPA's Cyber security Evaluation Programme will measure the adoption and growth of cyber security risk management using a common capability-based evaluation framework. In the second phase, US-CERT will analyse institution-provided data for evidence of malicious activity. If malicious activity is found, US-CERT will provide the institution with targeted strategies to mitigate the activity and protect against similar activity in the future.

National Cyber Incident Response

The President's *Cyberspace Policy Review* called for "a comprehensive framework to facilitate coordinated responses by government, the private sector, and allies to a significant cyber incident." To address this presidential priority, DHS created a working group of stakeholders from the public and private sectors that drafted the *National Cyber Incident Response Plan* (NCIRP). The NCIRP provides a framework for the NCCIC's response capabilities and for coordination of Federal, state and local governments, the private sector, and international partners during significant cyber incidents. The plan specifically addresses the role of the Treasury and the FS-ISAC in providing for coordination of national response capabilities by providing flexible, adaptable synchronization of response activities across jurisdictional lines. In September 2010, DHS tested the NCIRP during a response exercise in which members of the domestic and international cyber incident response community addressed a scenario of a coordinated cyber event.

The NCIRP working group is now completing the final stages of plan revision using observations from the exercise and experience from real world events.

National Strategy for Trusted Identities in Cyberspace

DHS also worked closely with our public and private sector partners on, the Administration's National Strategy for Trusted Identities in Cyberspace (NSTIC), which seeks to increase the security of online transactions through the development of more trustworthy digital credentials. The adoption of more trustworthy credentials will help to reduce account takeovers and raise overall consumer safety levels. Trusted identities are a key part of the Department's vision for a healthy cyber ecosystem. The voluntary adoption of credentials envisioned by the NSTIC will make online transactions faster, more convenient, safer and more private.

DHS Technical Assistance to the Banking and Finance Sector

Over the past year, DHS has demonstrated its ability to assist financial institutions with cyber intrusion mitigation and incident response while building on lessons learned. Initiating technical assistance with any private company to provide analysis and mitigation advice is a sensitive endeavour that requires trust and confidentiality.

In June 2010, for example, US-CERT partnered with the Federal Bureau of Investigation (FBI) to address a specific threat impacting a U.S. financial institution. By providing remote operational support following a formal request for technical assistance from the financial institution, US-CERT was able to analyse the threat, develop near-term mitigation recommendations, and identify strategies for preventing similar activity. In this instance, malicious actors used a combination of legitimate and illegitimate data to create false online accounts, ultimately giving them access to sensitive systems. A rapid cross-sector and interagency response effort prevented any known financial losses from this event.

As a result of knowledge gained during this engagement and from the collaborative relationship built with this particular financial institution, US-CERT was better able to assist another financial institution that experienced a similar event. In June 2011,

US-CERT partnered with the Secret Service to assist the second institution with their detection and mitigation efforts and leveraged its relationship with the initial institution to bring the two entities together to discuss the vulnerability.

During an unrelated event in December 2010, US-CERT partnered with FBI and the National Security Agency to provide on-site and remote assistance and support in response to a significant cyber security incident involving financial entities. Upon formal request, US-CERT was able respond to this incident with specialized technical insight, support, and assistance. Specifically, US-CERT conducted interviews and briefings with high-ranking company officials, served as the lead for a skilled technical team of network analysts, and coordinated the development of a mitigation strategy with other agencies and financial sector institutions. Through our analysis and unique capability to coordinate cross-sector and interagency response efforts, we discovered other potential and actual victims of this threat. US-CERT aggressively worked to publish alert and awareness products for the wider community.

5

Information Technology and Terrorism

Information technologies are a powerful set of enabling technologies. They are flexible enough to play a supporting role to traditional terrorist activities as well as to provide an alternative medium for conflict. However, the use of IT is double edged. In adopting IT-enabled means and tactics, a terrorist organization also assumes some significant risks.

ENHANCED TERRORIST COMMUNICATIONS

IT gives individuals and groups a reach and influence that was previously reserved for well-organized, state- funded terrorist organizations. It represents, in many respects, the "death of distance." Physical distance and national borders that once separated terrorists from their co-conspirators, their audience, and their targets cease to exist in the world of modern telecommunications and the Internet.

Terrorist groups have been known to share information and collaborate with each other. Documented cases include Italy's Red Brigades collaborating with Germany's Baader-Meinhof gang in the late 1970s, the Red Army Faction (Baader-Meinhof's successor) with the French group Action Directe in the mid-1980s and the Japanese Red Army with the Popular Front for the Liberation of Palestine in the late 1980s. Such collaborations were inherently risky because the international, inter-group communications could have been intercepted by law-enforcement or national- intelligence agencies. By using strong encryption techniques for security, however, terrorists could communicate among themselves in a variety of ways without fear that government agencies might be listening in and decrypting their messages. Encryption can also be used for anonymous communications and authenticating communications—a form of digital signature. The same techniques can be applied to intra-group communications, for security, anonymity, or to authenticate them.

Although encryption makes for seemingly safer intra- and inter-group communications, such communications can still be intercepted and possibly, decoded, especially if the terrorist group fails to implement a sophisticated key management system to protect its code keys. As terrorists are often fighting sovereign-state governments, their adversaries usually have vast resources with which to crack encryption codes. The percentage of encrypted communications around the world today is also still very small. By embracing this technology before it is more accepted and more widely used, terrorists may be drawing attention to themselves, making it more likely that their communications will receive greater scrutiny and perhaps even be decoded. Thus, encryption may lead to a false sense of security in the confidentiality, authenticity and integrity of communications, as well as drawing unwanted law-enforcement attention to the group.

Terrorist use of computers to store and transmit messages may also provide law-enforcement agencies with a dangerous, incriminating record if the terrorists are ever apprehended. Stored evidence on computer systems, even if encrypted, could be decoded and used to convict, and even information believed to have been erased may be recoverable. Hamas recently discovered the pitfalls of using computers to store critical contact information when 'Abd-al-Rahman Zaydan was arrested and sentenced by the Nabus Military Court in January 1995 and his computer seized. Zaydan apparently created and maintained a database for Hamas that linked dozens of terrorists squads and activists in Israel, Jordan, and Germany. Following Zaydan's arrest, Hamas' method of operation was uncovered, and terrorists were apprehended.

For those terrorists seeking to spread their terror or to publicize their cause, IT offers a new medium through which to communicate to a vast and growing world audience. These broadcasts may be directed at a specific individual or at the global, web-surfing populace. E-mail offers a tool for potentially safer, quicker communication with the terrorist support base, within the terrorist organization itself and even direct communication to the terrorists' target audience. Web sites and bulletin boards can spread propaganda and attract supporters. One recent example of terrorists using IT to disseminate information is the MRTA's website, which contains official communiques, press releases, interviews with leaders, background information on the organization and statements about its political objectives. The organization's website in itself generated additional international news media coverage for the group, although the impact of this additional attention, and that of the website itself, on the Peruvian government and international opinion is difficult to assess.

Adopting IT for broadcast purposes may help to change the nature of terrorism. Because terrorists may no longer be completely dependent upon the news media to disseminate their point of view, the indiscriminate violence that is so often employed to attract news-media attention may no longer be as necessary. The interactive capabilities of IT may also change the nature of the communications that take place. With the news media, communications are essentially one-way. With technologies like the Internet, however, terrorists can engage in dialogue with more people than ever before, including supporters, potential new recruits and critics, thereby allowing them to adjust their positions and tactics and, potentially, to increase their support and general appeal.

But the use of IT to disseminate information can also have significant, undesirable effects. Unless the terrorists are careful in their usage of the Internet for e-mail, website maintenance, or other services, they may unwittingly supply law enforcers with an easy path to their door. Also, by putting its positions and ideological arguments in the public domain, a terrorist group invites opposing sides to disseminate their own propaganda. The ensuing war of words may be to the terrorists' disadvantage as supporters are drawn away. Indeed, absolute belief in their ideological position is often the glue that binds individuals in terrorist groups together. Cogent dissenting opinions could undermine group cohesion. Regular use of e-mail and the Internet could provide law enforcers with yet another means to locate the group. Mass-media attention provides other benefits beyond publicizing an act of brutality, such as a degree of legitimacy and the forced attention of a significantly larger audience. Thus, for terrorists, using IT is not a perfect substitute for international news-media coverage and may even have negative consequences.

New Targets

The global diffusion and integration of IT has effectively moved many national assets into, or created new ones inside, the virtual world of computer networks. These assets vary from the wires, computers, and other necessary telecommunications equipment to the information they contain to the capability for communication itself. As a consequence, they are vulnerable to a relatively new form of attack using IT- enabled means.

By using cyberspace as a new conflict medium, terrorists can obviate the distance between themselves and their designated targets. In the past, terrorists needed to be physically present at their target locations to prepare and execute acts of violence. In cyberspace, however, one node on the international computer network has nearly instantaneous access to any other. Exploiting this access, a terrorist might be able to strike at targets thousands of miles away from his operational base without ever leaving it.

Many U.S. infrastructure industries are, to varying degrees, vulnerable to attack and may offer attractive targets for terrorists. The public switched network (PSN) encompasses the U.S. public telephone networks and the Internet and, as the backbone of the United States' information infrastructure upon which millions of people and businesses depend every day, could be attacked to cause serious national disruption. A terrorist need only have a computer, modem, and the technical expertise to gain access to the U.S. long-distance telephone network or the critical servers of the Internet to create problems for the information infrastructure.

The problems may be as extreme as completely incapacitating a telecommunications system, as insidious as altering or stealing information being transmitted, or as relatively benign as pirating telecommunications services. Other targets might include assets that are connected to the PSN corporate networks, building environmental-control systems, financial transaction and record-keeping systems, medical and educational networks, transportation systems, manufacturing systems, utility monitoring and control systems, and government computer systems. The great diversity of the terrorist population makes each of the above mentioned infrastructures a potentially inviting target for some group or individual. For example, medical systems at abortion clinics might be threatened by anti-abortion terrorists; corporate networks might interest environmental terrorists; government systems—if the government is secular or dominated by another religion—could be threatened by religious terrorists, by anarchists, or by foreign governments; and all systems might be considered fair game for a nihilistic terrorist faction.

If a terrorist organization were to develop an electronic attack capability concentrating the necessary technical expertise and equipment to disrupt, damage, or destroy targeted information systems, it would first have to overcome a significant technical hurdle. Rumors persist that people proficient in network attacks are available for hire. Short of hiring such mercenaries, however, a terrorist group would need to foster the requisite technical expertise within its membership. The current trend towards easier-to-use hacking tools indicates that this hurdle will not be as high in the future as it is today, even as it is significantly lower today than it was 2 years ago. For example, a relatively new automated tool for performing system administration functions called "Netcat" was introduced in July 1996, at the annual "Def Con" hacker conference in Las Vegas, Nevada. Anyone may download a copy of Netcat from the Internet and obtain extensive documentation detailing how to use the tool to perform, in addition to legitimate system- administration functions, such sophisticated hacker attacks as "IP spoofing," "packet sniffing," and "SYN bombing." Netcat is one of the more recent examples of publicly available hacker tools that continue to lower the threshold of required technical expertise to conduct electronic attacks.

In developing and becoming dependent on electronic attacks, though, a terrorist organization may be assuming significant risks inherent in the relative novelty of the technology. Computer-security experts and systems administrators are locked in a seemingly eternal struggle with hackers, industrial spies, and others seeking unauthorized access to computer systems. The battlefield changes constantly as each side innovates and develops new techniques either to protect or break into systems. A terrorist group could thus find its newly acquired capability obsolete within a few months, unless its technical experts were able to keep pace. Terrorist computers and networks would also be no less fragile than the systems they seek to attack. Thus, in trying to exploit the weaknesses of a fragile IT infrastructure, terrorists would acquire the same vulnerabilities and weaknesses themselves. Similarly, a terrorist organization relying heavily on IT has a vested interest in keeping the international networks functioning. A certain amount of freedom and flexibility with respect to targeting could therefore be lost by adopting IT.

Anonymity

Using IT may complement the current trend towards anonymous terrorism. Because the terrorist need not physically trespass on the target site, personal identification becomes very difficult. Even the virtual identities often used on the Internet may be a form of deception. An attacker may have multiple electronic identities or may have appropriated someone else's identity. Many sophisticated computer intruders today can enter systems and damage them without leaving any clues to their identity or origin. Tracing has thus become a major challenge for law enforcement. Even if an attacker could be traced with audit logs that somehow escaped tampering, proving that the suspected terrorist was the person punching the keys and committing the act would require substantially more proof than that contained in an audit log.

Capturing cybercriminals to date has typically entailed an elaborate investigation, involving the use of electronic monitoring programs specifically set up to detect the cybercriminal's movements. These investigations require months of surveillance and, more important, the continued perpetration of similar illegal activities by the target criminal. If the criminal were to cease his normal patterns of behavior or otherwise stop engaging in such activity, tracking him down would be impossible. Thus, provided terrorists are careful about covering their electronic tracks, change their patterns of behavior after each attack, and destroy any evidence on their computers that might implicate them, they may control the degree of anonymity and visibility that their activities give them. If they were so inclined, they could conduct their terrorism in quiet obscurity from virtually anywhere. Conversely, if the terrorists are not careful, they may unwittingly supply law enforcers with a trail leading directly to their door.

State Sponsorship

IT may also help to end the need for state sponsorship of terrorism. Tehran and Tripoli are believed to provide terrorists with sanctuary, bases of operation, secure communications through diplomatic channels, training, financial support, weapons, and intelligence. These "rogue" states, with their hostility towards the United States and other Western countries, may also support IT-enabled terrorism. While such terrorism may benefit from state sponsorship, it does not require it.

Using encryption to secure communications, and skillful, untraceable network attacks to strike targets, a terrorist may evade detection and identification, avoiding the need for state sanctuary. Terrorists operating in this way would be able to work from almost any country in the world—provided they had access to the necessary telecommunications infrastructure— even from the United States, in relative safety.

Foreign bases of operation might be useful for intelligence-gathering activities, but, again, they are not required for IT-enabled terrorism. The open societies of Western democracies offer ample opportunity for discreet information-gathering by terrorists posing as tourists, journalists, or ordinary civilians. In addition, information about various systems' vulnerabilities is often shared on-line between hackers on computer bulletin boards, websites, news groups, and other forms of electronic association, and this information can be obtained without setting foot in the target country.

Finally, terrorists engaged in IT-enabled forms of terrorism may escape the need for state funding. Compared to the costs modem terrorists incur for armaments, international travel, and training facilities, IT terrorism is relatively inexpensive—the basic hardware is available for a few thousand dollars. Also, if the terrorists become proficient at network attacks, they may be able to extort or steal money from large, IT-dependent financial institutions by threatening to shut down their corporate networks or by more direct means. Rumors abound of organized criminal elements conducting technologically sophisticated bank protection rackets, but financial institutions deny that such extortion has taken or is taking place. In the final analysis, state sponsorship may no longer be the essential ingredient it once was for terrorists as IT effectively renders the many advantages of state sponsorship obsolete.

Domestic Terrorism

The face of U.S. domestic terrorism may already be changing given the massive infusion of IT into the economy and society. U.S. law-enforcement officials have blamed the Internet for spreading bomb-building information and contributing to the rise in domestic bombings. In terms of electronic attacks, individuals and small groups have emerged as potent menaces, capable of wreaking significant havoc. On November 24, 1994, General Electric, the National Broadcasting Corporation, and other U.S.-based companies suffered a significant breach of network security. For several hours, these corporate networks—supposedly protected behind "firewalls"—were in disarray as administrators sought to repair the damage wrought by intruders. The perpetrators of the attack issued a manifesto. Calling themselves the "Internet Liberation Front," they denounced corporations for turning the Internet into "a cesspool of greed" and declared "cyberwar."

IT appears to lower the threshold for participating in illegal acts. People who might shun an activity if physical involvement were required may be willing to try it via the safety of a computer. How many hackers would be willing to scale a fence, cut through barbed wire and risk being shot to steal information from a military base? Yet, hackers routinely break into U.S. Department of Defense computer systems to steal information and cause mischief. From interviews with hackers, computer-security expert Donn Parker found many of them to be incapable of personal confrontation, much less inflicting personal injury upon another. Given a computer and network to insulate them, however, they are able to steal and harm people without reservation. By lowering this threshold, the potential pool of individuals willing and able to conduct terrorism might grow and may help to broaden the spectrum of political motives and organizational structures found among potential terrorists today.

Digital communications and the Internet have enabled geographically dispersed people to meet and share their opinions in electronic settings that promote such interaction. They may even move their dialogues and discussions to a more private venue by changing the virtual locations of their meetings or using encryption. These forms of association have naturally led to the creation of clubs and groups. As the Internet Liberation Front example shows, some of these groups appear to be formed to do mischief. Some scholars consider these new types of associations the precursors of what will become a dominant social organizational form and, ultimately, the center of future conflicts.

Hackers as Terrorists

The ability to predict when political groups will turn to terrorism to advance their agenda remains elusive. Studies of terrorists and terrorist psychology essentially conclude that, although certain common traits can be inferred, no generic terrorist personality profile exists. Among the traits that many terrorists have been found to share are stress-seeking, risk-taking, low self-esteem, and patience. In 1977, Charles A. Russell, Chief of the U.S. Air Force's Acquisitions and Analysis Division in the Directorate of Counterintelligence, and Captain Bowman H. Miller of the Headquarters Air Force Office of Special Investigations, Washington, D.C., went so far as to propose a 'typical' terrorist description as: "male (although there are many notable exceptions) in his early twenties, single, from a middle-to-upper-class family, well- educated, with some university training, although he may be a university dropout, who often joined or was recruited into the group while at university."

During their research, scholars also debunked some commonly held beliefs, including the myths that terrorists must be mentally ill and necessarily violent. Apparently, some terrorist leaders were so averse to violence that they would block out the consequences of their actions while performing terrorist acts. To maintain group cohesion and motivation, terrorists have often used powerful, absolutist ideologies: "the ideology becomes a holy writ and dictates what is morally acceptable...members of a terrorist group submerge their own individual identities into the group identity, and the group ideology becomes the determinant of individual morality."

Hackers as a group exhibit several similarities to terrorists. Most hackers are twenty-something males who have difficulty with inter-personal relationships; they may have college degrees, or they were unsuccessful in school, but self-educated to a comparable level; and they are patient when working with computers. They seem willing to continue their activities even though the risks may be increasing as law enforcers bolster their efforts to apprehend and prosecute computer criminals. Ideologically, many hackers feel passionately about the freedom of information and the free flow of electronic information within cyberspace.39 These principles were at the core of the Internet Liberation Front's declaration of cyberwar against corporations attempting to profit from the flow of information, and the bonds between the group members were apparently strong enough to enable the concerted attack.

Despite the personality similarities that can be drawn between terrorists and present-day hackers, the fact remains that terrorism is extreme, and far more aberrant than prankish hacking. And, although hackers have demonstrated that they are willing to bring down computer networks to cause functional paralysis and even monetary loss, this propensity for expensive mischief is not conclusive evidence that they would be willing to jeopardize lives or even kill for a cause. One would hope that the threshold for willfully causing deaths is high enough that the vast majority of, if not all, hackers would refrain from such behavior.

Hackers, however, may unwittingly cause deaths by disrupting telecommunications, altering data, or crashing computer systems.

If, for example, a group of hackers were to shut down a part of the PSN for a period of time and during that time someone died as a result of the network being down—because a doctor could not confer with a specialist, appropriate emergency help could not be dispatched, or any other failure attributable to the communications system's failure—then those hackers would be indirectly responsible. Thus, regarding the question whether hackers today will be the terrorists of tomorrow, one can only point to the fact that some hackers have been willing to act in concert to attack the telecommunications infrastructure, and insofar as an infrastructure attack constitutes terrorism, hacker terrorism has already occurred.

Terrorist Use of Information Technology

Significant controversy exists over whether terrorists would be interested in using IT. Recalling the diversity of contemporary terrorists, credible generic statements about who would be interested in IT-enabled terrorism are difficult to make. Four variables, however, influence the likelihood of terrorists adopting any new tactic: the attractiveness of available targets; the effect of strategy on target audiences; the level of technical challenge; and the group's perception of its current methods. Examining the current practitioners of terrorism and the characteristics of IT-enabled terrorism in relation to these variables gives an insight into the probability that terrorists will adopt IT-enabled terrorist tactics.

Terrorism experts make a strong case that modern international terrorist groups that crave mass-media attention would be unlikely to employ IT-enabled terrorist tactics. For example, Brian Jenkins believes that modern terrorists see their current tactics as sufficient and are not interested in branching out into new forms of conflict such as network attacks. He points out that disruptive terrorism like IT-enabled attacks are "technically demanding and do not produce immediate, visible effects. There is no drama. No lives hang in the balance. There is no bang, no blood. They satisfy neither the hostility nor the publicity hunger of terrorists." Computer-security experts concur that IT- enabled means are too technologically challenging and too undervalued by the media to make them attractive tactics for terrorists. These arguments, however, do not make a compelling case for modern terrorists refraining from using any form of IT. In fact, many modem terrorist groups are already using IT to enhance their communications capabilities. Former Central Intelligence Agency (CIA) Director John Deutch testified before the U.S. Senate Permanent Subcommittee on Investigations in June 1996 that Hizbollah and other terrorist groups were already taking advantage of modem digital telecommunications systems. Thus, while these established organizations may be reluctant or unwilling to employ IT as a primary offensive means, they may use it to support their present operations.

In contrast, single-issue and nihilistic terrorists, specifically those not yet using IT-enabled means, may not be as hesitant to adopt IT as the terrorists mentioned above. For example, many right-wing militias in the United States have already been actively using the Internet to communicate and share propaganda and other information. As far as such groups adopting IT as a primary medium for conflict, this is highly unlikely. IT lacks drama; it requires a high level of technical expertise; and the media tends to undervalue IT-enabled incidents.

As long as the current tactics of these groups are sufficient to accomplish their short-term goals and move towards their long-term goals, why should they change? The assets available via cyberspace may not be the kinds of symbolic targets that these groups may want to attack. And, even if they were, the fragility of computer hardware may make a physical attack more attractive because it is significantly less technically challenging than attempting a network attack. For these reasons, many in the computer-security field question why any terrorist would want to conduct a sustained campaign of terror using IT. As Donn Parker noted, "Computers are fragile things; if you want to destroy them, then blow them up. Who needs to use network attacks?" Or, as Marcus Ranum surmised, "If a terrorist wants to bring down Wall Street, he won't do it with computers, he'll do it by blowing up the power grid. If a terrorist wanted to bring down the [New York Stock Exchange], he'd get a bomb onto the trading floor."

The current environment thus does not appear to encourage adopting IT-enabled terrorism, but identifiable trends indicate that adoption could become increasingly likely. With respect to the availability of desirable targets via cyberspace, terrorists are likely to choose to employ electronic attacks only if the reachable assets are attractive targets, and as infrastructure industries continue to modemise their information systems to take advantage of the benefits of IT, this situation will become more likely. Until the impact of an electronic attack upon the target audience breaks the current stigma of being perpetrated by delinquent adolescents, terrorists will probably shun such tactics. A change in this public perception is essential if legitimacy-seeking terrorists are to adopt them. For anonymous terrorists this stigma is not a serious issue. Although electronic attacks still present terrorists with a significant technical hurdle, the trend towards more-user-friendly programs to aid hackers will clearly lower this barrier in future. Finally, terrorists are unlikely to change their tactics and innovate new ones unless they come to see their old methods as somehow inadequate. As most terrorists view their current tactics as sufficient, a move to adopt IT- enabled terrorism appears unlikely. In light of this assessment, the fact that IT-enabled terrorism has not emerged as a significant problem is understandable.

Predicting when the conditions favouring a transition to IT-enabled terrorism will occur is complicated by other factors. For example, if efforts to improve the robustness and security of the United States' information infrastructure are successful, the technical challenge may always remain beyond terrorist capabilities. If, on the other hand, the infrastructure remains vulnerable, automated tools for electronic attacks continue to become easier to use and readily available, and systems responsible for public safety— such as air-traffic-control systems—become accessible, then some terrorist might succeed in an electronic attack.

Is This Terrorism?

Are the new breeds of "terrorists" really terrorists or simply a derivative of the ordinary criminal? As discussed earlier, distinguishing a terrorist from a common criminal is important because governments deal differently with each. Certainly, single-issue terrorists who use violence to affect policy on their single issue qualify as "real" terrorists, as do the nihilistic and anarchistic groups who launch general attacks against society and symbols of government. But can network attacks like shutting down a long-distance telephone network or a company's internal network be considered terrorism? No violence is used; no life-threatening terror is instilled. The stated reason for the attack on General Electric was more of a social than a political challenge. Non-lethal network attacks such as these must fall into a gray area between ordinary crime and terrorism. They are illegal acts motivated by a pseudo-political agenda that can cause significant disruption, but they are non-lethal and, as such, are not truly terrorist in nature. But this analysis does not preclude the possibility of IT terrorism either now or in the future; it only suggests that the aforementioned acts of IT sabotage do not constitute terrorism as it has been understood thus far.

In considering such attacks, however, it is important to keep in mind that criminal organizations are differentiated from terrorist groups by their pursuit of profit rather than overtly political objectives. Unfortunately, this is also an area where there is considerable hyperbole. In 1998, for example, the New Republic ran a story about teenage hackers who were extorting money from corporations. The story turned out to be almost completely fabricated. Nevertheless, there are several important and substantiated cases of criminals targeting computer systems for theft—of either data or money—and for extortion of companies by using threats to destroy or degrade their computer systems and the accompanying data.

It was revealed in January 1998, for example, that hackers had succeeded in obtaining access to confidential records of the customers of the Tokyo- based Sakura Bank Ltd. Information on up to 20,000 customers was stolen, some of which was subsequently made available to a mailing-list vendor Although customer accounts were not compromised, the episode illustrated the vulnerability of some financial institutions to forms of electronic infiltration. In other cases, of course, money not data is the target. Reportedly, Russian hackers made almost 500 attempts to access computer networks of the Central Bank of Russia between 1994 and 1996. During 1995 the criminals succeeded in stealing 250 billion rubles ($4.7M) in 1995. Russian criminals were also successful in what has become an infamous attack on Citicorp. After gaining access to the bank's cash management system in June 1994, a hacker, Vladimir Levin, who lived in St. Petersburg, began to wire money to accounts in Argentina, Indonesia, Finland, Russia, Switzerland, Germany, and Israel. Ultimately he moved about $10 million. Arrests of some of the collaborators were made in Tel Aviv and Rotterdam and all but $400,000 of the money was eventually recovered. Lenin himself was arrested in February 1995 by Scotland Yard during a visit he made to Britain. There was speculation that theft of this kind was only possible with inside information provided by an accomplice working for Citicorp. It has also been claimed that tighter security will prevent any repetition of such activity. Such claims notwithstanding, cyber- theft could become a very important activity for at least some criminal organizations in the future.

Equally if not more attractive will be cyber-extortion, an opportunity for organized crime that stems from the vulnerabilities of computerized data-storage and communications systems on which many firms are increasingly reliant. Threats to destroy data or even to destroy the computer system itself, with everything stored on it, can have a chilling effect. In cases where their credibility is demonstrated through some kind of warning or symbolic action that reveals both their capabilities and their willingness to use them, criminal organizations engaged in extortion are likely to have their demands met. According to the Sunday Times (London) in June 1996, successful extortion of this kind had become evident: in the previous 3 years there had been more than 40 attacks on computer systems in London, New York, and other European banking centers, as a result of which around 400 million pounds ($650 million) had been handed over to criminal extortionists. Companies in Britain had given in to extortion demands in order to prevent the destruction of computerized information systems. In one case in January 1993, trading ceased at a brokerage house after a threat was followed by a computer crash. Ten million pounds ($16 million) were apparently paid to the extortionists via a bank account in Zurich. In March 1995 a defense firm paid a similar amount to prevent implementation of a threat to its computer and information systems. The operations were believed to be the work of well-organized crime groups (at least one of which was believed to be from Russia). The threats were made to senior management and were given credibility by actions which demonstrated the capacity of the extortionists to destroy critical data. The money was sent to offshore bank accounts from which it was quickly removed.

Providing fully adequate verification of such reports is difficult, since most companies are reluctant to divulge information about their vulnerabilities, their susceptibility to extortion, or their willingness to meet the demands of criminals. One of the concerns, of course, is customer confidence. Another is the possibility of encouraging imitators—who might or might not be genuine. In 1997, for example, a series of telephone calls was made to banks in Portland, Oregon and Boston, Massachusetts claiming that they, along with other financial institutions, had been targeted by an environmental group which had penetrated their computer systems and would disrupt or destroy them unless the banks made a $2 million donation. A subsequent telephone call was traced to a public pay phone and the person who had made the threats was arrested and subsequently sentenced to 6 months in jail. Other cases have been more serious.

If criminal organizations threaten information systems primarily for profit, there might also be conditions that provoke such threats for purposes of deterrence and defense. It is not inconceivable that a major transnational criminal organization, facing a threat to its very existence by United States law enforcement and intelligence agencies, will threaten U.S. information systems. Whether such threats would provide sufficient deterrence would depend on a variety of circumstances, including, on the one side, the willingness and capabilities of the organization to cause damage, and one the other side, the commitment of the United States to dismantling the organizational structure of the group. It is worth emphasizing though that such a contingency is not far-fetched. In many respects it would simply be the cyber-space equivalent of the kind of developments which occurred in both Italy and

Colombia in the 1980s and early 1990s, when organized crime, for a variety of reasons, declared war on the state. In both these cases, of course, the state ultimately proved victorious. Cyber-space, however, is the ideal environment for asymmetric warfare and provides unprecedented opportunities for criminal organizations to confront the state in ways that dramatically raise the stakes. Moreover, for countries like the United States with a high level of dependence on computerized information and communication systems, sophistication is a source of vulnerability.

The capacity to confront the state in cyber-space is not something that transnational criminal organizations will use often. Their preference is for co-option and corruption. Nevertheless, the possibility of cyber-war gives them a weapon of last resort. Moreover, the capabilities to degrade the state's information systems can also be a useful tactical tool. This was evident in Amsterdam in 1995 when "police found themselves locked into an information battle with hackers employed by a criminal organization. The hackers managed to cause serious disruption to the police investigation by hacking into their communication system, thereby gathering operational intelligence and disrupting their command and control net." Such episodes which, in effect, are exercises in defensive information warfare are likely to become increasingly frequent. So too is the use of cyber-threats by criminal organizations—both to acquire wealth and to protect themselves.

INFORMATION AGE TERRORISM

Terrorism will change in the 21st century. Information warfare, the current "hot topic" for the military, along with Command and Control Warfare (C2W) are two concepts that some argue will create or accelerate a "Revolution in Military Affairs." These ideas also suggest the possibility of a "Revolution in Terrorism Affairs." Information age terrorism may take on three distinct forms: conventional terrorism, technoterrorism, and cyberterrorism. While conventional terrorism will still rely on physical violence, terrorists acquisition of high technology information warfare capabilities will allow a shift toward tactics focused on disruption rather than destruction. Information age terrorism, while continuing to use "conventional" weapons, will also employ weapons radically different from those used in conventional terrorism. This shift toward disruption in cyberspace, though the use of new weapons and without the use of violence in the physical world, may force a redefinition of the classic conception of terrorism.

INFORMATION WARFARE

The definition of Information Warfare has been extensively debated in the open press. The Department of Defense has a classified definition of Information Warfare contained in DOD Directive T$3600.1, but the public debate on the subject will be sufficient for the purposes of this thesis. Drs. John Arquilla and David Ronfeldt capture the broad nature of information warfare in *Cyberwar is Coming!* In this work, they address the military and civilian, as well as the offensive and defensive components of information warfare. The spectrum of conflict is split into "netwar" and "cyberwar".

Netwar refers to information-related conflict at a grand level between nations or societies. It means trying to disrupt, damage or modify what a target population knows or thinks it know about itself and the world around it. A netwar may focus on public or elite opinion, or both, It may involve public diplomacy measures, propaganda and psychological campaigns, political and cultural subversion, deception of or interference with local media, infiltration of computer networks and databases, and efforts to promote dissident or opposition movements across computer networks.

Cyberwar is the military cousin of netwar. While a diverse group of actors can conduct netwar at a variety of levels, cyberwar exists exclusively in the military realm.

Cyberwar refers to conducting, and preparing to conduct, military operations according to information-related principles. It means disrupting, if not destroying, information and communications system, broadly defined to include even military culture, on which an adversary relies in order to know itself: who it is, where it is, what it can do when, why it is fighting, which threats to counter first, and so forth. It means trying to know everything about an adversary while keeping the adversary from knowing much about oneself.

Cyberterrorism, while utilizing some cyberwar tactics, lies in the realm of netwar, Through an examination of cyber and netwar, Arquilla and Ronfeldt highlight the increasing importance of information control for military victory in the information age. In the future, information control may also be critical for successful terrorism or counter-terrorism.

The National Defense University (NDU) has posited a working definition of Information-Based Warfare that outlines the offensive and defensive components of information warfare. It highlights the applicability of information as both a target and a weapon across the conflict spectrum:

Information-based Warfare is an approach to armed conflict focusing on the management and use of information in all its forms and at all levels to achieve a decisive military advantage especially in the joint and combined environment. Information-based Warfare is both offensive and defensive in nature — ranging from measures that prohibit the enemy from exploiting information to corresponding measures to assure the integrity, availability, and interoperability of friendly information assets.

While ultimately military in nature, Information-based Warfare is also waged in political, economic, and social arenas and is applicable over the entire national security continuum from peace to war and from 'tooth to tail.' Finally, Information-based Warfare focuses on the command and control needs of the commander by employing state-of-the-art information technology such as synthetic environments to dominate the battlefield.

Martin Libicki of NDU has also examined the concept of Information Warfare and its implications for the future. In his Advanced Concepts and Technology paper, "What is Information Warfare?" Libicki outlines seven specific forms of information warfare: command and control warfare, information-based warfare, electronic warfare, psychological warfare, hacker warfare, economic information warfare, and cyber warfare. While most of these forms of conflict fall into the military realm, each of them is applicable to terrorism in the emerging information age. The form described as hacker war (warfare against computer networks) is split into three areas by Libicki the physical, the syntactic, and the semantic. The physical attack of computer networks is classified as technoterrorism by my typology. The attack of computer systems at the syntactic level (attack on the flow of electrons within the network) and at the semantic level (attacks on the veracity of a network's information—fooling the computer into producing an output that is incorrect) are defined as cyberterrorism because they exist exclusively in the realm of cyberspace.

There are two components of Information Warfare. First, your own information must be protected and trusted at all levels. During collection, the accuracy of the information received must be verified. During processing, information must be defended against theft, destruction and modification. Finally, during distribution of information to other elements, the means of transfer must be secure to ensure that information arrives at its destination in an unaltered format. The defensive portion of information warfare aims to ensure information confidentiality, integrity, and availability.

Second, an effort to disrupt the information gathering, processing, and distribution functions of the enemy must be undertaken. The effort to manipulate the information of the enemy while protecting your own takes place on several levels. Information warfare is not just about computers sending electrons from point A to point B. It is not only the hardware and software but the "wetware" (computer slang for a human brain) that is critical to information warfare. The fundamental goal of warfare is to change the mind of the enemy and convince him to do your will. The goal of information warfare is to accomplish this through the manipulation of the enemy's ability to control information. This places information warfare in the camp to Sun Tzu. Michael Handel captures the essence of information warfare by quoting both Clausewitz and Sun Tzu who states, "For to win one hundred victories in one hundred battle is not the acme of skill. To subdue the enemy without fighting is the acme of skill." This effort to win without fighting runs counter to Clausewitz, who believed that combat and bloodshed were an integral part of warfare. "Kind-hearted people might of course think there was some ingenious way to disarm or defeat and enemy without too much bloodshed, and might imagine this is the true goal of the art of war. Pleasant as it sounds, it is a fallacy that must be exposed." While contradictory, both quotes apply to terrorism in the information age. While perceived as "less bloody," and "not really fighting," physical destruction can play an important role in information warfare. One of the tools of information warfare is infrastructure warfare, in which the infrastructure of an enemy is targeted with both "regular" technology (bombs, missiles, troops on the ground) and "information" technology, the attempt to utilize malicious software to disrupt and alter enemy telecommunications without physical destruction and to induce a psychological state in the enemy that will lead him to "do your will."

Information warfare is the quest to disrupt, disable, destroy, or modify an adversary's information and information systems while simultaneously protecting your own. While electronic attacks of a network via computer and modem are the "cleanest" means of information warfare, physical attacks on the network's infrastructure are also possible and should always be considered as an option open terrorists.

Command and Control Warfare (C2W)

Chairman of the Joint Chief's of Staff Memorandum of Policy Number 30, "Command and Control Warfare," identifies Command and Control Warfare (C2W) as the military component of information warfare. Both terrorism and information warfare cover a larger spectrum of conflict than simply command and control, but the fundamentals of both are rooted in the ability to affect the thinking of the enemy. As a result, there are several useful parallels between C2W and terrorism in the information age.

The "five pillars" of C2W (electronic warfare, physical destruction, operations security, psychological operations, military deception) are designed to help classify a military operation. Each of these pillars is also applicable to terrorism. An understanding of C2W is useful in examining both the internal and external working of terrorist organizations. Properly performing in all five areas enhances the ability of a terrorist organization to mount an offensive against its opponent. If one of the areas is weak, it can be exploited by the organization under attack and used to disrupt or destroy a terrorist organization. While the defending group targets the weakness of a terrorist group, the terrorist group will target any perceived weakness of the defending group. This continual targeting and retargeting of actual and perceived weaknesses is the basis for determining the type of strategy that a defending group will use. If a terrorist organization is seen to have several glaring weaknesses in its C2 structure, the defending group may find it most effective to pursue an offensive strategy in an effort to destroy the terrorist. If, however, the terrorist' C2 networks are hard to identify, target, and attack, the only option open to the defender is to establish a defensive strategy in cyberspace whereby the costs of attack are increased, and the benefits reduced. New technology has affected the C2W "balance of power" between terrorists and authorities. Counter-terror forces now have the capability to more closely monitor communications channels using increasingly sophisticated computers. Terrorists, however, can also use increasing computer power and publicly available encryption technology to secure their member's communications. Terrorists, in the past, operated in what J. Bowyer Bell described as a "dragonworld," where they were forced to live in fear of constant government surveillance. With the rise of secure voice and data communications (i.e., Pretty Good Privacy (PGP for E-mail and PGPphone for Internet voice communication encryption), terrorists can emerge from the dragonworld. Conventional defensive C2W restrictions no longer exist for the information age terrorist, who can devote more time to offensive C2W and other acts without constantly worrying about secure communication.

Defense in cyberspace bears some resemblance to defense in the physical world. The most effective defense is to isolate a computer or network completely from the rest of cyberspace. If there is no access into a computer system because it has been removed from all networks, defending it will be easier. The primary concern for such a "stand alone" computer is the possibility of an authorized user inserting some form of malicious software. The problems associated with trusted individuals "going over" to the enemy camp have existed throughout history and are hardly unique to the information age. The second form of defense is similar to a point defense with access to a computer system challenged by an authentication and identification procedure. In this case, the computer asks for and verifies the password provided by the user. While "static" passwords that do not change are vulnerable to attack by random guessing, technology, such as the "smart card," exists to provide a constantly changing set of passwords that are nearly impossible to crack. Increasing the transmission paths available to data is akin to a defense in depth. As the data paths increase, the ability of an enemy to attack all of them successfully decreases. When one communication path is destroyed or degraded (by accident, natural causes, or malicious action), data will instantaneously switch to one of the other available paths with no impact to the end user. The use of encryption to ensure the confidentiality and integrity of data consists of electronically scrambling, and thus armor plating, the data that is to be sent through cyberspace. Even if the data is intercepted and copies, its contents remain unknown to the enemy until they can decrypt it, which may take years.

The ever shifting nature of conventional terrorism causes difficulty for defender states who attempt to pursue an offensive strategy against terrorism. The inability to target and attack small terrorist groups, plus the myriad of defensive techniques available to both state and substate actors will only increase the problems associated with countering conventional terrorists as the exploit the principles of information warfare.

INFRASTRUCTURE WARFARE

Infrastructure Warfare is an attack against the physical components of a state's networks, such as power and water distribution, telecommunications networks, rail lines, and roads, As related to information warfare, infrastructure warfare is defined as a physical attack on system components that would subsequently influence the ability to process or transmit information. As such bombing the telephone switching building that serve a specific location to isolate it from the rest of the world or destroying the electrical grid that supplies power to a targeted system would constitute infrastructure warfare. Terrorists have already proven that they are capable of physical destruction via numerous airline, building, and infrastructure bombings. Terrorists design these events to "send a message" to the world and to terrorize specific target audiences. Terrorist infrastructure warfare may utilize the same tools, such as bombs, with which the terrorist is familiar, but for a different purpose. Instead of attempting to "make a statement" by bombing a physical target for a physical impact, a terrorist group can bomb infrastructure targets to cause cascading failures (loss of electricity leads to loss of computers which leads to loss of communications, etc.) within a targeted system. These secondary effects of the bombing, which may only destroy equipment without causing personnel casualties, are the primary goal of the terrorist in infrastructure warfare.

CYBERSPACE

Cyberspace is a term coined to capture the essence of "where" computers work. While the physical components of computers and their networks are necessary for cyberspace to exist, it is more than merely the sum of these parts. Winn Schwartau defines cyberspace as follows:

Cyberspace is that intangible place between computers where information momentarily exists on its route from one end of the global network to the other. When little Ashley calls Grandmother, they are speaking in Cyberspace, the place between the phones. Cyberspace is the ethereal reality, an infinity of electrons speeding down copper or glass fibers at the speed of light from one point to another. Cyberspace includes the air waves vibrating with cellular, microwave and satellite communications. According to John Perry Barlow, cofounder of Electronic Frontier Foundation, Cyberspace is where all of our money is, except for the cash in our pocket."

The Defense Information Systems Agency, a branch of the Department of Defense charged with conducting defensive information warfare defines cyberspace as: The electronic environment formed by the aggregate of global computing and telecommunications resources. Cyberspace is a virtual 5th dimension characterized by: no geographic, national, or temporal boundaries, no ownership, laws, or identity cards.

Cyberspace does not have a physical reality. One cannot physically "enter" cyberspace. It consists of the "virtual world" through which all electronic transactions take place. It is in this realm that the cyberterrorist will operate.

CYBERTERRORISM

The term cyberterrorism refers to the use of information warfare tactics and techniques by terrorist organizations to affect cyberspace. The cyberterrorist will operate exclusively within cyberspace and will not physically destroy any of the infrastructure that supports the existence of cyberspace. While cyberterrorists wish to have an impact on the actions of real people in the real world, they operate within the virtual world of cyberspace to manipulate these actors. Thus, if cyberterrorists wished to take down a telephone system or an electric grid, they would attack the computers controlling the system and not its subsidiary physical components.

Weapons of the Cyberterrorist

The weapons of the cyberterrorist are not designed to kill people or break physical objects. Rather, they exist exclusively to destroy or modify computer data. The weapons and the targets are the electrons moving within cyberspace. While it is possible to attack this data without any human interfaces, the human is usually the weakest link in a computer system.

Joseph Seanor of CIBIR Corporation, a computer crime investigative group, recently discussed the "Methods of Operations" of Cyberterrorists. His definitions provide a useful starting point to examine how cyberterrorists may attack their targets. The critical element in cyberterrorism, and information warfare in general, is knowledge. While the "tools" of the cyberterrorist (computer modems, phone connections) are nearly universally available, the knowledge of computer systems and their weaknesses (while becoming increasingly common is not as easily obtained. Individuals who have the requisite level of knowledge to become cyberterrorists fall into three main categories. The first is a "hacker" defined as a "person that breaks into computers to prove that it can be done. Some are destructive in nature, others are purely joyriders." The second category is the cyberpunk, "a harder edged computer hacker, one that enjoys technology and uses that technology to make money or act as an anarchist." The third category is the cypherpunk, "a person that is interested in the use of encryption to protect the privacy and the use of decryption methods to access other protected files." Paul Strassmann notes that, with the skill resident in these groups, several risks to computer systems exist:

Pest Programs

- Trojan horse attacks- implanting malicious code, sending letter bombs.
- Logic bombs-setting time or event bombs
- Malevolent worms- denying access to distributed resources
- Virus Attacks- attaching code to programs and replicating it

Bypasses

- Backdoor attacks- using existing flaws in software for exploitation
- Authorization attacks- password cracking, hacking control files

Active Misuse

- Creating, modifying, denying service, entering false or misleading data
- Incremental attacks- using salami tactics
- Denials of service- launching saturation attacks

Passive Misuse

- Browsing- reading and copying with apparent authorization
- Interference, aggregation- exploiting database searches, traffic analysis
- Indirect misuse- preparing for subsequent misuses, off-line pre-encryptive matching, factoring numbers to obtain crypto keys, autodialer and voice-mail scanning.

To achieve these results, the cyberterrorist cannot use the weapons commonly employed in conventional terrorism. While a conventional terrorist finds a fertilizer bomb effective in blowing up a building or other symbolic target, a technoterrorist will find the same bomb useful in destroying a critical node in a network to cause disruption. Cyberterrorists have no use for physical explosives. Their weapons exist nearly exclusively in cyberspace. These new weapons are unique in that they can simultaneously be more powerful and weaker than the weapons of the conventional terrorist. This apparent dichotomy exists because the laws of physics do not operate in cyberspace in the same manner as the physical world. A conventional bomb will have some effect every time it is exploded in the real world. A software bomb when exploded in cyberspace may have an extraordinary effect the first time it is used as it normally exploits an existing weakness in a computer operating system. After that weakness has been corrected, an identical software bomb will do no damage to the targeted computer or its data.

Several cyberterrorist weapons can have an impact on the networks of today and tomorrow.

Viruses. One of the most heralded weapons of a cyberterrorist or a hacker is the computers virus. Computer viruses are programs designed to perform actions not intended by the operator. These actions include erasing or modifying the data in a computer's memory or storage with or without malicious intent. A virus is so named because it "lives" within a host system or program and cannot spread without some actin., often unwitting (such as using an infected disk), by the system operator. Viruses can be used in an attempt to shut down a computer or even hold it hostage. The front page publicity granted the "Michelangelo virus" every march serves as an example of the publicity power generated by hostile virus. This particular virus was written to check the computer's internal clock/calendar and destroy the data on the infected computer on Michelangelo's birthday, March 6. The virus was widely publicized when released in 1992. The ease of identifying and removing the Michelangelo virus has resulted in publicity about it *not* attacking computers:

MICHELANGEL0 VIRUS FAILS TO SURFACE: The Michelangelo virus, a nasty bit of high-technology vandalism designed to break out each year on March 6, the great artist's birthday, failed to cripple the world's computers. The Michelangelo virus was front-page news in 1992.

To compete against virus detection and removal programs, virus writers have created a subset of the virus, known as a polymorphic virus. This type of virus changes itself slightly every time it is replicated or executed, thus denying a virus detection program a fixed set of "indicators" that the virus has infected a computer. The battle between virus writers and virus fighters will continue into the future, with each trying to outsmart the other. The sheer explosion in the number of viruses (in 1991 where were approximately 500 known computer viruses, by 1995 that number expanded to more than 5,000) is evidence of this threat. This exponential growth suggests that virus writers hold the initiative in the battle for cyberspace. For existing operating systems that are infected with viruses, a cure cannot be developed until the virus is released into the system. Once released, the virus can be studied to find a method to prevent its further spread and remove it form the system. The computer community is striving to regain the initiative by developing operating systems that are more resistant to viruses. Despite these developments, those that attack computer systems will generally hold the initiative.

Trojan Horses. The second type of weapon is a trojan horse. True to its name, it is a program that does not appear to be destructive but releases a second program to perform a task unintended by the system operator. A trojan horse can be used to install a password "sniffer" program that collects the passwords of valid users and stores them for later use by an intruder posing as a legitimate user. Cyberterrorists can utilize this type of weapon for espionage to gain the information needed to access a system by impersonating legitimate users, thus compounding the problem of intrusion detection.

Worms. Worms are programs originally developed to travel through systems and perform mundane tasks, such as data collection or ensure of old data. While they can be useful, if misprogrammed or programmed with malicious intent, they can be extraordinarily destructive. A virus attaches itself to a host program, but a worm is designed to spread across a computer network independently. While normally programmed to perform a task on a network, a worm may also simply replicate itself on target computers while it continues to spread across a network. The Morris worm discussed in Chapter IV serves as an example of the damage a "non-malicious" worm can cause.

Humans. Computer operators are the vehicles by which viruses, trojan horses, and worms are initially programmed and then inserted into computer systems. In addition to utilizing software attacks on a computer system, a cyberterrorist or hacker can attack a computer system through the vulnerability of its operators. The hacker community commonly refers to this as "social engineering." Using a social engineering tactic, a cyberterrorist may impersonate a computer technician and call individuals within the targeted organization to obtain information to penetrate a system. Once in possession of legitimate log on information, cyberterrorists will have "legal" access to a system and can insert viruses, trojan horses, or worms to expand their control of the system or shut it down.

Electro-Magnetic Pulse Weapons. While not nearly as widespread as viruses, there exists a class of weapons that destroy computers and electronics through an electromagnetic pulse, The capability now exists to generate an instantaneous electromagnetic pulse that will overload and destroy the sensitive circuitry in advanced electronics and computer systems without the previously required detonation of nuclear weapons in the upper atmosphere. Any system that is within the limited range of these weapons will be disrupted or have its electronic components destroyed. While there have been reports of the military using such weapons in the GulfWar, there are no indications that any terrorist organization possesses or has used these weapons against computer targets. Press reports from Japan indicate that the AUM Shinrikyo cult, incriminated in the sarin gas attacks on Tokyo's subway was attempting to develop a high powered microwave weapon, ostensibly for use against humans. While suspected of being powerful enough to incinerate a human body, they may have intended this weapon for use against electronic targets as well.

An electromagnetic weapon does not leave a crater like a conventional bomb, nor does it modify the operating system of a computer. As such, detection of an attack becomes more difficult.

These weapons have been names HERF (High energy Radio Frequency) Guns and EMP/T (Electro Magnetic Pulse Transformer) Bombs by Winn Schwartau in testimony before Congress.

In the same manner as a fertilizer bomb can be assembled by a conventional terrorist, a cyberterrorist can manufacture an EMP/T bomb out of readily available electrical and electronic components.

TECHNOTERRORISM

Technoterrorism is the intermediate step between "conventional" terrorism and "cyberterrorism." The technoterrorist understands the importance of high technology networks and C2 systems to a "third wave" state.

Unlike the cyberterrorist, the technoterrorist will target and attack those systems that exist in the physical world to disrupt cyberspace.

Thus, the computer itself (hardware rather than software) is the target of the technoterrorist. The technoterrorist will use "conventional" weapons such as bombs and physical destruction to destroy or disable those systems that control cyberspace.

TERRORISM

The debate over the definition of terrorism is as old as the term itself. As the world moves into the information age, expanding the definition of terrorism to include actions taken inside cyberspace as well as the physical world may be necessary.

There are several elements that run through the many definitions of terrorism. The first critical element is physical violence. At some point in terrorism, an individual or group must believe that they are being threatened with violence. The second element is the political nature of terrorism. The violence caused by a terrorist action must have some larger political goal than the physical action itself.

The debate surrounding the definition of terrorism is addressed in Appendix B, which contains an overview of some of the more popular definitions in the literature. An understanding of the violent and political elements of terrorism are most important for this study.

One of the popular selling points of information warfare is that it is a less violent and destructive form of warfare in which the combatant states wage war with electrons in cyberspace. While the ability of states to wage relatively bloodless war is yet to be seen (the Persian Gulf war began to approach this standard in terms of allied casualties), the potential to create mass chaos and insecurity in a society via information warfare techniques may appeal to terrorists.

The definition of terrorism must be adapted and applied to those events that extend beyond mere physical violence and include what can be called "cyberviolence," or violence in cyberspace, where electrons, not people are destroyed. In addition, disruption, not destruction must be included as a tool to be utilized by cyberterrorists.

The evolving concept of information warfare will influence terrorism in the information age. Every advance in computing power continues to increase the usefulness of computers and their associated networks to law-abiding citizens. Simultaneously, these computers increase the power of the weapons available to cyberterrorist and criminals. The implications of computer technology's dual nature, as both a tool and weapon, must be understood in the information age. The military information warfare tactics that exploit this dual nature may be used against the United States by future cyberterrorists. As such, it is important to include information warfare as a potential component of information age terrorism.

WAR AGAINST INFORMATION-AGE TERRORISM

In a time when insurgency and terrorism have blended into a single entity, and the distinction between a full-fledged confrontation and a low intensity conflict has blurred, the relevance of the concept of a Dharmic war is circumspect. While classical nihilist viewpoint saw violence as a means of struggle, post-modern terrorists today often regard violence as an end in itself that generates identity or damages the adversary's identity. The actions of the Pakistan sponsored terrorist groups in Kashmir reflect this growing trend.

Causes for Terrorism

Military theorists have traditionally held three causes for terrorism:

1. It appeals as a *weapon of the weak* and the subjugated – a shadowy way to wage war by attacking asymmetrically against an ostensibly stronger enemy. The action of the PLO and associated organizations against the Jewish state of Israel falls into this category.
2. *"I bomb, therefore I am"* has also been ascribed to terrorist motives. It enables a
3. perpetrator to publicize his identity, project it explosively, and touch the nerves of powerful distant leaders. Attack on the J&K legislature building illustrates this fact.
4. Terrorism has sometimes appealed as a way to *achieve a new future order* by willfully wrecking the present. Promises of an Islamic paradise after the Armageddon comes in this category.

While the importance of addressing the root causes of terrorism cannot be understated, it is imperative on every civilized nation on Earth to safeguard its citizens from the actions of a select group of misanthropes. In order to effectively neutralize the scourge of terrorism, it is essential to understand the chief characteristics of modern day 'Information Age Terrorism.'

Traditional Viewpoint of War

The traditional Newtonian paradigm of war has upheld the following characteristics of any conflict:

1. It is *deterministically predictable* i.e. given the initial conditions and having identified the 'universal laws of

combat', we should try to resolve the problem and predict the result.

2. *Linearity* of the system is assumed as it imparts stability to the system. In layman's language, a direct and proportional connection is established between each cause and effect.
3. Newtonian viewpoint is *reductionist*. Surprisingly here, Carl von Clausewitz seems to disagree as he clearly states ' But in war more than in any other subject, we must begin by looking at the nature of the whole; for here more than elsewhere the part and the whole must always be thought of together.'
4. The military operation is treated as a *closed system* not susceptible to perturbations from its surroundings. The focus is also on optimization on the Cartesian assumption of existence of an optimal solution.
5. *Synchronization* is upheld as sacrosanct in the *microscopic command* and control operation.

Emerging Trends

The three main attributes of emerging terrorist activities are as follows:

1. *Organization*: Terrorists will continue moving from hierarchical toward information-age network designs. While Arquilla et al hold hybrid/symbiotic structures to be of ancillary relevance, the perception of the undersigned is different. The structure I postulate is as follows: At the core is a council in an all-channel network. In the intermediate step, a star network is formed with each primary node as its epicenter. In the periphery are chain type links to each secondary node.
2. *Doctrine and strategy*: Systemic disruption may become as much an objective as target destruction. After 9/11 attacks, the NYSE was closed for several days. Some experts have been ascribed an economic motive for the Aug 25 Mumbai Blasts.

3. *Technology*: Terrorists are likely to increasingly use advanced information technologies for offensive and defensive purposes, as well as to support their organizational structures.

Technological Advances

The terrorist in his search for 'Weapons of Mass Disruption' is aided by technological advances like

1. Novel *communications technologies* ranging from satellite phones to the Internet.
2. Information-processing technologies like *advanced encryption* techniques.
3. *Steganography* to embed messages into digital photographs or music clip.

Tiers in Terror

The corrosive proxy war waged by ISI against our country has two tiers of terror. Hard-core professionals based in Islamabad characterize the principal layer, but the actual implementation is left to amateur cutouts.

The deniability gained by ISI operating through willing amateurs is viewed as an excuse by the US dispensation to exculpate the Pakistani dictatorship.

The archetypal master of statecraft, Kautilya mentions in Arthashastra that any intelligence setup should keep the permanent and fixed employees at a bare minimum.

In the present context, it translates to the simple equation that

Number of Agents in Layer One + Number of Agents in Layer Two << Number of Agents in Layer Three

NETWORK DESIGN CLASSIFICATION:

The present terrorist groups have incorporated a decentralized decision making and operations structure making it difficult for the armed forces to eradicate the terror by means of a single surgical strike.

Thus the design may sometimes appear either as

1. *Acephalous (headless) design*: After the Houdini act by Bin Laden in the Tora Bora caves, the Al Qaeda ("The Base") is functioning with out a central command unit.
2. *Polycephalous (Hydra-headed) design*: Kashmir terrorist groups have incorporated this strategy. The Abdul Majeed Dhar controversy in the Hizbul Mujahideen (HM) is illustrative of this pervasive phenomenon.

Societal Networks

Modern societal networks have displayed three vital characteristics in the recent past namely:

1. *'Positive feedback' loops producing vicious cycle*: What started as a trickle of Kashmiri Pandits leaving their ancestral villages transformed into a large-scale emigration.
2. *Tight coupling between the nodes of the network causing Domino Effect*: Indian cricket aficionados and motor race enthusiasts would relate more to this point.
3. *Nonlinear behavior*: A small shock or perturbation to the network produces a disproportionately large disruption illustrated by the 9/11 attacks bringing the airline industry in the whole western world to its knees.

Counter-Terrorist Unit Architecture

To counter the decentralized network of the terrorists, it is essential for intelligence agencies to adopt a similar organizational framework. I postulate the following basic schematic to illustrate several points.

At the core lies the centralized command A, which manipulates the macroscopic parameters leaving actual decision taking to the man in the field. In other words while command is top-down guidance, control is bottom-up feedback. The nodes in the sub-net A are fully-connected to each other and are equal to each other in rank and status.

Each node in A , which could a person or an institution, is the epicenter of a star network. This network of agents designated B can be called the executors of the plan. This agent network is also fixed and is protected in the present case by a 1+ 1 protection scheme. Redundancy options and techniques are out of scope of our present discussion.

From agent C, we reach the actual implementers of the scheme. C is again the epicenter of a star network D. Each node in D leads to a chain network E. The agents in E who could also indulge in HUMINT are to be kept in a Mobile ad-hoc network scenario.

The tradeoff in counter-espionage network design is between connectivity and security. Ideally speaking, a network is maximally effective if the number of hops to the centralized command is limited at say 2. The Al Qaeda bombers attacking the WTC demonstrated this principle.

6

Modern Technology of Digital Warfare

Each age has seen war transformed by modern technologies and concepts. The Information Age promises to be no different. Some have called the Gulf War the first "Information War" - others have called it the last "Industrial Age" war. The power of information was clearly demonstrated in the context of traditional conflict. Information was leveraged to significantly improve the effectiveness of all aspects of warfare from logistics to command, control, communications, and computers, intelligence, surveillance, and reconnaissance (C4ISR).

The effectiveness of the U.S. and its allies in the Gulf War has surely deterred potential adversaries from taking on our forces in the rather symmetrical manner that Iraq attempted and has stimulated thinking about other strategies for countering conventional forces. Digital war, enabled by advances in technology and its widespread adoption as well as the globalization of economics and commerce, is surely a strategy that potential adversaries are thinking about to achieve some of the objectives that have previously been sought by means of traditional warfare.

Digital war, a subset of what we call information war, involves non-physical attacks on information, information processes, and information infrastructure that compromise, alter, damage, disrupt, or destroy information and/or delay, confuse, deceive, and disrupt information processing and decision making.

Digital war intrinsically possesses in ultimate form some of the same characteristics that traditional military planners are striving for, including low-cost precision, standoff, and stealth. Digital war threatens the ability of a nation state's military to interpose itself between its population and "enemies of the state," thereby causing a loss of sanctuary. The importance of sanctuary can be inferred by our willingness to spend significant resources on air, sea, and missile defenses to provide our citizens with a workable sanctuary with respect to territorial intrusions.

Another characteristic of information attacks stems from the loss of sanctuary. Attacks of this sort, particularly when they consist of more than an isolated incident, create a perception of vulnerability, loss of control, and loss of confidence in the ability of the state to provide protection. Thus, the impact can far exceed the actual damage that has occurred. This non-linear relationship between actual damage and societal damage makes the problem of digital war a particularly challenging one because it creates a mismatch between rational defense responses and their effectiveness.

How does one respond to a serious set of information attacks? Responding with traditional military forces may be politically unacceptable or in fact, may be ineffectual. Currently there is no consensus, even among those in the defense establishment who think about these issues, regarding how to deal with such an attack.

Given the potential effectiveness of digital war, particularly as an instrument of power for niche competitors and non-state actors, we need, as a society, to take this Information Age form of war very seriously. If we do not, and if we rely solely on traditional weapons and concepts of war, we may be building our own 21st Century Maginot line that can be flanked with the speed of light.

MERGING LEVELS OF WAR

The American public's lack of stamina to endure a protracted conflict and their abhorrence of battlefield casualties requires quick, decisive, strategic results. It is the warfighter's quest for immediate strategic results that will force the restructure of the three levels of war. With the help of information technology, joint commanders of the Twenty-first century will be able to efficiently command and control geometrically greater battle spaces at a far greater tempo and confidence level. The amount of uncertainty will be less. The virtually seamless flow of information from the lowest echelons--conceivably individual battalions, ships or aircraft--gives joint commanders a significantly increased knowledge base from which to coordinate, synchronize, and employ forces. This knowledge will be shared nearly simultaneous throughout the chain of command. The force multiplying effect of shared information will be to achieve a greater coherence and unity of effort with significantly fewer casualties. Consequently, actions at every level will instantaneously effect the other and will have the affect of reducing the time between decisions. Furthermore, the trend toward more powerful weapon systems will give rise to tactical elements being employed more often in direct support of strategic objectives. Situational awareness will permit the conduct of simultaneous offensive operations allowing the capability to convert tactical success immediately into decisive strategic results.

In the pursuit of more decisive operations, a great shift in the power to make operational and tactical decisions at one echelon will occur. The desirability of this shift will depend on how senior leaders adapt to the greater responsibility. A goal of joint digitization is to provide a greater assimilation of more information into the warfighting process. This implementation goal will ultimately expand the strategic level's span of control with the streamlining of the operational chain of command. Today, military organizations are generally sized by how much one commander can effectively control. By design, each echelon's commander is better informed to make appropriate decisions concerning his responsibilities. During the late 1980's and early 1990's, an evolution in business management led by the integration of information systems caused an increase in the span of control for a typical senior manager; this subsequently resulted in a flattening of the management structure. Likewise, digitization will provide more senior leaders the information that will permit them to feel comfortable making more judgments that were traditionally left to operational and tactical commanders. As in business, digitization will cause an increase in the span of control at the strategic level and a subsequent greater centralization of command. In the future, digital technology may render our current structure obsolete.

A flatter structure may not be always beneficial. The disadvantage of centralization is the magnitude that each decision potentially has. Mistakes in simple judgment can lead to greater, longer lasting consequences. Since the influence of a strong commander permeates throughout, there may be cases where trusting a single individual's perceptions may be, in the end, very costly in terms of resources, lives, and continued public support.

Another important reason for the merging levels of war is that communication between all echelons is expected to shift dissemination and collection of intelligence, targeting, and other data from hierarchical to a non-hierarchical command structure.

Hierarchial Structure Non-Hierarchial Structure

This internetted command structure undesirably leads to an "diffused command authority." Even today there are indications of just how future technology can alter command approaches within the military. Electronic mail (E-mail) has created a formal, as well as, informal dissemination structure within the Department of Defense. The ease at which an individual can send a courtesy copy or a message to anyone, regardless of position, has placed unusual demands upon an organization's hierarchy. It is easy to interpolate how the future and its promise for "smarter" systems, which are better able to assimilate and display information, can change the traditional needs for hierarchical levels. What is not clear is the effect that these informal lines of communications will have on a command structure during times of conflict.

As technology increases the strategic echelon's span of control, there will be a predictable gravitation to coordinate tactical weapons at the highest possible level; thus, more pressure to flatten or merge the levels of war. Improved war-fighting capabilities which have increased the mobility, dispersion, lethality, and tempo will drive control measures at least to a joint theatre level. Centralized control is needed for synchronization of combat power in order to conserve assets, and prevent fratricide and civilian collateral damage. Weapon systems could be enabled or disabled remotely whether they are on a ship, land or aircraft. It will be possible to control tactical fires and the maneuvers of combat elements to optimize the direct obtainment of the strategic goal. These combat elements will be armed with far more sophisticated direct and indirect munitions with ranges that exceed line of sight. Military professionals saw just a glimpse of technology during Desert Storm. By Twenty-first century standards, Desert Storm will look antiquated, but it illustrates just how complex and how important synchronizing forces are in order to prevent friendly casualties and to insure decisive strategic results.

The significance for future military organizations is that traditional tactical and operational levels will have the same information and same battle space concerns. The need for separation based upon capability to command and control will likely cease to exist in the Twenty-first century. The overall disadvantages of this merging has yet to form. How the senior leadership adapts and structures the resulting organizations will determine the magnitude of the drawbacks.

Diminished Command Prerogatives

Like many problems, the solutions often have undesirable consequences. It is quite possible that digitization upon Twenty-first century military organization will be detrimental to the concept of execution at the lowest level and could lead to over control. With the shared vision resulting from digitization, every one within the chain of command could have access to the same situational information. Theoretically, everyone from the White House, the Joint Staff and CINC Staffs, down to the tactical levels could have access to the same facts. Potentially it could become normal for some operational and tactical level decisions to come from the White House or the Joint Staff. The United States military requires leaders that possess boldness and initiative to act on one's own judgment. These traits within our leaders make the U.S. military a formidable force. Digitization may unintentionally affect the relationship between echelons by limiting the organization's initiative, ingenuity, and inventiveness through constant monitoring by superiors.

No one likes to have someone looking over their shoulder as they work. Increased theatre awareness and the ability to automatically transfer databases will result in the expansion and availability of on-line information. This may very likely result in a great deal of second guessing by senior commanders and staff. Invariably during a crisis, a subordinate commander who is closer to the action will select a different course of action than that of the senior commander. Should the superior commander second guess and redirect the effort or sit on his hands and wait it out? The challenge for senior leaders in the future will be curtailing their inclinations and allowing subordinate leaders their prerogatives. When a commander thinks he has all the facts, allowing a subordinate his prerogatives by not interfering goes against the "zero defects" culture that permeates the military today; unfortunately, there is no evidence that the future culture will be any different.

Information technology will also find it hard to digitize what is in the commander's head and what he feels--the kind of intangible awareness that comes from being close and near the area of operation. Our forces will fight the way they train. There is a danger that factors that cannot be quantified will be disregarded and our commanders not near the action will be "partly conditioned" by the technical tools available to them. For example, during a peacetime exercise, based on intuition or other undigitizable information, a commander may want to deviate from a plan during its execution. How many times will a commander accept corrections or challenges, by a "all-knowing" higher commander or superior's staff. Echelons above may believe they understand and have the "correct" bigger picture and demand adherence to previously coordinated plans or only minor tweaks to an existing plan.

There are very few commanders, believing they have the right situational information, that can allow a subordinate to act contrary or independently to their expectations without at least making an inquiry. Sure, the subordinate commander could explain and defend his actions and even prevail; however, a sense of autonomy, pride and creativeness is predictably lost by a subordinate each time it occurs. It doesn't take many real-time corrections or constant challenges by a boss to stifle boldness and initiative. It might be hard for today's leaders to appreciate the loss of initiative and boldness caused by digitization, since they have had these traits nurtured into them throughout their careers. The concern should be about the generation of leaders who grow up with extensive and perhaps constant oversight and monitoring.

The Marines "Warfighting" manual, FMFM 1, has recognized this concern and has succinctly stated, "Equipment that permits over control of units in battle is in conflict with the Marine Corps's philosophy of command and is not justifiable." The digitization technology of the Twenty-first century, by obtaining massive situational awareness, may have the unintended consequence of permitting commanders too much control. The military services could be entering into a new era of electronic micro-management.

The pressure to micro-manage, to ask questions, and to second guess field commander's decisions will be very high. Consider a CINC or a Joint Task Force commander, with the military and civilian leadership in Washington D.C. and the media doggedly pursuing in "real time" their individual stories, demanding to know status and planned intentions. The pressures will be enormous for information. With instantaneous civilian global information networks, such as CNN and broadcast network news, our civilian population has become more addicted to war news. For the future, the "CNN war leads public and leaders to define political events in terms of the video clips and sound bites that compose TV news images." A causal effect of this coverage is that the available reaction time to events for civilian policy makers is going to decrease because of amplified public interest. The American people are going to demand more information from their senior civilian and military leaders. Accordingly, policy makers are going to want to know more and want to know it sooner.

The pressure upon senior military leaders to supply only the most accurate information and not to publicly embarrass themselves, as well as their civilian leaders, will be immense. The future joint leader and corresponding staff are going to be forced to make larger number of inquiries to satisfy the media and public. Situational awareness through digital technology will be the enabling technology for maintaining public support for the military, as well as keeping the political leadership from embarrassment.

A good counter argument might be that unintrusive electronic queries will be extensively used and the distraction will be very minor. This argument holds well, if the question is strictly qualitative in nature, is an acceptable answer, or doesn't require explanations. Unfortunately, it is more likely that one answer will precipitate several more questions that may or may not be available unobtrusively through an electronic data base. Digitization might inadvertently and unanticipatedly increase outside distractions through the answering of endless questions up the chain of command. On the positive side, it is easy to see how this kind of uncontrolled eavesdropping by a higher level staff can lead to better situational awareness and better serve a joint commander. Sadly, it is hard to imagine how unencumbered, direct access to planning and execution information by a superior and his staff, without the subordinate's personal spin, could have a positive effect on the hard-charging, self-motivated commander.

One could argue that the higher echelons will not be interested in information that is specific and in detail. It is more likely that the smaller Twenty-first century force structure will limit the options available to our senior leaders. Consequently, leaders will require more specific information in order to make decisions. For example, the Joint Staff is currently in the process of developing and fielding the first phase of the Global Command and Control System (GCCS). ADM Owens, Vice Chairman, Joint Chief of Staff was given a demonstration of the Global Status of Resources and Training System (GSORTS). While being impressed with its capability to easily understand air base and other readiness ratings, he indicated it would be nice to also receive the aircraft availability by individual weapon's load, including Precision Guided Munitions (PGMs), and by sensors in a particular area of responsibility. What is significant is not that the Admiral wanted to know this information, but how the information going to be used at the strategic level. What if the information is not as expected or quantifiably correct? Very few leaders like to be surprised, and with the relatively smaller force structure, specifics are becoming very important.

Another concern is whether our warfighters will be prepared for the avalanche of questions. It cannot be discounted that routine questions from higher echelons tend to increase exponentially in importance the farther down the chain of command they propagate. So the lower echeloned, smaller staffed, war-fighting organizations are less prepared to handle queries and are distracted disproportionately.

Often in discussions about digitization and automation, it is surmised that staff sizes will decrease in numbers. It is quite possible that staff sizes may need to increase--not decrease. The requirement for information is compounded by the problem that during peace there is a tendency to become over organized and more bureaucratic in structure. This tendency can be summarized as the "need-to-know everything" syndrome. The propensity to explain and track data is gradually taking up more of the commander's and staff's time. As our services become more complex, more records and information are required to be processed and the demand for support staff increases. Large bureaucratic staffs do not normally foster and facilitate initiative and boldness in subordinate organizations.

The military has already experienced the unintended consequences of automation when it comes to bureaucratic staffwork. Consider how the word processor has streamlined typing and the electronic mailing of documents and messages. As stated before, automated offices are able to effortlessly and with efficiency send documents and E-mail via Local Area Networks and, through MILNET, between organizations. These tools obviously save time through simplifying distribution, increasing information transfers between organizations, thereby decreasing the number of secretaries and military clerks. However, the demand for more usable information by senior decision makers has also increased, requiring staff officers to spend greater portions of their time typing questions and answers.

With the increase in productivity, automation has fostered an increase in reporting and information generation. It is true that reports and briefs are now written easily on computers, but organizations tend now to spend more time reworking letters and briefing charts to achieve limited gains in redrafts and minor formatting. The reworking does not necessarily result in better content but only ensures cosmetically perfect documents. The labor saving and time saving office computer has the unintended consequence of creating more work. Computers have increased the military staffs work load and have unintentionally required more staff, not less.

Increased Fragility

General Sullivan, Chief of Staff, Army, states technology driven battle space awareness "can provide us with lighter, more effective and more lethal weapon systems to offset our smaller force structure." But, one also must consider that as these force multiplying systems are effected by attritions of war, their corresponding impact upon the force is an equally multiplying loss. Digital technologies provide a tremendous capability, however, they must be weighted cautiously against their vulnerabilities.

The use of digital technology has consequences that are paradoxical in nature. While it is true that the implementation of more advanced sensor-to-weapon systems will give better situational awareness, help minimize fratricide and better focus combat power, they can also be our Achilles heel. There is the concern whether the new electronic systems will have the resilience to absorb shocks and withstand perturbations associated with the realities of modern war. The more advanced the equipment the more complex it becomes. Generally, the more complex the system, the less reliable, and the harder or longer it takes to repair.

A possible solution to the attrition issue is the use of redundancy in the digital architecture. Redundancy is not likely to protect the force as technology is being looked upon by our senior leaders to help mitigate the smaller force structure. It is a reality that the U. S. military will always be dependent upon finite amounts of specialized electronic equipment that will invariably not be easily replaced nor repaired.

There are other compounding effects of attrition, such as the digital technologies dependence upon reliable communication architectures. It is the dependence and reliance of electronically synthesized data from widely dispersed systems that makes communications the most vulnerable segment. The greatest threat to the entire digitization architecture is the lack of robust, redundant communications paths. For example, Desert Storm validated the notion that a CONUS based force projection strategy, with its anticipated tempo is dependent upon assured satellite communications for both inter- and intra-theatre communications irrespective of use on land or sea. Above the tactical level of war, it is anticipated for the Twenty-first century that medium data rates for the military, as well as civilian satellite systems, will be vulnerable to jamming by today's low cost technology. Since digital communications demands are going to be predictably greater than their capacity, there will be no redundancy nor unused capacity. Even today, it is doctrine not to normally keep communication equipment in reserve. Also, key communications equipment is subject to targeting through old-fashioned direct or indirect fires. An unsophisticated enemy sharp-shooter could easily fire a well placed bullet and take out the feed to a critical satellite or a microwave antenna. This would effectively disrupt the digital architecture with devastating consequences to the command and control process. Communications will be the weakest link for the future's dispersed digitized systems.

There is a trend growing within the U.S. military to use commercially available off-the shelf technology that is generally not designed to Military Standards nor for ease of trouble shooting. An unintentional result of using the less rugged commercial electronic equipment is it will require warfighting organizations to have near-by repairmen and large stocks within theatre of specialized electronic repair parts. Otherwise, replenishment could become a problem since strategic mobility will always be at a premium during a crisis.

Repair parts may not always be available. A CONUS based support structure assumes that the tempo at which critical items are used and destroyed will not exceed the rate at which they are being replaced. If tradition holds, then the military will keep electronic equipment beyond normal commercial applications. CONUS depots will have to have on-hand the repair parts since industry does not normally keep the production lines of specialized nor dated electronic designs operating. Leaders will need to take into account and understand the perishability and limited availability of electronic equipment.

Lack of timely repair could contribute to the increased fragility of the force. The advanced equipment of the future, whether it be built to commercial or military standards, will require a greater level of maintenance expertise. The philosophy of using built-in diagnostic and automatic check-out equipment does design complexity away from the operator; however, repair responsibilities dramatically shift to maintenance personnel. Repairing systems in the forward areas will be more difficult and there will be a greater tendency to evacuate equipment for repairs to the depots; thus increasing the time to repair. Based on complexity, it can be anticipated that digital electronic systems are going to have a much longer logistics tail than we have today.

Our force structure will likely have a critical shortage of qualified electronic technicians. Consider the same scenario of equipment damaged by a "low-tech" sharpshooter. What if the shooter decides to wait around to kill the skilled operator or maintenance person conducting the repair? Skilled repairmen will not be replaced easily. Maintenance personnel of the future will require more extensive and sophisticated training than today's technicians, since the systems will be more intricate. As the armed forces continue to compete against educational institutions and private corporations for the limited number of qualified 17-24 year-olds, it is going to be a challenge to keep qualified personnel skilled in electronics. Even the reliance on dedicated and first-rate National Guard and Reserve units is optimistic. Units meant to augment during national emergencies may not be able to keep operator and repair personnel up to warfighting standards.

The implication--"there will be time for training after the troops are assembled--is virtually over." It is not quantitatively known whether the rate of replacement of critical specialty skills will be able to keep pace, but one has only to look at where we are, traditionally short of technical specialists today. As during Desert Storm, it will be common for the Services to depend upon civilian technicians in forward deployed areas for maintenance and repair, due to the maintenance complexity of electronic equipment and the lack of qualified military personnel. It is possible that demographics, and sociopolitical educational realities, might just be the limiting factors of the Twenty-first century digitized force. The demand for "high-tech" personnel is going to go up--not down.

Another concern for the future is that we will depend more upon our allies for support. As the United States modernizes its forces with the latest electronic gadgetry, will our allies be willing to invest in the same kinds of equipment, or will we be willing to sell or give it to them' By digitizing everything from Command and Control to weapons systems, they might make it impossible to be electronically interoperable within a theatre with our coalition partners.

INADVERTENT ROBUSTNESS

There are some who have suggested that we are not as vulnerable to information attacks as has been claimed because the collection of our legacy systems provides a certain amount of inherent robustness and resiliency. They point to the overlaps and duplications in these systems and argue that it would be very hard for anyone to completely disrupt a given set of services. They point to the lack of interoperability among legacy systems and the firewalls that are thereby created and argue that it would be impossible for attackers to get very far by penetrating the weakest systems and using them as launching pads for attacks on other systems. They argue that our current legacy systems and their interrelationships are difficult (even for us) to understand, so it must follow that potential adversaries will also be confused.

Clearly there is some truth in each of these arguments. But this unruly collection of legacy systems also carries with it significant disadvantages. As far as security considerations are concerned, five points need to be made. First, this issue is not whether or not an attack could totally destroy or disrupt a particular system or type of service, but whether or not there could be sufficient damage to trigger the perception of a failure and result in panic behavior that could in turn create a significant national problem. Second, the redundancies in the systems are only partial and unplanned. Hence, they are neither complete nor reliable.

Third, our legacy systems, many having been designed and built with little or no attention to security, are difficult to protect and secure. Fourth, as the need for interconnectivity and interoperability increases, more and more systems are being lashed together with "work-arounds." These patches, in many cases, compromise security. Lastly, the lack of security that these systems provide is dampening the demand for services that could make operations more effective and efficient in many areas. Our current collection of legacy systems has other disadvantages as well. For example, the lack of interoperability wastes resources and impairs operations. Thus, it should be clear that the disadvantages of our current collection of legacy systems are not a blessing in disguise but rather the source of problems that need to be addressed so that we can take full advantage of the opportunities that information technologies can provide.

Formulating the Problem

The first step in tackling any problem involves developing an understanding of the possible environments that may be faced (or the "states of nature"), one's options, and the objective that is being sought. This requires an identification of the variables that are relevant, that is, those that can significantly influence the outcome as well as the subset of these relevant variables that are controllable, which form the basis for designing options. In a problem as complex as IW-D, working to formulate the problem accomplishes three things. First, it provides a useful framework for discussion. Second, it serves to keep the focus on those specific areas that are either unknown or in dispute. Third, it serves as a benchmark for measuring progress.

In this case, the states of nature correspond to the nature of the threat that will be faced vis-a-vis the vulnerabilities of our information infrastructure while our options correspond to the strategies we adopt and the actions we take to defend ourselves. The objective being sought corresponds to a level of infrastructure performance, its definition and measure being a major challenge in and of itself.

A good place to start is to try to develop an understanding of the nature of the threat, or more accurately the spectrum of relevant threats. This involves the identification of potential threats and the estimation of their likelihoods. Normally one would construct a set of states of natures that are mutually exclusive and collectively exhaustive so that a probability density function could be used. For the purposes of this discussion, the states of nature referred to correspond to potential threats grouped in some logical fashion to facilitate analysis of how well each defensive strategy deals with each of these threats.

Having an initial concept of the nature and range of potential threats, one can develop alternative defensive strategies and corresponding sets of action to counter one or more of these threats. A great deal depends upon what variables we believe we can and should control.

Each defensive strategy, with its corresponding set of actions, then needs to be analyzed with respect to each of the threats. The results of these analyses will be a characterization of the results or outcomes from pursuing each of the defensive strategies with respect to each of the threats. These outcomes, which are basically descriptions of results (e.g., number of penetrations and their consequences), then need to be translated into value measures that represent their impact. These costs and benefits provide a rational basis for determining an appropriate defensive strategy. Much will depend upon how we measure success. Given the central role that the threat topology plays in problem formulation, we will now turn our attention to examining this topology.

Threat Topology

The irregular nature of the space is meant to indicate that its boundaries are not well defined. Nevertheless, one can group threats in order of the seriousness of their consequences (from left to right). The consequences associated with a failure to counter a specific attack range, on the one hand, from isolated and limited consequences to, on the other hand, consequences of catastrophic proportions.

There are a relatively small number of threats that most everyone would agree have strategic implications and must be defended against with considerable vigor. Attacks against our systems that control and safeguard weapons of mass destruction

(WMD) and our minimum essential emergency communication network (MEECN) clearly fall into this category. Others that fall into this category would include the information and communication systems associated with the National Command Authority (NCA), some of our command, control, communications and intelligence (C3I) systems, and some of our intelligence systems, particularly information regarding sources and methods. A review of other Government information and information systems would result in additional information and systems that should be added to this list.

Beyond those sets of threats that clearly fall into either the Everyday or Strategic categories, there are classes of threats that span the threat spectrum.

Attacks on our national, or for that matter international, infrastructure do not fall neatly into one area of the threat topology but in fact populate all three classes of threat. These attacks on our public safety, energy, financial, and communications systems and services have different implications and consequences depending on the specific nature of the attacks and the circumstances surrounding the attack.

The vast majority of attacks on infrastructure are by hackers whose motives run the full gamut from financial motives, to having some fun, or to more serious forms of antisocial behavior. While some of these attacks may have serious consequences in the form of significant losses of data, interrupted services, or stolen assets or services, only a small number of these lone perpetrator attacks are likely to have potential strategic consequences. This is not to say that it is impossible that some set of circumstances would result in the snowballing of one of these hacker attacks into a national security concern, but rather that this outcome is unlikely.

However, infrastructure attacks can be quite serious if they are well planned and coordinated. Arguably this would require an adversary with seriousness of purpose and with some sophistication and organization. This kind of attack would be better named digital warfare rather than be included as part of the group referred to as hacker attacks. Depending on the level of sophistication of a digital warfare operation, its consequences could range from a "high-end" hacker attack to an attack with strategic consequences.

A key point to be made involves the chaotic nature of the transition between topological boundaries for infrastructure attacks. Chaotic behavior involves a non-linear relationship between input and output where prediction becomes extremely difficult if not impossible. Two distinct scenarios serve to illustrate the chaotic nature of infrastructure attacks. In the first case, a particular infrastructure attack may trigger a series of proximate consequences that are difficult to predict and that greatly magnify the effects of the attack. In the second case, a series of attacks will exhibit chaotic behavior when the sum of their consequences can not be determined by adding up their individual consequences, or when their cumulative effect far exceeds the sum of the individual effects of a series of independent events. These are not uncommon patterns. Valid scientific disciplines of complexity, catastrophe, and complexity theory have been developed because these patterns occur throughout nature.

It is much the same story for attacks on commercial targets. In the Everyday category are attacks that amount to Information Age versions of fraud and theftùa continuation of white collar crime and a transformation of some more violent crime into a non-physical form. As Dr. Horton (PDASD (C3I)) has pointed out, one of the more notorious bank robbers of the 20th century, when asked why he robbed banks (given that they were often so well defended), was purported to remark, "that's where the money is." Well, digital money (assets and services) is where the money is in the Information Age. As with attacks on infrastructure, attacks on commercial targets can range from Everyday threats to Strategic ones depending on the circumstances. Attacks on commercial targets by competing organizations usually do not target money directly, but rather target vital information (e.g., trade secrets) and have the potential for more serious consequences than isolated thefts or embezzlements. These attacks, in the form of commercial espionage, have Potentially Strategic consequences, particularly when key industries are targeted by foreign companies.

Commercial espionage turns into economic war which could have Strategic consequences when it involves concerted efforts by state actors, international organizations, or other foreign-controlled groups.

Threat Characteristics

As can been seen from the series of graphical depictions of the threat topology presented above, the threat we face is multidimensional, somewhat messy and, with respect to the consequences of information attacks, can behave in a chaotic manner. The dynamic and interactive nature of the threat makes defending against attacks all the more challenging.

Unfortunately, the attackers possess some inherent advantages. For example, the attacker can pick the time, place, medium, and method of the attack. The technology edge also goes to the attacker, for it is very difficult to develop perfect defenses at an affordable cost. Therefore, there will always be "holes." Which ones will be exploited are unknown until attacks occur, thus the offense usually is one step ahead of the defense. Those who choose to orchestrate coordinated attacks on infrastructure also have the advantage that comes from being able to control their attack more easily than can a number of loosely coupled defenders.

In any event this is a learning environment for both attackers and defendersùa dynamic one at that. In this organic environment, attackers learn from undetected attacks, whether successful or not, while both sides learn from detected attacks, whether successful or not. Both attackers and defenders make adjustments and the "game" continues.

This aspect of the threat means that defense is not a one time thing. It must be a continuous activity. It also means that collection and analysis of information about attacks is vital to maintaining parity with attackers. Finally, it means that defenders must be proactive and undertake efforts designed to anticipate methods of attack so that timely defenses can be developed.

IW-D CONSIDERATIONS

The problem of how best to defend against a variety of potential digital information attacks is exacerbated by the following three characteristics of the problem: our inability to develop a simple relationship between a type of attack or threat and an organization, the essentially non-linear relationship between outcome and value, and the fact that key variables are not within our control.

Being able to decompose a problem often helps us to make progress, at least on some fronts, by facilitating the delegation of either functional or jurisdictional responsibility along organizational lines. As we have seen, the problem of IW-D resists decomposition along organizational lines. This is because there is a weak mapping between threat and organization from two perspectives. First, the organizational target of the attack is weakly related to the threat topology, that is, an attack on a given organization may result in a set of consequences that span the threat spectrum. Second, there is no clean mapping between organizational responsibility and the threat topology. This is particularly true of the area identified as Potentially Strategic.

It is always easier to solve problems with well-behaved or predictable objective functions or measures of value. As we have seen, the IW-D problem has situations where the relationship between events and variables behave in a chaotic manner. This introduces a large dose of uncertainty into the equation.

If these first two characteristics of the IW-D problem did not present significant challenges in and of themselves, we are also faced with the fact that some of the key variables that have an influence on outcomes and the values of these outcomes are only partially controllable. For example, each of the following variables, if fully controllable, could significantly either reduce the number or severity of attacks and/or the impact of the attacks: proliferation of technology, level of awareness and training of personnel, availability of computer expertise, system defenses, and public perceptions. We have come to the end of the discussion of the nature of the problem and its characteristics that will drive the search for a solution. Next, a proposed solution approach is presented and discussed.

Proposed IW-D Strategy

The proposed solution to IW suggested here is a "Defense-in-Depth" strategy, a strategy that involves a series of successively stronger or "higher" defensive barriers that work together to decompose the spectrum of threats into manageable pieces. While implementing this concept still involves considerable challenges, it provides some structure for efforts to defend ourselves against information attacks.

Following a discussion of this IW-D strategy, the nature of a division of responsibility, some of the critical prerequisites for progress, key challenges that lie ahead, and the elements of an action plan for organizations with IW-D responsibilities will be addressed.

Defense-in-Depth

The proposed "defense-in-depth" strategy, consists conceptually of three lines of defense. Each line of defense is designed specifically to counter the threats associated with a particular region of the threat topology.

The first line of defense is to defend against Everyday attacks, which constituted most of the threat topology. Based upon the information available, the vast majority of these attacks can be handled with basic defenses.

The higher hurdles associated with the Potentially Strategic and Strategic attacks are then responsible for handling more sophisticated but far fewer attacks from fewer potential sources. For example, attacks with strategic implications would need to get through the first two lines of defense that should filter out all but the most skilled, resourced, and persistent adversaries. This means we can concentrate our intelligence and monitoring efforts on a smaller population, which in turn increases the chances of successful defense. This defensive strategy also means that we can take different philosophical approaches with each line of defense depending on the nature of the threat. The two endpoints of the philosophical spectrum can be thought of as the "information first" and "security first" approaches. In the Everyday region of the threat topology our approach has been to emphasize access to information. In the Strategic region, we put security first by restricting access and connectivity to the point of degrading performance and efficiency.

Division of Responsibility

A suggested division of primary responsibility for IW-D between the public and private sectors as a function of the threat topology. The modifier "primary" is used to make the point that, despite the assignment of responsibility in a particular area to either the public or private sector, both public and private organizations have responsibilities in each area.

The topological regions associated with either Everyday or Strategic threats are the most straightforward. Primary responsibility for the everyday threat should be the responsibility of the private sector. Handling such threats is simply the cost of doing business in the Information Age. With the availability of relatively low-cost defenses against these threats, the burden placed on the private sector is affordable. Furthermore, organizations are clearly in the best position to understand their own systems and the needs and concerns of their customers.

Responding to strategic threats is clearly the job of the public sector, although an adequate defense will involve some coordination with private sector and international organizations, particularly when it comes to the region of the threat topology that contains threats associated with attacks on the national information infrastructure or other institutions providing vital services.

Where to assign primary responsibility for defenses against threats in the Potentially Strategic region of the threat topology is less clear. This area could be called a "zone of collaboration," where the public and private sectors need to work closely together to understand the threat and develop mechanisms designed to counter it.

PERSPECTIVES ON INFORMATION SECURITY

Efforts to achieve effective collaboration will need to overcome the understandably different perspectives that organizations bring to the table.

Commercial organizations traditionally treat events such as Everyday attacks as simply a cost of doing business not significantly different than pilferage euphemistically referred to as inventory "shrinkage." Countermeasures have a definite expected value and are employed when their costs are less than their expected value. Private sector organizations traditionally respond to relatively low probability events with potentially large costs by either purchasing insurance or providing self-insurance.

The perspective on information security taken by organizations entrusted with information and systems deemed vital to our national security is quite different. Unlike many information attacks on private sector systems, the cost of a breech in security of national security information can not easily be determined. Overshadowing the actual costs of a particular incident is the fact that the very protection of the integrity of national security information and the systems that handle it is considered to have intrinsic value in and of itself. Risk avoidance is the ingrained response in these situations.

Given the nature of the IW threat topology, national and private sector information security are now inexorably intertwined. Attacks on the national or global information infrastructure can seriously affect private sector organizations and attacks on key private sector organizations that provide vital services have definite national security implications. These situations are contained in the Potentially Strategic region of the threat topology.

It is proposed that, in this region, rather than take a simple "dollars and cents" approach as in the Everyday region or a risk avoidance approach as taken in the Strategic region, we should take a collective risk management approach. This is clearly an area which requires defenses to be closely coordinated.

Managing the Solution

Given what we have seen about the nature of this problem as we have considered the different areas of the threat topology, it should be clear that any attempt to try to manage IW-D using a centralized approach is doomed to failure. If one has any doubt, they should be reminded of the weak threat to organizational mapping which prevents effective delegation of the problem with clean "chains of command" and the considerable limits on the ability of the Government or any single organization to control significant relevant variables.

Given the urgency and importance of this problem, a proactive stance is required. Therefore, it should be equally obvious that a laissez-faire approach is also doomed to failure.

A form of collective orchestration is needed to develop the degree of awareness and understanding of the threat and to develop the necessary defenses. The Government needs to lead by establishing what I have called a "framework for progress." The specific roles and responsibilities of the private and public sectors will vary as a function of the threat as we have seen in our brief look at each of the three major regions of the threat topology. While this discussion has focused on the roles, responsibilities and need for collaboration among U.S. players, the problem of IW-D transcends national boundaries. Without appropriate international agreements and cooperation among nations and international organizations, our collective ability to handle threats will be severely hampered.

Framework for Progress

While we have come a considerable distance in our journey to better understand the nature of this problem, many of us have been frustrated by the lack of a supportive environment for progress. Although we can continue to make progress, even on the rocky path we are currently forced to travel, progress in the six areas identified in the graphic will greatly smooth out our path and accelerate our progress.

First, one of the key prerequisites for progress is to create awareness of the problem and its complexities, as well as to foster a climate that will facilitate discussion and cooperation among the many groups and organizations that need to be a part of this effort. Given recent events surrounding some aspects of information security, we need to start by rebuilding bridges between some public and private sector groups and organizations.

Second, it is important that we work toward a well-defined vision that clearly lays out what we are trying to achieve and the appropriate role of the Government.

Third, the "rules of the game" need to be developed and promulgated. Many of our current laws and regulations have not caught up with the realities of the Information Age. A set of rules needs to address the establishment of information security standards, or a minimum level of defense to be associated with different kinds of data and information services. These would be similar to the recent development of privacy standards.

Fourth, self-interest, even enlightened self-interest and the desire of individuals and organizations to be good citizens, are not enough to ensure that appropriate actions and defenses will be developed and employed. Resources need to be provided for government organizations to help implement this framework for progress and to develop and implement the needed defenses. We also need to provide incentives that encourage public sector organizations to do what is collectively needed. In some specific cases, the Government will need to actually provide funds to private sector organizations to implement enhanced security.

Fifth, the solution to this problem depends on a great deal of cooperation among disparate groups and organizations. Mechanisms to facilitate and enhance cooperation (including the establishment of panels, groups, and clearinghouses) need to be developed.

Sixth, we need to fix responsibility for the many tasks involved in IW-D. We need to decide questions of jurisdiction. We need to make liabilities known and well defined. Finally, we need to clearly establish the responsibility of each organization. The nature of organizational responsibilities is discussed in more detail below.

None of these six aspects of the framework for progress is likely to be accomplished anytime soon. One only need review the legislative process and experiences with the translation of privacy concerns into a set of rules of the game to realize that it will be quite a while before each of these foundational pillars is in place. However, we must begin now to foster discussion of these issues and try to keep attention focused on this subject.

Allocation of Responsibilities

The responsibilities of public and private sector organizations differ as a function of the threat region. In all regions of the threat from everyday to strategic, however, each sector of society has some responsibility.

Responsibilities for Everyday Threats

The primary responsibility for the Everyday region of the threat topology falls upon the private sector. First and foremost, private sector organizations must assume responsibility for the protection of their own systems. When security laws and regulations are legislated and formulated, these organizations will, of course, also be responsible for adhering to these rules of the game.

Given the time it may take to develop and put in place a legal and regulatory framework to deal with the myriad of information security issues, it is proposed that on a voluntary basis, private sector organizations assume the responsibility for reporting incidents.

It is hard to overstate the importance of the collection of information related to information attacks and their analysis. Without the development of a body of knowledge concerning these attacks, efforts at building defenses will be severely hampered.

The Government (including the federal, state, and local levels) must assume certain responsibility for this region of the threat topology as well.

Clearly, the Government bears the responsibility for protecting its own systems and for the enforcement of appropriate laws and regulations. Given the importance of gaining international cooperation on this problem that knows no state boundaries, the Government must take on the negotiation of the necessary treaties and agreements.

Clearly, the collection of incident data with respect to its own systems is also a Government responsibility. But given the importance of pooling information to gain a more accurate situation assessment, the Government must also put in place appropriate mechanisms for data sharing, analysis of data, and the dissemination of results.

Issues related to classification and security of these data and the products of these analyses will need to be addressed. A way must be found to get the information that individuals and organizations need to defend themselves to those involved in the effort.

RESPONSIBILITIES FOR STRATEGIC THREATS

The Federal Government has the responsibility for the defense of the Strategic region of the threat topology, albeit with some support in selected areas from the private sector and state and local governments.

Given the dynamic and interactive nature of this situation, it is important that the current and emerging threat be as fully understood as possible. Therefore, utilizing information collected as well as information reported by others, the Federal Government has the responsibility to perform strategic threat analyses on an ongoing basis.

The Federal Government also needs to develop an appropriate deterrence strategy designed to dissuade potential attackers. Strategic systems must be monitored and surveillance operations must be mounted.

Obviously, the Federal Government has the responsibility for protecting strategic information and the systems that collect, store, process, and disseminate this information.

Finally, the Federal Government needs to develop plans for reconstitution of damaged or disrupted systems and lost, compromised, or damaged information and for implementation of these plans should an event occur.

The private sector also has a role to play in this region of the threat topology. First, many strategic systems depend to some extent on the availability and integrity of private sector or state and local government information and systems. Second, some private sector or state and local government information and systems may be so critical that they are, for all intents and purposes, strategic. In both these cases, organizations need to cooperate with the Federal Government to protect these systems and the information they handle. Developing an adequate understanding of the threat requires that all organizations report incidents and share data related to attacks, whether successful or not. Thus another responsibility that must be assumed by private sector organizations is the prompt reporting of incidents and related information.

Responsibilities for Potentially Strategic Threats

The division of responsibilities for this region of the threat topology is not as clear-cut or as familiar as for the other two regions. In this zone of collaboration, public and private sector organizations need to find ways and create mechanisms that foster a shared perception of the nature of the threat, particularly those aspects of a situation that increase the likelihood of strategic consequences. In addition, ways should be found to enhance our defenses and improve our ability to mitigate the effects of attacks in this region to prevent them from having strategic consequences.

In this region, the Government needs to take the lead in helping to develop the necessary understanding of the threat, while the private sector needs to support Government efforts by providing incident data. The Government also needs to take the lead in developing coordinating mechanisms designed to both support improved understanding and the coordination of defenses.

The two biggest challenges associated with this pivotal threat region are first, the recognition of when an attack of strategic significance has begun and in characterizing the nature and scope of the attack and second, in the effecting of a transition from a "peace time" to a "war time" footing. The success of the processes and mechanisms developed to coordinate this transition will be critical to the success of any IW-D strategy.

The private sector needs to take the lead in this region by turning improvements in understanding into more effective defenses. This includes not only enhanced detection tools and techniques but also an improved ability to contain an attack, thereby limiting its spread, damage, and consequences. The Government needs to assist the private sector in these efforts by providing resources and technical support. Resources might take the form of tax incentives, or as was recommended in the case of some private sector systems that were deemed to be strategic, direct payments.

IW-D CHALLENGES

For anyone who thrives on challenges, defending against information warfare is a great line of work. There are five key challenges we face. The first challenge involves the development of a better understanding of the nature and characteristics of the threat among society and its institutions. Success requires that everyone be on board. Therefore, it is important that we continue to work to increase awareness of this problem and to develop a better understanding of both the nature of the threat and our vulnerabilities.

The second challenge is to develop a strategy for deterring digital information attacks. The first line of defense is deterrence. Not enough effort is being devoted to developing and gaming possible strategies. In February 1996, ACTIS sponsored a workshop on this subject. This workshop was a highly successful endeavor, giving those who attended a better idea where the latest thinking is on this subject, stimulating more thinking about the subject, and bringing some key issues into sharper focus. (The proceedings of this workshop, "IW and Deterrence," have been published and are available from ACTIS.)

The third and fourth challenges involve developing means of providing warning for attacks and ways of successfully defending against attacks that do occur. Improving our ability to see an attack coming, or providing indications and warning (I&W) of attacks in a timely fashion, is perhaps the most single difficult challenge we face. Developing an I&W capability involves not only the traditional strategic and tactical warning capabilities, but also the ability to know that an attack has begun and to ascertain the likely scope of such an attack. Given that currently, in many cases, an attack in progress is not even recognized, this will be a tall order. This is not only a technical challenge, but it is, as mentioned earlier, an organizational challenge. This is because of the information necessary to provide warning of an imminent action or an attack in its early stages would most likely need to come primarily from private sector organizations whose "peace time" reporting structures may not either require reporting of all relevant incident data or require it in near real time. Thus an attack of strategic significance may be well underway before we realize it and are able to move to a "war time" footing, which would bring with it the increased reporting requirements and coordination necessary to assess the situation and respond accordingly.

As a result of my participation in a series of "day after" games developed by RAND for ASD(C3I), I have concluded that we will not be able to respond to such attacks in a timely and effective manner unless there is 1) more awareness and understanding of the nature of strategic IW capabilities and our own vulnerabilities among not only key officials in public and private organizations but also among Congress, the Media and the Public; 2) more understanding of the offense arsenal at our disposal, particularly the direct, indirect, and collateral damage they might cause; 3) a pre-agreed systematic system of alerts similar to the DEFCON system, each level of which carries with it known, understood, and practiced processes and actions; and 4) a "battle damage" assessment process suitable for IW.

The construction of a DEFCON-type system for IW-D will require the investment of a considerable amount of intellectual capital as well as a considerable amount of coordination among a wide variety of Government departments and agencies, the Congress, industrial associations, and private organizations. Given the nature of the problem, time will be of the essence should problems with our information infrastructure begin to appear. Well thought-out options that address both the need for increased collection and analyses and the need to take measures to prevent or control damage are essential to countering this threat. Given the trifurcated threat topology and the very different nature of each of the three threat regions, implementing the proposed "defense-in-depth" strategy will be a considerable undertaking.

The fifth challenge is to develop appropriate and effective responses to such attacks. Responses to attacks include identification, interdiction, apprehension, and punishment (possibly including retaliation).

IWS Awareness and Understanding

We have much to learn and many to educate. When many of the individuals who need to become more aware of the threat and its potential consequences are exposed to the subject only by reading novels or going to the movies, we cannot really expect to develop the degree of understanding required. When the only exposure to the subject is through fiction, it is no wonder that the threat may be dismissed as fictional. There are still many individuals in key positions in both the public and private sector who need to have a better appreciation for this problem and to be more motivated to address the issues. On the other hand, admittedly we do not possess a great abundance of factual information. While we have clear indications that some potentially serious attacks, even crippling attacks, are technically feasible, as has been pointed out, there is no "smoking keyboard" to show. Yet it should be pointed out that the time it took to create a working atomic bomb from the time its theoretical feasibility was recognized surprised many, even the most knowledgeable scientists.

Our ignorance about the nature of potential attacks is mirrored by a lack of knowledge about the effectiveness of current and developing defensive techniques and strategies.

When our systems are not being adequately monitored and incidents are not being adequately recorded and investigated, it is hard to see how we can develop the vastly improved understanding of both the threat and the effectiveness of defenses we require. Increased collection and analysis is clearly needed to provide the empirical foundation required to a) increase awareness, b) increase our understanding, c) support planning, and d) develop effective defenses. Given our tendencies to value privacy, both in terms of individuals and corporations, and the limitations we have imposed upon the collection of domestic intelligence, it is unlikely that sufficient information will be collected and analyzed by the Government to quickly determine the nature and extent of an ongoing IW attack in its early stages. Therefore, it is extremely important that when it appears that such an attack may be imminent or in progress, that "peace time" data collection and analysis arrangements be quickly shifted to a "war time" footing. In designing a DEFCON-like process, it will be important to define "trigger" events that will automatically cause information to flow to a situation assessment organization. This is because of the time criticality of providing up-to-date information to the decision makers who will be considering appropriate DEFCON-like decisions involving potentially costly actions to safeguard the NII and prevent further damage to our information infrastructure and the key public safety and economic functions that it supports.

IW Deterrence

With the dawn of the atomic age came the recognition that developing strategies for deterrence and counter proliferation needed to be pursued with a sense of the utmost urgency. IW differs from atomic warfare in a number of significant ways, and therefore lessons learned from our experience in developing a workable strategy for deterrence may not apply directly to the problem of deterrence of IW attacks, but certainly may provide a starting point or checklist for consideration.

Some of the compelling issues related to the development of a deterrent to IW attacks include various means of raising the attack threshold, using offensive IW, dealing with non-state actors, taking preemptive actions, and developing potential forms of punishing attackers.

While raising the defensive threshold, thereby making attacks more difficult and costly as well as limiting the damage they can do, is widely recognized as an important component of any deterrence strategy, an issue that needs to be addressed relates to the "height" of the threshold. For example, what is more defense? When does more defense become counterproductive?

Another critical issue is whether or not having and indicating a willingness to employ a potent offensive IW capability would be an effective deterrent, and if so, in which particular set(s) of circumstances.

Given the low cost and small footprint required, non-state and even individual actors may gain the wherewithal to pose a strategic threat. How can one gain the leverage on these kinds of adversaries to deter them from launching such attacks?

Other key issues include the nature of preemptive actions that could be employed and the relationship between punishment (or retaliation) and deterrence.

Building a Defense-in-Depth

Our ability to defend individual systems and the information they handle is the foundation of any IW-D strategy or approach. In order to achieve the requisite level of defenses, we need to 1) revise our approach to system design and acquisition,

2) understand the dimensions of defense, and 3) support the development of critical enabling technologies.

SYSTEM DESIGN AND ACQUISITION

The current trend in designing systems is to provide vastly increased access to increasing amounts of information at all levels of an organization and to provide for more external connectivity. We in government are joining the move to separate the flow of information from the management or command structure. Our new approach to information systems involves "reach back," that is, individuals are not "pushed" information but rather "pull" the information they require from distributed databases. In response to the sheer amount of information available, more and more sophisticated presentations (displays) are being developed. Driven by the reduced life cycle of information technology and shrinking budgets, we are becoming more and more reliant on commercial-off-the-shelf (COTS) equipment and software. These trends make it more and more difficult to ensure the integrity of information or recognize when it has been compromised.

If we are to build the level of defenses to IW attacks we need and provide users with the level of assurance required to give them confidence in their systems, we need some changes in our approach to system design and acquisition. For a number of reasons, not the last of which is security, we need to focus more on providing quality information, that is on moving up the "data-information-understanding-knowledge" continuum. In evaluating system designs and in setting standards for systems to meet, we need to augment the current set of measures of merit (MOMs) for information. In addition to attributes such as timeliness and accuracy, we also need to focus on authenticity, integrity, and availability.

Connectivity is important to achieving the levels of functionality desired, but increased emphasis on secure interoperability is needed to achieve IW-D objectives. Fixing and patching systems and installing new releases offer many opportunities to bypass or disable system defenses. Operations and Maintenance (O&M) activities also provide opportunities to prevent intrusions and strengthen system defenses. System operators and software maintenance engineers are often the least experienced and lowest paid in their professions. They also typically receive the least training. Given the critical nature of O&M for maintaining system defenses, O&M practices need to be reviewed.

Dimensions of Defense

In addition to how a system is designed, these dimensions of defense include system operations, methods, and procedures employed to limit the attractiveness of an attack and/or the consequences of an attack. Some of the dimensions of defense that need to be considered in constructing and "tuning" each system to its unique set of circumstances. Each dimension offers a range of choices that provides either more or less protection. More protection always comes at a price (although surprisingly the price may be quite low, particularly when compared with the security gains that can be achieved). Achieving higher levels of protection either actually costs more to build into a system or exacts a cost in terms of operating overhead or in loss of functionality.

CRITICAL TECHNOLOGIES

Building defenses into systems presumes we have the means to do so. Many of the defensive capabilities we currently have are not adequate for certain known levels or types of attacks, not to mention technically feasible but undocumented attacks. The following are some areas in which we could use some advances in technology.

Real-time intrusion detection is clearly a key element in any set of defenses. Our ability to detect, in real time, intrusions into our systems and the identity of the intruder is currently very limited. In does not take very long to carry out an information attack. Damage can occur in an instant. Clearly an automated capability to respond to an intrusion that can prevent or limit the damage would be highly desirable.

Given our increasing reliance on COTS, we need ways to cost-effectively make sure that the software we buy does what we want it to and only what we want it to. Any Information Age organization buys millions of lines of code each year whose exact origins are not known with any degree of confidence. Automated tools for performing quality assurance (QA) and for verifying and validating (V&V) the code would be an immense help.

Knowing for sure that data were not altered or compromised and that the source of a piece of data or a message was verified would go a long way in the effort to combat certain types of IW attacks.

Organizational Action Plan

The cornerstone of our efforts to combat IW will be the efforts of all organizations to protect their own systems and information. Some organizations have been worrying about this for a long time and have developed and implemented plans to keep on top of this increasingly serious set of threats. Other organizations have more work to do.

It might be helpful, even for those organizations that feel they are well prepared, to review the following list of suggested actions to determine what they need to do to be better prepared for the future.

The first suggested action involves a review of the organization's mission in light of the emerging threat. A few organizations may find that IW-D adds a mission or increases the importance of an existing mission.

New relationships with external organizations may be required, or perhaps existing relationships may need to be modified. Thus, a review of these relationships is in order.

Who is responsible for IW-D in the organization? Perhaps the organization has a Chief Information Officer (CIO) and it would be appropriate for the CIO to take on this responsibility. Perhaps the responsibility for IW-D is spread out among several individuals. In any event, a clear allocation of responsibilities is required.

Not all information or all systems should be considered equal with respect to the protection they merit. It is important, given resource constraints, to identify which information and systems (and functions of these systems) are critical and which are not critical. How vulnerable are the information and systems? What is the specific nature of the vulnerabilities? Answers are needed to provide a basis for planning and developing defenses.

It needs to be remembered that vulnerabilities are relative to the threat, the nature of which is constantly evolving. Thus, vulnerability analyses are not a one-time task but must be part of a continuing effort.

Isolated actions to improve security are helpful, but they are no substitute for the development of a comprehensive IW-D strategy for an organization. Since it is not possible to avoid all the risks associated with IW, each organization needs to develop a plan to manage these risks. In the course of developing and articulating an organizational IW-D strategy and risk management plan, many issues will be raised and discussed. These discussions will create a greater awareness of the problem within the organization and improve the organization's ability to meet the challenges associated with IW-D.

Combatting IW is a long-term proposition. There are many long poles in the tent. An organization's investment strategies need to be reviewed and investments in defenses and supporting technologies must be made. Some reallocation of resources may be made necessary by changes in the operating costs associated with introducing new procedures and safeguards.

INFORMATION WAR ATTACKS ON THE UNITED STATES

Workshop participants divided discussion of this topic into two very different topics: deterring attacks directed through computers and their connectivity (cyber-war attacks) and those directed at the general public through public media such as television, radio, and print. Indeed, one of the most profound dimensions of disagreement among workshop participants was the degree to which the Department of Defense ought to consider media attacks at all. However, because media messages can influence, and arguably have (Beirut bombing, Mogadishu television pictures, etc.) influenced, both the tasking of military assets and mission accomplishment, both types were examined.

CYBER-WAR ATTACKS

Considerable discussion was required for the group to agree on the wide range of types of computer attacks that must be considered. Initially, some felt the discussion should focus only on protection of internal DoD systems, while others wanted to include broad strategic or operational attacks on the banking system or other commercial or quasi-governmental arenas. The workshop was aware, however, of an ACTIS analysis of Defensive Information Warfare that differentiates attacks by their targets and implications into:

- Day-to-day or routine attacks with limited or diffuse impact on U.S. interests. These include ônormalö hacking for fun and profit, typical white collar crime, and other attacks with discrete impact.
- Potentially strategic (catastrophic) attacks. These are limited attacks with unpredictable consequences that could, under some circumstances or in some combinations, have catastrophic implications for U.S. interests. For example, an attack on a single bank, even if the losses are large (millions), is no threat to the U.S. banking system. However, an orchestrated and publicized series of successful attacks on individual banks could undermine confidence in the banking system and create a much more serious problem, even though the specific attacks were each quite limited.
- Strategic (catastrophic) attacks are those which, if successful, will in themselves do great harm to the United States. Destruction of the systems that control systems in key industries and leave them so they cannot be repaired promptly would fall in this category.

In addition, workshop participants stressed that not all information warfare attacks on computer systems need take the form of computer intrusion. Physical destruction of crucial telephone switching stations or other national information infrastructure assets would, themselves, be very damaging.

One significant finding was that the workshop participants consistently found themselves assuming that a visible set of defenses was the beginning point for deterring attacks on important computer systems. In essence, the argument was that information attacks are instrumental acts and will not occur if the attacking party perceives little opportunity for success.

At the same time, the workshop also noted that "success" has very different meaning for different types of actors and that some individuals, particularly those with ôtypicalö hacker attitudes, would be likely to perceive a more robust defensive posture as a challenge, not as discouragement.

This, of course, is a lesson in the need for specific contexts when discussing deterrence and IW. What works in some circumstances may be very wrong in others.

Regardless of whether good defenses necessarily deter attacks, there was consensus that the set of defenses now in place is inadequate for discouraging any but the least well prepared intruder. Not only are systems poorly protected, very few intrusions are detected (reportedly about 5%) and few of those (another 5%) are actually reported, even within the Department of Defense.

If these figures are correct, the likelihood of knowing about an attack is .0025 (one-quarter of one percent) and the risk of being caught must be, by definition, even lower. Improved indications and warning (I&W), as well as improved reporting of detected attacks, are essential elements of improved defensive systems. In this context, the workshop also concluded that assessing the ability of DoD or others to deter attacks will require a sound understanding of the pattern of attacks being experienced. Better data collection as well as I&W was also a priority.

Finally, a variety of defensive measures were identified for computer systems. These are not unique to the deterrence arena, but rather reflect the workshop participants' assumption that some attacks will be deterred by effective defenses.

The technical representatives in the workshop also stressed that for the foreseeable future the advantage in the cyber-war arena will lie with the offense. Hence, building defenses does not guarantee success. Creating redundancy as well as the capacity to contain, recover from, and reconstitute in spite of successful attacks are essential elements of a successful deterrence strategy. Vice Admiral Cebrowski, the JCS J-6, argued, in his luncheon presentation to the workshop, that decoupling information attacks from their purpose is an effective deterrent.

MEDIA WAR

The workshop explored the potential for media attacks to deter effective military action in a Middle Eastern context. The scenario involved a campaign aimed initially at public attitudes in friendly and other regional countries whose cooperation is essential for major U.S. operations in and around the Persian Gulf, and later at public attitudes in the United States. The thrust of the argument was that prudent, even essential, military actions could well be called into question through media attacks with primarily political messages. Several conclusions emerged from these discussions.

- First, because of its democratic traditions and freedom of speech considerations, the U.S. is almost certainly going to be placed in a reactive mode if a media war campaign is launched.
- Second, foreign powers will find it difficult to intimidate U.S. leaders or to put forward obviously false information toward the U.S. public without effective U.S. media responses, but may be able to communicate quite inaccurate images to selected foreign publics who are predisposed to believe them.
- Third, the infrastructure to deliver television images into distant regions may not be readily available within DoD, particularly in a non-warfare situation where the sovereignty of foreign states must be respected.
- Fourth, wargames and seminars are needed involving not only DoD, but across the range of civilian agencies and industry representatives necessary for effective television imagery and counter-imagery in media wars.

Media warfare can put enormous time pressure on U.S. and allied decision making, particularly when the adversary is an authoritarian state with little or no necessity for either internal or international consultation.

Core Conclusion About Deterring Information Warfare Attacks on the United States

While recognizing that the variety of potential attackers, attack contexts, and arenas where information warfare attacks may take place is vast and too complex for simple solutions, the workshop participants were confident that the United States already has basic policies in place that serve as effective deterrents in many circumstances. In essence, some information warfare attacks on the United States are deterred by the same policy that deters other types of attack. Acting under its rights as a sovereign state, the U.S. stands ready to respond to any attack on its interests with all appropriate means, including law enforcement as well as military capacity.

Finally, the workshop recognized that considerable legal work needs to be completed in this arena. First, U.S. law (both state and federal) needs to be clear about the definition of crimes in the information arena. Second, international agreements and treaties are needed to ensure that foreign attackers can be prosecuted effectively and that acts of war are clearly identifiable.

Using Information Warfare to Deter Foreign Governments

In large measure because the discussion on defending against information operations was so rich, but also to a certain extent because of the relatively low level of classification for the meeting, this topic was addressed more quickly and in less detail than the others.

Some limits on U.S. offensive activities were noted. First, media manipulation that involves government personnel providing false information is neither politically wise nor consistent with U.S. policy and law. Second, information attacks are attacks and therefore subject to international law.

Those limits having been noted, the workshop participants also recognized that the technical capacity to render an adversary "ignorant," poor, uncertain of the capability to control its own forces, unable to communicate with its population, or uncertain of the quality of its basic information, could have a profound effect on its willingness to undertake a military adventure and thus equate to a powerful deterrent.

Moreover, while barely unveiling the true potential of highly leveraged information and superior battlefield awareness, Desert Storm has provided the world with a demonstration of the potential advantage of information dominance. Finally, the workshop concluded that research and development into tools and techniques that can impact potential adversaries' knowledge of the battlefield, control of their own forces, resources necessary to support armed conflict and deliver services to their populations, or leverage uncertainty about their own information, should go forward.

A series of more focused roundtables (smaller working groups with selected expertise) is planned to follow up on significant issues left unresolved or where more sensitive issues need to be considered.

The Workshop on Information Warfare and Deterrence was held at the National Defense University as the sixth in a series sponsored by the Directorate of Advanced Concepts, Technologies, and Information Strategies (ACTIS). The topic arose both from (1) issues that surfaced in earlier workshops on subjects as diverse as Coalition Command and Control (C2), Technologies and Operations Other Than War (OOTW), and Command Arrangements for Peace Operations; and (2) interests expressed by ACTIS sponsors in the Joint Staff (J-6) and the Office of the Secretary of Defense, Assistant Secretary of Defense for Command, Control, Communications and Intelligence (ASD/C3I).

As with past ACTIS workshops, this one brought together senior analysts and technical experts, as well as active military leaders and action officers with operational responsibilities in the affected areas, for a non-attribution discussion working toward consensus or clear articulation of alternatives and their consequences. The list of attendees is included as Appendix A. The overall goal of the workshop series is to conceptualize and develop Mission Capability Packages (MCPs) that will support effective decision making and command and control in arenas where DoD has significant responsibilities. MCPs are coherent blends of doctrine, command organization, education, training, systems, and force structure that increase the likelihood of mission accomplishment across a range of anticipated situations and threats. Workshops are a beginning point for MCPs, suggesting novel concepts for later revision and analysis. As this process develops, the MCP is refined and its implications become better understood until an implementable concept emerges which can be passed from the research and development community to the practical world of implementation and action.

Workshop Objectives

When exploring new or relatively new concepts like the relationship between IW and deterrence, analysts can be fairly certain that outcomes will likely be different than expectations. With this in mind the workshop sought to bound the initial explorations to those that might logically be achieved in a two-day effort. The workshop focused on three principal issues:

- What, in today's world, do the terms "deterrence" and "information warfare" mean and how are they related?
- How might IW attacks on the United States be deterred, if at all? This issue was broken, for practical analysis, into "cyber-attacks" and "media warfare" attacks.
- Can the United States use IW to deter other kinds of attacks on itself, its allies, or its interests?

This workshop was conducted at the Secret level (except for one unclassified discussion of media war). Being restricted to classification levels no higher than Secret inhibited discussion of some topics largely by preventing discussion of particular systems and examples. However, the participants were still able to engage in a rich give-and-take and achieved a high degree of candor. A series of more focused roundtables (smaller working groups with selected expertise) is planned to follow up on significant issues left unresolved or where more sensitive issues need to be considered. Evidence Based Research, Inc. served as workshop organizer and rapporteur for the discussions.

Key Concepts and Implications

On one level, deterrence and information warfare are well matched. Both belong to the world of robust ideas with broad implications. Both are highly relevant to the post-Cold War era in which conflict has been transformed from bipolar global structures to multi-sided, local and regional contests in which the military element is a crucial part of, but not the driving force for, competition and conflict. On the other hand, the two topics can be seen as orders of magnitude apart. IW is a huge domain, ranging from media wars to electronic combat and from economic competition to strategic conflict waged against civilian populations. Deterrence is actually a narrow topic that only applies when a set of quite restrictive assumptions apply. Not surprisingly, therefore, the workshop participants found the relationship between the two concepts to be spottyùhighly relevant on some topics, marginally so on others, and not at all relevant in many areas.

Deterrence as a Concept

Many of our common notions of deterrence arise from the recently concluded Cold War. Strategic deterrence was equated with deterring both a Soviet invasion of Western Europe or a first strike on the United States, by the assured ability to reply with a devastating nuclear attack on the Soviet Unions homeland. The workshop participants were well aware that most 'deterrence theory' is largely a product of that Cold War era. This suggests that those whose experience is from that era may bring extraneous concepts or baggage to the topic. Hence, they also heavily agreed that deterrence applications outside the nuclear war arena must be thought through carefully and should be exposed to domain experts from the appropriate arenas before they are considered mature. Throughout history the primary form of deterrence has been defenses. These defenses have been both passive and active. Passive defenses include fortifications, moats and natural features such as rivers, oceans and high ground, and serve to deter by making attacks more difficult and costly. Active defenses and their ability to deter can best be summed up by the quotation frequently attributed to President Theodore Roosevelt: "Speak softly and carry a big stick." In the aggregate, this involves military defense forces.

Military capability or force is obviously not the only way to deter. For example, economic self-interest may deter. Just as an employee is restrained from insulting his employer or a businessman from annoying his customer, nations may be restrained from some information adventures either by the direct cost of the adventure or by the harm to future trade and other economic activity that may result. Building economic interdependency can therefore be considered as a form of deterrence. Likewise, information actions and interdependency might also be a kind of deterrence.

In any sphere, the retaliatory capability need not be real; but it must be perceived as real. Conversely, capability to deter may be insufficient if the adverse party is unaware of the capability or is not persuaded that the capability might be used. Military examples include the Strategic Defense Initiative as deterrence through perception management, and the reverse, when the perception of U.S. military might did not deter Iraq's 1990 invasion of Kuwait. Saddam Hussein either underestimated our power or our willingness to use that power.

DETERRENCE IN THE INFORMATION AGE

The workshop readily reached consensus on a basic definition of deterrence as "prevention or discouragement, by fear or doubt, from acting." Clearly this definition implies an actor and a target. Moreover, the group also agreed on a simple set of conditions necessary for successful deterrence. These were seen as:

- A threat to something of value that exceeds the perceived gain of non-compliance.
- A clear statement of the behavior to be avoided or performed.
- Clear and unambiguous communication of the threat and the desired or proscribed behavior to the target.
- Credible threat, meaning that the actor is perceived by the target to have the will and capability to execute the threat.
- Situational constraints that make it impossible for the target to avoid punishment.
- Controllability of the threat and its implications by the actor.

The Domain of Information and Information Warfare

The simple, but crucial, step of defining what is encompassed by the term "information" is all too often ignored by those who write about its importance and its future.

Three relatively independent dimensions were required to capture and describe the information warfare arena: the degree of conflict/cooperation, substantive focus (political, military, social, economic, and so forth), and the nature of the actors involved (individuals, private organizations, nation states, international organizations, the general public, media, etc.).

The workshop participants generally accepted the broad nature of the information warfare domain and the central role of information systems and processes in the world today. However, they inferred several very important implications from this broad characterization of the relevant domain.

- First, the term "information warfare" is used to mean many things, but is often focused on the military domain or the cyber-war domain dominated by computers. This narrow definition is inconsistent with the broad policy questions relevant to competition and conflict using information media.
- Because information warfare is really a broad and diverse arena, analysis of it must be focused on selected elements, which must be clearly defined in each application. Overall, the field is so broad that virtually no meaningful generalizations can be drawn about it.
- Isolation (except in rare instances), of military, national, public, and private information systems is all but impossible today. Even very important military traffic is likely to be carried on national infrastructure systems. Public and private information sectors are heavily interdependent, and this linkage will continue to grow.
- A whole raft of information systems make potential targets -- banking systems, control systems for railway operations, air control systems, control systems for pipelines, media systems, and others. Only a fraction of those are primarily

military or under the direct protection of the Department of Defense.

- As has been stressed by ADM Owens, Vice Chairman of the Joint Chiefs of Staff, the civilian sector is no longer a sanctuary that can be protected by interposing military forces between adversaries and their targets. Traditional military forces can be flanked at the speed of light by information age attacks on the general population or key economic systems.
- More profoundly, there is no consensus on the appropriate boundary between the military and Department of Defense roles and missions, those of the law enforcement and intelligence systems, and those of the commercial sector.

Workshop participants were aware of a variety of policy initiatives to create interagency working groups and coordinating mechanisms as well as public-private dialogues and mechanisms for both exchanging information and developing plans for dealing with information age threats that cut across communities. Considerable progress has been made in generating better awareness of the threat and there is some effort toward cooperation. However, the general consensus was that these helpful activities were only now developing momentum and were far from successful completion.

7

Information Warfare in State Sponsored Espionage and Crime

The advanced information warfare techniques of computer penetration, surveillance, and exploitation developed by the following states can be utilized for terrorism as well as espionage and crime. There is a long history of state sponsorship of terrorism in the 20th century. Often the goal of computer penetrations is to provide easy access for future penetrations. In effect, foreign states are conducting information warfare espionage to have "turn key" access to U.S. systems in the future. The only difference between these acts of computer espionage and terrorism is the addition of a political motive or goal to the criminal nature of the penetration. States may, in the future, choose to provide this information to a sponsored terrorist group for use against the United States. As such, a careful examination of past and current information warfare activities at the state level is important as it may identify future terrorist targets or tactics likely to be used by state sponsored terrorist groups.

Who can perpetrate an organized "computer attack" against the United States? A study of the threat by Wayne Madsen addresses these issues. He classifies foreign nations into one of four categories of computer advancement:

(1) highly advance, (2) operationally advance, (3) basic development, and (4) initial development. France, the United Kingdom, Japan, China, and the United States represent the first category, and their intelligence agencies are highly advanced in

the science of electronic eavesdropping and computer intelligence gathering. Russia, India, Ukraine, and Colombia represent the second category. While Russia and India, arguably, have first-rate intelligence-gathering organizations, their high technology capabilities still lag behind those of the first category but are improving steadily. Libya, Ghana, and Bolivia fall into the third category. Their intelligence agencies will soon have high technology capabilities. Zaire, Ethiopia, and Tanzania represent the fourth category: their intelligence organizations lack high technology capabilities and their embryonic computer and data communications systems are vulnerable to the capabilities of the nations in the first three categories.

While this is a comprehensive list of states, the threat continues to grow. This is due to the increasing rate of computer power and technology available to sub-state actors, such as hackers." In the past, one needed to have the power and resources of a state behind them to conduct an effective worldwide SIGINT operation. Now, a few people can conduct a computer intelligence (COMPINT) effort with limited funds. Whereas access to remote sites to place antennas or military overflight of territory was a prerequisite for SIGINT, the most critical element of COMPINT is the knowledge of how to exploit a computer system. As cyberspace is a nonphysical reality, borders and geographic location of the target system are meaningless in a COMPINT effort. Since the world's computers are becoming increasingly interconnected, a modem to connect to the Internet and a desktop computer, coupled with a talented computer user, are all that is required to start intelligence gathering. With the power of desktop computers doubling every 12-18 months, the computing power that previously only a government or large corporation could afford now sits in homes across the world. While state powers have exploited these assets in the past, substate actors may exploit them easily in the future.

Definitions

The cited 1997 STC Report emphasised the distinction between the use of information in warfare and the newer concept of information warfare, the first being recognised since ancient times and referring basically to tactical and strategic deception, war propaganda, and destruction of command and control systems. In the current conceptualisation, information warfare "extends far beyond the traditional battlefield, and its possible perpetrators and victims are by no means confined to the military". A few definitions were reported then, to which your Rapporteur would like to add some new ones. The first is proposed by the Institute for the Advanced Study of Information Warfare:

"Information warfare is the offensive and defensive use of information and information systems to exploit, corrupt, or destroy an adversary's information and information systems, while protecting one's own. Such actions are designed to achieve advantages over military or business adversaries."

The International Centre for Security Analysis of King's College, London suggests that information warfare "is about struggles for control over information activities" and distinguishes three levels or categories: ideational struggle for the mind of an opponent, struggle for information dominance, and attacks on, and defence of, information flows and activities. The first, highest level "encompasses the whole range of psychological, media, diplomatic and military techniques for influencing the mind of an opponent, whether that opponent is a military commander or a whole population". The second level could be assimilated with the Revolution in Military Affairs (RMA), whose theorists and advocates see, as the future evolution of armed forces, the goal of dominating the "information spectrum". The ultimate objective of this level of information warfare would be to render physical conflict "either unnecessary or at worst short, sharp and successful". At the third level the focus is on any kind of electronic attack upon military or civilian information infrastructures, including criminal hacking (or cracking), data disruption, illegal systems penetration, and also physical destruction, deception and psychological operations.

The Washington based Center for Strategic and International Studies (CSIS) recently published a comprehensive study on these issues and admitted that so many different activities have been classified under the label "information warfare" that it is now difficult to understand exactly what it is. Nonetheless, this study classifies information warfare activities according to the source, the form, and the tactical objectives of the attack. Thus, information warfare can be viewed as a combination of these three dimensions.

First, an attack could originate either from outside or from within the targeted organisation or system. Second, four categories of attack can be identified:

- Data attacks are conducted by inserting data into a system to make it malfunction.
- Software attacks, similar to data attacks, are conducted by penetrating systems with software causing failure or making them perform functions different from those intended.
- Hacking or cracking is seizing or attempting to seize control of an information system (or a vital part of it) to disrupt, deny use, steal resources or data, or cause any other kind of harm.
- Physical attacks are the traditional form of attack (bombing, assaulting, and destroying) directed against information systems. An electromagnetic pulse (EMP) produced by nuclear explosions can also be included in this kind of attack.

All these different forms of information warfare attack can be categorised by their goals or tactical objectives: they could be aimed at exploitation, deception, disruption or destruction of information systems.

The French Ministry of Defence has also offered an interesting definition of information warfare. It has singled out three types:

- War for information (guerre pour l'information): to obtain information about the enemy's means, capabilities and strategies in order to defend ourselves;
- War against information (guerre contre l'information): at the same time to protect our information systems and to disrupt or destroy the enemy's.
- War through information (guerre par l'information): to conduct misinformation or deception operations against the enemy in order to achieve "information dominance".

All the above are accurate and acceptable definitions, but for the sake of clarity we can try to summarise them into a simpler and more limited formula. Information warfare could be then defined as defensive and offensive operations, conducted by individuals or structured organisations with specific political and strategic goals, for the exploitation, disruption or destruction of data contained in computers or transmitted over the Internet and other networked information systems.

ASSESSING THE THREAT

In general terms, a threat can be defined as the combination of acapability and a hostile intent. According to many analysts, the reason for concern about attacks upon information systems, or information warfare, is that the means of offence are widely available, inexpensive and easy to use. In a world where even governments and the military tend to rely on computer hardware and software available commercially off-the-shelf (COTS), virtually anybody with a computer and the technical skills could become a cracker or a cyberterrorist. Moreover, the progress in information technology makes the electronic tools available to conduct such attacks more sophisticated every day and, through the Internet and the interlinked computer world, easier to acquire. But the most potentially dangerous feature of information warfare is that it can be conducted from anywhere in the world and the possibilities of discovering the attack's origin, or even its presence, are extremely difficult.

Who can conduct such attacks? A recent analysis has listed the potential "enemies" according to the levels of threat. At the lower level are the crackers, or "hackers with malicious intentions", sometimes highly knowledgeable in technical matters and very determined, but often isolated and without a clear political agenda. Then we have some pressure groups, organisations that fight for specific political causes and might decide to acquire the technology in order to attack the information systems of other organisations or even of states. Terrorists come next in the scale: some groups are becoming increasingly sophisticated in the use of technology and can conduct strategic offensive information warfare. At the highest level are the states, many of which now have access to extremely sophisticated technology and can acquire the necessary organisational infrastructure to conduct both offensive and defensive information warfare. In fact, some experts doubt the effectiveness, capability, or even willingness of the non-state actors to conduct attacks that can seriously threaten other nations' security.

In the last fifteen years, both the private and public sectors' information systems have been subjected to attacks that have substantially increased with the growth of the Internet. Computer viruses have been a primary concern of information security experts. These are generally very small programmes, often with destructive capabilities, designed to invade computer systems or individual PCs by attaching themselves to other bits of executable programme codes. Created by hackers, computer science students or disgruntled programmers, these viruses have been extremely destructive to many computers and networks, but have not proved to be particularly effective as weapons to date. Because of their non-professional origins, the viruses often contain errors and, moreover, their authors are often incapable of envisioning the complexity and variety of the systems they are attacking.

Of course, it is still possible that a state or a terrorist group can assemble a team of experts capable of creating malicious viruses and using them to conduct information warfare attacks. But computer viruses are extremely unpredictable and far from precise in their behaviour, and they might eventually damage the attacker as much as the victim. In addition, the international anti-virus industry is mature and is well positioned to create necessary antidotes to almost any new virus.

Other, more dangerous attacks on information systems have been conducted by criminal hacking intruders. Private corporations, particularly in the financial sector, are regularly penetrated by cybercriminals: the FBI estimates that these electronic intrusions cause yearly losses of about $10 billion in the United States alone. This is probably only the tip of the iceberg. In fact, concerns about protecting shareholder value and customer confidence may keep many firms from reporting all the attacks to law enforcement agencies.

Electronic intrusions into the military information infrastructure cause deep concern in the United States. According to the CSIS, probe attacks against the Pentagon number in the tens of thousands every year. John J. Hamre, Deputy Secretary of Defense, recently stated that from January to mid-November 1998, the National Security Agency (NSA) recorded more than 3,800 incidents of intrusion attempts against the Defense Department's unclassified computer systems and networks. Over 100 of these attacks reached root-level access and many were even able to break down some kinds of service. This reflects only what has been reported to NSA, but "the actual number of intrusions probably is considerably higher".

The literature and the chronicles are full of examples of successful network intrusions at the US Department of Defense (DoD) and other Western defence institutions. One of the most interesting is the break-in at the Air Force's Laboratories in the town of Rome, in New York State, when two British boys hacked into the system with the help of what is called a "sniffer" programme, able to capture passwords and user log-ins to the network. The case served as a learning experience for the Air Force Information Warfare Center, which then developed the advanced technical skills to counter these intrusions. Similar hacker intrusions are regularly experienced by all other US military services and government agencies.

While most of the attacks in the last few years were generally conducted by individuals or by small groups of intruders, with little or no political purpose, recently some cases suggested the possibility of state-sponsored hacking or cracking. Additionally, some anti-state, politically motivated activity has occurred. In October 1998, China launched a new website to publicise its efforts in human rights. A few days later, hackers replaced the home page of that site with a message condemning Beijing for its poor record in human rights.

Another, more revealing case occurred in Ireland, where refugees from East Timor had set up a website to protest against the occupation of their country by Indonesia. The Irish Internet provider even created a new domain name ".tp", as if East Timor were an independent country. In January 1999, a concerted attack against the East Timorese server started, originating from 18 different places as far apart as Australia, the United States, Japan, the Netherlands and Canada. The attackers managed to render the web server useless and forced the Irish provider to disconnect its entire system. Clearly, this was not an ordinary cracker intrusion, though many doubt that the Indonesian government had the capability to conduct such a concerted information warfare action. The most probable culprit is a group of politicised hackers sympathetic with the Indonesian position.

The NATO information system was also indirectly threatened in October 1998, when a Serbian group of hackers known as Black Hand penetrated a Kosovo Albanian web server and threatened to sabotage the Alliance's information system. The organisation temporarily closed all foreign access to its web server and its web site was down for two days. Realising that the electronic defences of the NATO web server were extremely weak, experts took some countermeasures, which proved to be insufficient in the light of subsequent events.

During the Kosovo crisis, hackers attacked the NATO web site, causing a line saturation of the server by using a "bombardment strategy". The organisation had to defend itself from macro viruses from FRY trying to corrupt its e-mail system, which was also being saturated by one individual sending 2,000 messages a day. These attacks were possible because NATO was using the same server for the e-mail system and its web-pages. When these tasks are done by separate servers, as is now the case at NATO, the threat is reduced. Allied governments' web sites have also been targeted during the war, and according to US Air Force sources the attacks came not only from FRY, but also from Russia and China. It is unclear, however, whether these attacks were state-sponsored or the work of groups of hackers. Conversely, FRY's information systems were severely damaged by NATO bombings and electronic operations - although Belgrade itself dismantled communication systems to deprive its people of outside information. In addition, thousands of Western civilian hackers conducted online attacks against the FRY government's web servers.

Such cases might not prove the existence of state-sponsored information warfare or cyberterrorism, but they offer good examples of what could happen if the capability is coupled with a hostile intent. The subsequent question is: could a group of state-sponsored terrorists or individual crackers damage the information infrastructure of another nation so as to cause a major strategic disruption? The US Department of Defense seems to think so.

In the summer of 1997, a simulation exercise called "Eligible Receiver" was conducted at the Pentagon, ordered by the Joint Chiefs of Staff, to test the ability of the nation's military and civilian infrastructure to resist a concerted information warfare attack. A team of fictional hackers, the Red Team, was allowed to use only COTS materiel and information available on the Web and had to act within the US law. So far, the results of this exercise remain strictly "top secret". Nonetheless, many officials have referred to it in public declarations and some have partially revealed the outcome. James Adams, a journalist based in Washington DC, claimed in a book to have interviewed senior officials about "Eligible Receiver":

"The [simulated] attacks focused on three main areas: the national information infrastructure, the military leadership and the political leadership. In each of these three areas, the hackers found it exceptionally easy to penetrate apparently well-defended systems. Air traffic control systems were taken down, power grids made to fail, oil refineries stopped pumping - all initially apparent incidents. At the same time, in response to a hypothetical international crisis, the Defense department was moving to deploy forces overseas and the logistics network was swinging into action. It proved remarkably easy to disrupt that network by changing orders [S] and interrupt[ing] the logistics flow [S]. The hackers began to feed false news reports into the decision-making process so that the politicians faced a lack of public will about prosecuting a potential conflict and lacked detailed and accurate information [S].

In conclusion, according to Adams' sources, a team of skilled hackers, using standard equipment and publicly available information and playing by the rules, was able to cause a "serious degradation of the Pentagon's ability to deploy and to fight". In other words, they demonstrated that an "electronic Pearl Harbor" was possible.

Many things have changed in the last two years due to the fast pace of progress in information technology. Moreover, the policies and actions taken by the US government may have reduced the vulnerability of the nation's infrastructure. Nonetheless, if technology is helping Western governments establish better defences, it also helps potential enemies improve their capabilities to attack. A recently announced new breed of hacker software, that can learn and adapt to the network environment it attacks, may represent a new threat. According to information technology experts, the new programmes can change their mode of operation, or their targets, based on external stimulants. Pre-programmed to search for specific types of files common to most networks, such software, once in the system, can target data or files of interest to the intruders, even those marked secure or for internal use only.

In addition, many nations are trying to acquire the capabilities needed to conduct information warfare operations and new terrorist groups like Osama bin Laden's are known to use computers and satellite telecommunications. China has recently intensified its information warfare programmes, both to protect its own military infrastructures and to enable the People's Liberation Army to conduct electronic attacks. According to James Mulvenon, a defence specialist at Rand Corporation, Beijing "is seeking the ability both to interfere with Taiwan's command system, and ultimately to Ohack' into US military networks which control deployment in the Asian region."

A serious physical threat to information systems can be posed by the effects of the electro-magnetic pulse (EMP) produced by nuclear explosions. The immediate energy release from a detonated nuclear device produces intense, rapidly varying electric and magnetic fields that can extend for considerable distances and severely affect all electronic equipment and electrical or radar transmissions even to the point of destroying equipment circuits, microprocessors, and other components. Therefore, a single, very high-altitude nuclear blast above Europe or the United States, which may cause no physical damage to structures or people, could disable or disrupt all non-hardened information systems. While few nations currently have both nuclear weapons and the missiles capable of delivering them in space, the increasing number of "rogue" nations with nuclear weapons that are also developing or acquiring long-range missiles may present an extremely serious EMP threat in the near future.

EMP effects from nuclear explosions and non-nuclear weapons, such as HERP (High-Energy Radio Frequency) guns or EMP/T (Electro-Magnetic Pulses Transformer) bombs, may be much more dangerous for civilian information systems than for military ones, most of which are now EMP hardened. Shielding of iron or other materials such as copper mesh or non-magnetic metals is generally available only for the protection of sensitive military technology.

TARGETING THE UNITED STATES

Soviet Union/Russia

The first computer hacker incident to garner national attention was sponsored in part by the Soviet Union to gain access to Western technology and defense information. This incident was the subject of a book, *The Cuckoo's Egg,* by Clifford Stoll. A group of West German Hackers, who were operating on their own, approached the KGB in East Berlin and began to sell the "product" of their hacking. Later touted as a "KGB spy ring," the hackers attempted to break into scores of military, government, and business computers to provide information to the Soviets. While the hackers thought that military items would be high on the KGB shopping list (some were), most of the requests centered on high technology computer programs and equipment design. The Soviets desired the "source code "for sophisticated and widely used computer operating systems. With this knowledge, the Soviets could create their own team of "hackers" to penetrate systems in the West.

The operating system that runs a computer exists in two forms, the "source code" which a human can read, analyze, and understand when printed, and the "compiled" version, which translates the operating system "source code" into "machine language," the actual ones and zeros that the computer understands but is completely unintelligible to humans. The process of compiling the source code is similar to encryption. The machine language can be decompiled (decrypted) with the result being only similar, not identical, to the source code. Thus, any "source code" is one of a computer programming company's most closely held secrets. Knowledge of the "source code" makes it easier for a hostile competitor or state to identify what bugs exist in the program or even insert its own bugs, recompile the code, and replace the operating system with their altered version, all without the knowledge of the end user. In this manner, the Soviets were attempting to "get the keys to the filing cabinet rather than its contents" via their computer hackers. There are indications that the Soviet efforts to acquire this information were far more extensive than using the "amateur" hackers as their KGB contact told them that they had "competition" and may of its desires were met without the hackers providing the product. This knowledge, exploited by terrorists, could result in massive disruption of computer systems on the worldwide basis.

The computer penetration attempts by the Soviets/Russians continue. Wayne Madsen observes that "the Institute of Automated Systems (IAS) in Moscow hosts the National Center for Automated Data Exchanges with Foreign computer Networks and Data Banks (NCADE). During Soviet rule, NCADE had a special program to broaden linkages between Soviet computer users and foreign data networks and databases to obtain valuable software programs that the Soviets could not normally obtain because of Western export restrictions." Using these channels, the Soviets penetrated a German computer and obtained production information on the Tornado fighter aircraft in 1984. As recently as 1989 a Soviet Attaché, LtCol Yuri Pakhutsov, was expelled from the U.S. for allegedly attempting to acquire information on government computer security practices and capabilities. While the KGB of the Soviet Union was well organized and ran its "information warfare" attacks from several directorates, the current state of organized Russian computer espionage efforts is not clear. Statements made by retired Russian intelligence officers, even after the KGB-Hannover Hacker spying scandal, leave open the possibility that computer espionage efforts continue.

Colonel Barkovsky was not hesitant to state that the Russian Federation has embarked on a major programme of establishing information service networks throughout the country. Not elaborated upon was whether the Russian intelligence services will take advantage of the information-gathering capabilities provided by these networks.

One can only assume that the Russians are continuing their programs to acquire and target high technology in the United States.

Claire Sterling, in her book *The Terror Network,* claimed that the Soviet Union was a major sponsor of terrorism across the world. While the dissolution of the Soviet Union and the economic problem of Russia have clearly limited its ability to fund large terrorist operations, the cost involved in sponsoring cyberterrorism is significantly lower. The knowledge gained by the Soviets during Cold-War espionage efforts may (with or without the approval of the Soviet leadership) find its way into the hands of cyberterrorist organizations. This flow of information is potentially more damaging than the flow of arms and explosives to conventional terrorist organizations.

Bulgaria

Bulgaria has been a "breeding ground" for computer viruses during and after Communist rule. In the early 1990s, the Bulgarians had developed thirty unique viruses with more than 100 different variations and were releasing them at a rate of one per week. The "Hannover hackers" of *Cuckoo's Egg* fame also identify the Bulgarians as active in computer intelligence. Madsen cites the National Intelligence Service (foreign and domestic intelligence), and Razuznavatelno Upravleniye na Ministerstvoto (RUMNO) (Military intelligence) as the Bulgarian intelligence organizations most likely to be involved in computer intelligence gathering. It has also been rumored that a new "virus library" that allows anyone, not just a skilled programmer, to write a virus by "picking and choosing" among several options was first developed in Bulgaria. This system has the potential to produce thousands of new viruses to be unleashed at random or specific targets. A cyberterrorist bent on bringing a system down could single-handily generate a flood of viruses to infect the targeted computer. Even if virus detection software was installed, the chances are good that a virus could be created to evade detection.

France

France freely admits that it conducts intelligence operations against its allies and its enemies on the "economic front." As we move into the information age, the distinction between friends and enemies begins to blur. Madsen targets the Direction de la Surveillance du Territoire (DST) and the Directorate Generale de la Securite Exterieure (DGSE) as the agencies involved in COMPINT. In addition the Groupement de Communications Radio-electriques (GCR), the French NSA, maintains a close working relationship with France Telecom and, like the U.S. NSA, has strict rules on the use of encryption products within France, allegedly so that they can "break" the encryption and eavesdrop on communications within France.

Recently, the French government disclosed a document instructing the DGSE to gather intelligence on 49 U.S. aerospace and defense firms. The methods to obtain this information included bugging of Air France flights and breaking and entering of hotel rooms of visiting business executives to photocopy business materials. The Hughes Aircraft Company has been a favorite target of the French. The DGSE targeted Hughes for information on it HS 601 communication satellite, fiber optic anti-tank weapons, the Phoenix AIM-54 air to air missile, and various electro-optical sensors. The Hughes Corporation decided (ostensibly for business reasons) to cancel its attendance at the Paris Air Show after the revelations of French targeting. Another "aviation" scheme of the French involved the collection and exploitation of telemetry signals from a Boeing test flight of its new 747-400 aircraft. A French SIGINT and technical team were sent to Washington state to intercept and analyze the test flight data for the benefit of Airbus research. While not a direct computer controlled navigation and flight control systems. The knowledge gained from Boeing's telemetry data enabled them to develop similar systems for their own aircraft. Additionally, should the detailed knowledge of computer controlled aviation systems fall into the hands of a technologically sophisticated terrorist organization, the potential to create terror is substantial. A terrorist organization would only have to convince the public that it is capable of causing the controls of a particular type of airplane to stop responding to pilot inputs to create large concern over flying in that particular type of airplane.

Japan

The Japanese place a high priority on intelligence gathering through both "official" and corporate intelligence networks. Japan's international telecom carrier, NTT "routinely cooperates with Japanese intelligence to tap the phone lines of competitors." In addition Madsen asserts that the Japanese target U.S. satellite communications stations. "A 1987 classified CIA report, *Japan: Foreign Intelligence and Security Services,* claimed that the second most important Japanese intelligence priority was the gathering (in many cases by computer) of technological and scientific developments in the United States and Western Europe."

The efforts of Japan in the "high tech" sector are not simply related to "computer break-ins" but rather to acquire design specifications in an effort similar to that of the Former Soviet Union. While the Soviets were attempting to obtain source codes and hardware that they were unable to build themselves, the Japanese were working to save money on R&D by stealing advanced U.S. technology and then bringing similar products to market simultaneously with their U.S. competition.

Peter Schweizer outlines the story of a corporate spy who sold Hitachi copies of IBM's *Adirondack Workboods,* a series of books that held the secrets to future IBM technology. Hitachi was able to use this information to develop computer hardware that was nearly identical to IBM's but cheaper since Hitachi did not bear the development costs.

This case was "broken" by a Silicon Valley "sting" operation run by the FBI that initially targeted the Soviets. Japanese aggressiveness in pursuing this technology led them into the trap. The end result was an out of court settlement, reportedly for 300 million dollars between the Japanese and IBM. The information that an intelligence gathering effort obtains may be used by a sponsored terrorist organization to target a specific business or industry.

China

Chinese intelligence employs its large ethnic community abroad for many purposes. It is now clear that computer penetration was one of those functions. Andrew Wang, a Chinese immigrant, was arrested for stealing the source code of several programs from Ellery Systems. These programs were designed to "run" the emerging National Information Infrastructure. This source code, as previously discussed, would allow a foreign intelligence agency or terrorist group to identify and exploit loopholes in the "new information superhighway" that would carry everything from benign E-mail to national security data.

Germany

The Germans appear to have taken their cue from the success of such amateur hacker groups as the "Chaos Club" and the "Hannover Hackers" that worked with the KGB. According to Schweizer, the Germans created "Project Rahab," named after the biblical character who helped the Israelites infiltrate Jericho, in the mid 1980s to develop a "professional" hacking capability. The project was developed by the Bundes Nacrichten Dienst's (BND) Christian Stoessel, who wrote the initial "point paper" proposing hacking into foreign data bases for intelligence purposes. The project was joint effort between BND's Division I (HUMINT), Division II (SIGINT) and Division IV (HQ). In addition to the intelligence professionals, other technical experts from a variety of outside institutions were recruited, resulting in a staff of approximately 70 people. While focused initially on retrieving information, the Project Rahab staff soon turned to offensive measures that could be of use in a time of conflict, including a variety of viruses that could be inserted in to target computers. Schweizer claims that the Project has "accessed computer systems in the Soviet Union, Japan, France, the United States, Italy, and Great Britain," Included in the "hacks" of the Rahab staff is penetration of the SWIFT network, a dedicated international banking network that carries there majority of worldwide bank transfers. The implications of this information falling into terrorist hands are clear.

Iraq

Both sides waged information warfare, it appears, during the Gulf War. A Schweizer claims that a major computer penetration effort was launched during Desert Storm. A Government Accounting Office Report reinforces this claim as it outlines the efforts of Dutch hackers to penetrate U.S. unclassified military computers. The hackers exploited several well-known weaknesses and were able to penetrate a computer system that directly supported Operation Desert Storm. While the hackers did not attempt to shut down any of the penetrated systems, they did attempt to modify the software to provide easy access in the future. While the Dutch hackers have not been publicly linked to Iraqi intelligence efforts, a similar incident, involving a German citizen was detected during the GulfWar.

Lawrence Livermore Laboratories were used by "hackers" in an attempt to find information on the Patriot missile system. In this instance the actions of a third party "proxy" for Iraq had the potential to cause damage to the safety of troops on the ground, the integrity of air defenses in Israel and thus, cause a weakening of the allied coalition against Iraq. As Iraq is a known sponsor of terrorist organizations, it may turn to its proxies to carry out a cyberterror campaign against the information systems of enemy states.

Swiss

The Swiss, who have a long history in cryptography, may have perpetrated an information warfare attack against other nations. The Swiss firm of Crypto AG, which sells encryption technology and hardware to nations such as Iraq, Iran, Libya and Syria, has been accused of "bugging" their crypto equipment and listening in on "encrypted" communications. Further more, it is alleged that the Swiss firm is really owned by the German BND and that the U.S. National Security Agency has played a leading role in the bugging. While the firm has vehemently denied this charge, it raises several interesting information warfare possibilities. If supposedly "secure" crypto units were bugged without the knowledge of a client nation, the possibility exists that other computers or items of "high tech" equipment have been modified with less than possibility exists that other computers or items of "high tech" equipment have been modified with less than honorable intent. Several stories have appeared on the Internet discussing both software and hardware "flaws" distributed in products. One such flaw disabled a computer program after one month of use. The possibility exists that a program could "lock up" a computer after a certain time period or after it received a certain activation command. Computer hardware, such as printers and circuit boards could also be shipped with "logic bombs" in their programs that would cause the equipment to cease functioning. The known cases that have been discussed have all been "benign" errors by public companies that have been rapidly fixed once identified. If, However, a foreign power were to insert its own bug in the software's source code *before* shipment and not activate the program until hostilities were imminent, a substantial portion of an affected computer network could be disabled.

Seychelles

The island nation of the Seychelles has undertaken a high technology campaign against enemies of its government in England. The nation was able to exploit the British telephone system and conduct wiretaps against several targets. The information obtained with these wiretaps resulted in the assassination of an exiled anti-government leader. The Seychelles demonstrate the potential threat that even a small country can pose to a superpower by using information warfare techniques. In the information age, even the smallest state or terrorist group has a chance to impact the global network.

Israel

While not responsible for the creation of the "Friday the 13th" virus, (supposedly developed by a Palestinian to protest the 40th anniversary of the end of the Palestinian mandate) the computer links between Israel's intelligence service and the United States served as a conduit for the virus to spread to the United States. The Israelis used a "low tech" solution to enter U.S. databases- they recruited Jonathan Pollard. While unable to "break DIA's computers, Israel could obtain information that Pollard retrieved from computer systems and delivered to his handlers. This highlights the constant "human" factor in all of intelligence. Even if your computer cannot be accessed by any type of modem or network and is sitting inside a Tempest approved enclosure, an enemy agent can still physically break-in, or have an employee access the machine, copy the information from that computer onto a floppy disk and simply walk out of the building with it. Information that would have taken a wheelbarrow to get out of a secure facility now fits on a single diskette. While "hackers" may not "break into" some of their target computers, they are still able to analyze the type of information on the computer and possibly gain some information of the type of hardware and operating system that runs the computer. While this does not help the hacker, it may allow for mare "classic" espionage action to be taken by a foreign organization, such as bribing or blackmailing someone on the "inside." As jay Peterzell highlights, "NSA has figures that make the insider threat look soberingly real. An agency log of cases involving computer crime or computer espionage showed that up to 90% of know security breaches are the work of corporate or government insiders."

Israel was also involved in halting a second Patriot missile computer hacking operation. Israel detained an 18 year old for attacking U.S. defense computers to retrieve information on the Patriot missile system. Charges were not brought against the hacker, possibly to down play the incident and not highlight existing weaknesses in computer security.

INFORMATION WARFARE

The history of the Second World War offers great examples of the military and civilian leadership manipulating information, even in a very crude fashion, to achieve rather spectacular results. In those days, as we thought about dominating the information spectrum, we turned to the cryptographers who were on the leading edge of these efforts, the so-called "code breakers." These specialized folks focused intently upon breaking the Japanese and German codes. In Europe, the ULTRA project -- "ULTRA" for the

"ULTRA secret" -- produced spectacular results. Our code breakers literally worked miracles.

After the Normandy invasion, the German 7th Army attempted a counterattack to drive the Allied forces from the rather tenuous beachhead that they held. But with the help of ULTRA's ability to read the German mail and message traffic, we knew precisely what they were doing as they began to gather their forces to make this attack. We were able to put the British Second Tactical Air Force and the United States Ninth Tactical Air Force immediately upon these armor formations just as they massed. ULTRA gave us the critical information that allowed us to defeat the German forces before they ever came in contact with our ground forces.

By comparison, if you think to December of 1944 and the Battle of the Bulge, we see an example of where the Germans were able to catch us by surprise. They used an alternative communications network, and the Allies did not realize that the Germans had made this switch. It was our lack of information that really fueled the initial German success in the Battle of the Bulge. We had come to rely on ULTRA and had developed a little bit of self-delusion -- and the Germans took advantage of it very effectively.

Our ability to monitor the enemy's communications and use that information as an integral part of our operations is really nothing new. There is another example we should not forget. That's how we control the information that we allow the enemy to receive. Again, I am going back to the Second World War and talking about disinformation, particularly the disinformation campaign that centered on General Patton before and during the D-Day landings. At that time, the Allies understood the other guy's ability to intercept our open signals, so we devised a rather elaborate plan that played to this emerging capability on the part of the Germans. The Allies set up a fake Army headquarters and generated false communications transmissions in England. As a result, the Nazis ended up with a significant number of troops placed in the wrong positions.

Even as they started to pick up indications that there was this great Allied armada that was going to invade Normandy, the

Germans refused to believe that there could actually be an Allied invasion of Europe led by anyone but Patton. We played on that expectation in a way that kept Patton associated with his fake headquarters. Even as the Germans began to get higher and higher fidelity intelligence that indicated a real attack at Normandy, their leaders were frozen in indecision and, as a result, tied down considerable forces in France across from the shortest invasion route from England.

For instance, the aircraft we will fly over this time frame are fundamentally the same kinds of aircraft we are flying today. Some will have more advanced avionics, more advanced stealth characteristics or other features; but in the main, aircraft will remain fundamentally aircraft as we know them today. Ships will remain fundamentally ships as we know them today. The same holds true for tanks and armored personnel carriers.

Information warfare is not the exclusive domain of the Air Force, or any other service. I think information warfare has different meanings to a soldier, sailor, Marine, or airman. For instance, the soldier's focus may be on what happens at the corps level and below. The sailor's and Marine's focus is on the maritime and littoral regions. At the same time, an airman's focus is theatre-wide, from the front lines to the adversary's capital. You begin to see how IW covers the entire battlefield. But, because of these divergent views and unique needs, I think it's critical that all services come to grips with and develop capabilities for their respective mediums of operations -- that is land, sea, and air. Then, it falls to the joint force commander, or the regional commander-in-chief, to integrate these capabilities to accomplish the mission.

The Air Force has put considerable effort into developing our concepts. In fact, over the past four months, we have had a team travel to every commander-in-chief (CINC) of a U.S. unified command and brief them on our efforts to incorporate IW into our doctrine and to integrate these concepts into our force employment. Most importantly, we want to be sure that what we are doing and how we approach the subject as an institution will be consistent with the way the CINCs intend to fight. And we want to make sure that what we are doing will meet their needs.

As a practitioner of the profession of arms, I view information technology advances with a single-minded interest. I am motivated by the fact that throughout history, soldiers, sailors, Marines, and airmen have learned one extremely valuable lesson relative to engagement with an opposing force. That is, if you can analyze, act, and assess faster than your opponent, you will win.

The information explosion discussed here today is going to make dramatic changes in how this nation fights wars in the future. Such technology will allow a commander's vision and view of the battlefield to be shared at the lowest level -- to the flight for the airman, to the company on the ground, and to the ship's bridge. Simultaneously, soldiers, Marines, sailors, and airmen on the front lines will be able to see and exploit opportunities as they occur.

What this means is our joint forces may enjoy what some are calling "dominant battlefield awareness." We have some of this kind of capability today. We've made significant enhancements to our ability to leverage our forces with faster command and control and intelligence networks. Among other capabilities, these networks are dramatically reducing the time required to detect and destroy a target.

This process starts with how we gather data. Our intelligence, surveillance, and reconnaissance efforts have been significantly and dramatically improved since Desert Storm. If you are familiar with our TALON programs, you will appreciate what we are doing to reduce the sensor-to-shooter loop -- that is injecting what is detected by our space-based assets directly into the cockpit or a flight deck. We are making similar advances with the systems that operate within the earth's atmosphere. For example, our AWACS early warning aircraft have been greatly improved. Their current radar upgrade allows us to detect cruise missiles at twice the range that we could previously. The AWACS is being fitted with the Joint Tactical Information Distribution Systems, or JTIDS. We will start the initial JTIDS operational test this August. Expect that we will reach full operational capability before the end of the decade. JTIDS alone will give us some pretty significant capabilities. It is not restricted just to AWACS. It also gives our warfighters a secure and jam-resistant data link between Air Force, Navy, Army, and Marine units and future coalition partners -- on land, at sea, and in the air. What that really means is all the players will have a real-time picture and awareness of both what is happening on the ground and what is going on in the air above those forces. JTIDS will give us a tremendous capability to know, at a much higher fidelity, the location of both the enemy and our own forces.

We are also making similar improvements in how we plan and control air operations. Today, we are fielding CTAPS -- the Contingency Theatre Automated Planning System. CTAPS will connect our command and control from the joint forces air component commander (JFACC) to the air wings and the base-level planning cells. It will allow us to generate, disseminate, and monitor the progress of the daily air tasking order much faster than we ever have been able to do before. CTAPS also will tie in with the Combat Intelligence System which will provide us the enemy's order of battle through imagery and integrated threat data.

What does this really mean to us? During Desert Storm, it took us about 48 hours to plan and disseminate the ATO. That doesn't mean that it took 48 hours to execute a request from the field. But, it means that the deliberative process that planners went through to service targets was a 36- to 48-hour process. And you had to have someone manually intervene with an immediate air request to get inside those planning cycles. What the CTAPS system will do for us is take this 48-hour cycle and compress it to 12 hours. This really isn't some pie-in-the-sky system that we're dreaming about or visualizing. This is something that is in full use in exercises today and will be operational across the force next year. We have a similar planning tool that has been operational with our global air mobility forces for about three years.

These are a couple of examples of the kinds of tools we are putting in place. They are going to do more than replace the grease pencil and butcher block paper that (retired Air Force General) Chuck Horner and his staff had to use to run the air war during Desert Storm. These systems are going to help us dominate the information spectrum. I am convinced that this capability will be critical the next time our forces are employed in combat.

If you recall, I described information warfare in terms of how we deny, corrupt, or. destroy our adversary's information base while we protect our own. Much of this activity has a very offensive element to it. I think we have been doing this for some time, but perhaps we didn't use that term. For example, during Desert Storm, we targeted many of the Iraqi communications nodes and physically destroyed Saddam Hussein's ability to talk to his troops through normal channels. We forced him into sub-optimum modes of communicating.

In the future, we will approach this objective by viewing our adversary's information activities as a system, and we will engage that system in a variety of ways. In fact, rather than put a precision guided munition into the central telephone exchange in Baghdad and destroy it next time, we may elect to leave it standing so we can better exploit it through our advances in information warfare. So, there will be trade-offs between lethal and non-lethal dimensions in the IW arena.

In the same manner, we have been doing some things along the way that we could properly classify as offensive information operations. There are ways that we corrupt information available to the enemy to deceive him. They include using psychological operations and our electronic warfare assets, like the Compass Call aircraft. I think that these kinds of measures that are designed to corrupt information the enemy has are really critical tools that we provide to the CINCs today. They open the envelope for the potential of further operations tomorrow. Again, if you think back to what we did on D-Day with disinformation, and you consider the tremendous advances in technology since 1944, you begin to appreciate the tremendous potential that exists in this area.

If we recognize an adversary's information network as a lucrative target, an adversary will view our data banks and weapon systems the same way. Information security -- the classic OPSEC, COMSEC, and the more recently stressed computer security -- takes on a whole new level of urgency. As a result, the Air Force is taking some rather significant measures to safeguard our assets. This year, we are spending more than $80 million on defensive measures alone, including establishing a base network control center to protect access to computers and communications. This same center will permit us to see if someone has tried to gain access to our system and, hopefully, will allow us to track down who tried to intrude on the system. These initiatives are important because we run a tremendous risk if we look at information warfare as something that is unique to America. It is not, and by the same token, the U.S. military is not alone in this vulnerability.

Our commercial sector, other elements of the government, and our industrial sectors rely on information systems just as much, if not more, than the military. If you've read Tom Clancy's recent thriller, Debt of Honor, you're familiar with what may be plausible. In this fictional tale, Clancy describes the problems caused when someone infects the stock exchange's computers with a virus, literally bringing the stock market to a standstill. To me, Clancy's work reinforces how the information threat is more than just a unique military concern.

As I look at information warfare and how it relates to the services, I'm reminded of a story about a football team. It seems that during one of the games, the local team had to put in a back-up quarterback late in the fourth quarter. They were ahead, and they were just trying to hang on. So, they put this relatively untested young man into the game, and all he had to do was avoid making a mistake and the team would win. So, the coach grabbed the guy as he was about to go on the field and said, "OK, here's what I want you to do. Run the ball three times, and then punt." So, the kid understood that and goes out onto the field.

His first run gains 20 yards -- great. On the second play, he gains 30 yards. Now, this is going a lot better than he ever expected. On the third play, he gains 30 more yards. Now they are down on the 10-yard line, the fans are going crazy, and it appears they're going to wrap this thing up. All he has to do is score, and he'll seal the victory for sure. So, the center snaps the ball to him and he punts. Everyone is stunned by this. His coach pulls him over to the sidelines and asks him what he was thinking. And the quarterback replied, "I was thinking that since you didn't change that play, I must have the dumbest coach around."

It is not enough to make a game plan and go with it. You must act and react to what is happening around you. What we're doing today with information warfare is a little bit like that football game -- IW gives us the ability to plan faster with better information so that we can call the optimum play. It may allow us to know what defensive stunt the other team is going to use. It may allow us to give our opponent false information on what play we're about to use. And, most importantly, it may allow us to call an audible and adjust to a fluid situation.

But unlike the game that I just described, when America sends her military forces into action, we don't want a close, exciting game, and we don't want an inexperienced quarterback. This nation has come to expect in our military operations nothing but blow-outs -- 100 to nothing is a good score. And, I believe that exploiting this new and emerging information technology is going to be the key to making this happen. As we approach tomorrow, we need to do more as a service and with the other services. Let me touch just briefly on what we are doing in terms of changing the way we organize, train, and equip our forces.

First, in terms of organizing, in September 1993, the United States Air Force stood up the Air Force Information Warfare Center in San Antonio. This center has more than 1,000 men and women chartered to support IW planning, intelligence gathering, weapon system analysis, and related activities. This group will be a source of IW support teams to go out and assist the CINCs and JFACCs during crises or exercises. They will help build information warfare into the air campaign planning and execution. The Air Force is not alone in this. The Army has an Information Warfare Center at Fort Belvoir, Virginia, and the Navy has created a center at Fort Meade, Maryland.

Additionally, the Air Force is adjusting our training and education programs to include IW concepts. We have had a course for our major air command and numbered air force staffs to give them basic understanding of the issues. We are incorporating IW into our doctrine, so that airmen everywhere will share a common foundation and a common terminology. We're adjusting our mid- and senior-level professional military education schools at Maxwell

Air Force Base, Alabama. You see part of this effort here today. We have four Air Force officers attending the inaugural class of the National Defense University's School for Information Warfare.

Finally, and most significantly, we are beginning to procure weapon systems with a mindset that places high priority on maximizing their performance as an information warfare platform. One example of that is the United States' new air superiority fighter, the F-22. This aircraft is the first platform to be built around information technologies. This was an established objective when we started the program, not something added after the fact. A lot of people have heard about the F-22's stealth. You've heard about its supercruise capability -- that is the ability to cruise faster than the speed of sound in military power. And possibly you've heard about the fact that it has tremendous agility in the air-to-air arena. But, you cannot begin to appreciate its potential until you sit in the concept demonstrator and see how the F-22's integrated avionics work. The quality of the composite picture that's compiled from a variety of sources will literally water your eyes, particularly if you're an old-time fighter pilot. For the first time, you'll be able to sit with those flat glass displays and have tremendous situational awareness readily available to you. That is something we've needed for years, and we're finally in the process of getting it. It will allow our pilots to act and assess faster even when outnumbered. And I tell you it isn't just a concept -- it's being put into production today! The F-22 is just one of many Air Force programs that we're continuing to push forward. You see the same thought processes in the space-based infrared system, in our Joint STARS, and in our precision munitions program. As we move forward, we are establishing an additional requirement for our weapon systems -- that is security against the information threat -- that's being written into the requirements documents.

This new mindset is found throughout our acquisition strategy. We are changing how we view our modernization needs. We're taking another look at IW capabilities, like those associated with command and control, and we're treating them more like force structure than support structure. It's part of how we must change the way we do business to incorporate the fundamentals of information warfare.

This broad approach means that we must get the lawyers involved. When I first heard about bringing in the lawyers, I thought we had really slipped off the deep end one more time. I apologize if I offend any lawyers out there -- I always have held lawyers in fairly high esteem. The more I thought about bringing the lawyers into the equation, the more I realized we need their expertise. Because exploiting the information spectrum will readily cross international borders, we must be cognizant of what the law allows and will not allow.

When do you begin information warfare in the spin up to a conflict? When do you begin to go out there and intrude in somebody's banking system? When do you begin to get into somebody's telecommunications system? These are all very difficult questions. Clearly, information warfare is not something that is focused solely on the confines of a constrained battle area. While we will fight in a theatre, information warfare will force us to be engaged worldwide. Thus, we must have some good advice as we pursue this capability.

I appreciate this opportunity to share with you what the Air Force is doing to try and keep up with the information technology explosion. The American way of war has very strong roots in understanding the value of exploiting information to deny information to our adversary, to corrupt what data he has, and to exploit what we know.

World War II was filled with many examples of information warfare. Perhaps Winston Churchill offered the best summary of its importance. At the Tehran conference, when discussing the Allied plans to manipulate information before D-Day, many of these same ethical questions came up. When do we do it? How do we do it? Who are the innocent victims of this thing? And Churchill, addressing the other Allied leaders said, "In wartime, truth is so precious that she should always be attended by a bodyguard of lies" (Anthony Cave Brown, Bodyguard of Lies (New York: Harper and Row, 1975), p. 10). Something to think about. Later, there was a book written with that title by Anthony Brown. If you read his thick volume, it is rather chilling to see what was possible in that era, and then think about how much more is possible today with the technology that's available. Today and in the future, information warfare is, in fact, going to be this nation's bodyguard. It is essential for the success of our joint forces. To succeed, we are going to need help from a lot of people, including all the very interested people in this room. You understand the far-reaching implications of systems like LANDSAT or SATCOM which are readily available and widely employed at relatively low cost. You appreciate the potential for information technology to allow an adversary to build small, capable, autonomous, operating systems that can threaten U.S. forces on land, sea, or in the air. Such devices might operate relatively unseen and unobserved until they unleash their destructive power.

INFORMATION WARFARE AND INFORMATION STRATEGY

Information warfare is often thought of as being defined by a particular target setudecision makers, information, information processes, and information systems. The "battlespace" associated with IW has been a constantly expanding one, moving far beyond traditional military situations. In some quarters, IW has even been associated with the leveraging of information technologies to achieve greater effectiveness and efficiency. This has stretched the meaning of IW to the breaking point and has sowed more confusion than enlightenment. For this reason, this treatment of the subject uses the term "information strategies" to refer to the recognition and utilization of information and information technologies as an instrument of national power that can be independent of, or complementary to, military presence and operations.

The scope, or battlespace, of information warfare and strategy (IWS) can be defined by the players and three dimensionsùthe nature of their interactions, the level of their interactions, and the arena of their interactions. Nation states or combinations of nation states are not the only players. Non-state actors (including political, ethnic, and religious groups; organized crime; international and transnational organizations; and even individuals empowered by information technology) are able to engage in information attacks and to develop information strategies to achieve their desired ends. The term "war" has been used so loosely in recent times (e.g., War on Poverty, War on Drugs, War on Crime) that is should be no surprise that IW has evolved over the past several years to become a "catch-all" term that encompasses many disparate activities, some of which have long been associated with competition, conflict, and warfare, and others that are of more recent origin.

These include activities that range from propaganda campaigns (including Media War), to attacks (both physical and non-physical) against commanders, their information sources, and the means of communicating with their forces. Under this rather large umbrella that has become known as IW, one can find activities long associated with military concepts and operations, including deception, command and control warfare (C2W), and psychological operations (Psyops). Technological advances have added new forms such as electronic warfare (EW) and "hacker warfare."

The term "defensive information warfare" (IW-D) is used here to refer to all actions taken to defend against information attacks, that is, attacks on decision makers, the information and information-based processes they rely on, and their means of communicating their decisions. Strictly speaking, since these attacks can be launched during peace time at nonmilitary targets by nonmilitary groups, both foreign and domestic, the term IW-D should be IWS-D. However, IW-D is currently in wide use.

This overview of IW-D does not attempt to deal with the problems of defending against all of the different kinds of information attacks, but rather focuses its attention on the subset of IW that involves attacks against our information infrastructure, including what has become known as "hacker warfare" and in its more serious form, "digital warfare."

Analogies and Realities

Defending against information attacks has a number of characteristics in common with societal efforts to combat disease, drugs, and crime. Noting these similarities helps to put this problem into perspective, provides some potential useful lessons learned, and serves as a benchmark.

Before reviewing the specific similarities between combating IWS and these long-standing problems, it should be noted that, while eradicating information attacks may not be a realistic expectation, significant progress can be made in defending against all forms of information attacks, enough so that the risks can be kept at acceptable levels. Defending, as it is used here, includes preventing attacks, blunting attacks, and controlling the damage caused by attacks.

The problem of IW-D is similar to the problems encountered in the "wars" on disease, drugs, and crime in a number of dimensions. First, the solution to any of these problems requires the efforts of a number of organizations, both public and private. Second, it is unlikely, given the competition for resources, that any of these efforts will be fully funded.

Therefore, we can expect that there will never be what those who have IW-D responsibilities think are a sufficient level of funding for IW-D programs. Third, these are not static problems. Drug cartels and criminals certainly learn from their mistakes. Even viruses "learn." Thus, defense forces will be continuously locked in a battle to keep up with attackers. Fourth, public awareness and concern will reach peaks, often accompanied by frenzied efforts to solve the problem.

These relatively short periods of interest will be followed by longer periods when the urgency to solve the problem will give way to apathy. Maintaining funding and progress during these periods of waning public interest will be one of the key challenges of leadership in this area. Fifth, organizations and individuals will learn to make adjustments in their behavior to deal with IW attacks and their often unintended consequences. These adjustments will be made so that those organizations and individuals can accommodate some level of painùa dynamic equilibrium of sortsùas the cost of doing business in the Information Age. Finally, solutions will, of necessity, involve compromises. This is due to the natural tensions that exist among the various stakeholders. Tensions between the law enforcement and the protection of civil liberties are classic examples that have already arisen in the information domain.

Current Situation

Attacks on information systems are already a fact of life in the Information Age. Although a small portion of these attacks result in significant loss or damage, the vast majority of them result in little or no damage the crime equivalents of trespassing, public nuisance, minor vandalism, and petty theft.

It has been estimated that more than 90 percent of these attacks are perpetrated using available tools and techniques (based upon incidents reported to CERT), that only 1 attack in 20 is noticed by the victim, and that only 1 in 20 gets reported (these last two statistics were a result of a Defense Information Systems Agency (DISA) study and similar rates have been reported by others). However, it appears that reporting rates may be on the increase.

Of more concern is the presence of a technically feasible "strategic" threat. That is, the means exist to cause significant damage and disruption to U.S. public and private information assets, processes, and systems, and to compromise the integrity of vital information.

Analysts also have no difficulty identifying groups with the motivations and opportunities to launch such attacks. Given our present vulnerabilities as a nation, a well-planned, coordinated IW attack could have strategic consequences. Such an attack, or the threat of such an attack, could thwart our foreign policy objectives, degrade military performance, result in significant economic loss, and perhaps even undermine the confidence of our citizens in the Government's ability to protect its citizens and interests.

While no "smoking keyboard" has been found to validate such a threat, the very existence of the means to carry out such an attack, when coupled with the myriad of motives and opportunities that exist, results in our present state of vulnerability. These circumstances have created a situation that calls for prudent defensive actions to be taken in the public interest. We need to be proactive rather than be forced to react after an Information Age "Pearl Harbor." Moreover, a successful strategic attack would point the way and encourage others to plan similar attacks. Hence, we need to go on the offensive with a vigorous defense.

INFORMATION BASED WARFARE -THE NEW BATTLEFIELDS

Exiled to France, the Ayatollah Khomeni sought to maintain contact with the faithful. A cleric who espoused the return of his country to an Islamic theocracy-something: that many argued would move Iran back into the 16th century-the Ayatollah turned to 20th century tools to begin his crusade. Through the medium of cassettes, he began to record his message. After being mass-produced m 20th century studios, his 16th century message was smuggled back to Iran. Those tapes both planted the seed and inspired the flowering of a movement that brought Khomeni back to power m 1979.

For at least a decade, the American military had tinkered with devices for sabotaging enemy electrical systems. Some of the results were serendipitous. In the early 1980's, during a Navy exercise code-named Hey [Rube, long strands of rope chaff-glass filaments in which metal shards were embedded-had been dropped over the Pacific Ocean as part of a standard tactic to befuddle an opponent's radar. An unexpectedly skiff wind carried some of the chaff ninety miles to the coastline, where it got draped across power lines, shorting out transformers and causing power failures in parts of San Diego. The Navy quietly settled the damages- while carefully noting the effects of its unintended attack.

Information warfare has as many meanings as it has proponents, detractors and observers. Airpower theorists see it on the wings of Desert Storm; tank commanders see it in the American army's Force XXI; simulator designers see it in their virtual realities...and strategic-war planners see it as a way to lay waste to whole societies. Information warfare studies are proliferating within the American armed forces almost as quickly as the networks that carry them from desktop to desktop. The confusing planoply stems from the fact that the information revolution, whether it is in uniform or mufti, relies upon the fastest technology to do the oldest things. Thus it is always a peculiar mixture of the familiar and the shockingly new. In that war is all about strategies, command and morale, it has always been about information. All war is information war, and so every aspect of fighting wars in the information age can be called "information warfare" by someone. If information driven warfare means something new, it is the use of information as a substitute for traditional ways of fighting, rather than an adjunct to them. There are three ways that this might be achieved by:

- the high technology equivalent of brute force;
- subversion; and,
- a new form of deterrence.

For the purpose of this paper, we focus on the second element-subversion. It is our belief that because of the unique relationship between Americans and computers, IBW launched subversive acts-a prelude to, or the actual execution of "quiet wars"-may be accomplished.

The evolution and ultimate "blurring" of military and civilian sectors came about in large part because of the growth in hardware and software. It was not so long ago, in the early 1960's, that the Pentagon provided the market for sophisticated electronics. Today, it makes up less than 1% of that market. In many ways, the military is following the revolution, not leading it. In 1962 Paul Baran of RAND developed a concept that permitted the linking of computers from distant locations. It was designed to preserve the integrity of the military command and control network in case of a nuclear attack. In 1969, the Defense Advanced Research Projects Agency (DARPA) funded the first test of the concept, and the first node was installed at RAND. The test consisted of scientists from remote locations passing findings and research notes back and forth. However, a year later it was being used like a mail box for the users and it proceeded to grow rapidly in use. In 1983, the military part and the nonmilitary part grew apart and finally split, the nonmilitary section grew up into what is now called the Internet.

For the first time in our nation's history, technology is no longer the sole domain of the military. The speed of the growth and application of technology is clearly a concern for defense planners. While the US used some of the world's most advanced weaponry and technology in the Gulf War (much of which proved inaccurate) it also used a great deal of older technology, some of which dated back to the 1960's. As B.R. Inman and Daniel F. Burton

Jr. note in their article "Technology and US. National Security, "the 8088 microprocessor used in the Patriot missile was developed by the Intel Corporation fifteen years ago." This technology is not competitive today.

Opening and Closing Pandora's Box

In the center of Strike the battleship's commander, Captain David S. Bill, Ferched in his high backed padded chair. Although he occasionally glanced at the screens above, the captain's attention was largely fixed on the men clustered around four computers lining the far bulkhead. Something had gone awry with the ship's Tomahawk missile system.. For reasons no one could fathom, the Tomahawk computers seemed confused, refusing to transfer the necessary commands from the engagement-planning console to the launch console. The resulting impasse_"casualty" in Navy jargon_meant the missiles could not be fired...On Wisconsin, where the scheduled launch was now just moments away, the men in Strike were running out of solutions...As the request for additional time flashed up the chain of command, an excited voice from one of the nearby ships crackled through Strike: "Alpha, alpha." This is the Paul F Foster. Happy trails." Happy trails: the code phrase for missiles away. Operation Desert Storm had begun without Wisconsin.

As the most technologically vulnerable nation, the US defense planners must recognize several concepts about the technical end of the IBW battlefield:

It must be assumed that everyone has access to technology, therefore the US is the most vulnerable to attack;

As the US's ability to wage IBW increases, so to do the IBW capabilities, and response capabilities, of other nation-states and non-state actors;

While at first glance it would appear that IBW is most effective against adversaries with like technological capabilities and infrastructure-the top end of the IBW target spectrum-it must be remembered that technology comes in two forms-high and appropriate-and it is the latter that will always defeat the former. Thus, the benefits of IBW in arena's of conflict as found in the Gray

Areas are a target rich environment must be pursued alongside the force on force approach.

The technical realm of information based warfare can be split into two major areas: Netwar and Cyberwar. Netwar is the information related conflict between nations, societies, governments, or non-state actors with the targets being information systems and communications, and it consists of destruction of communications, acquisition of information, release of misinformation, and destruction or deletion of data. Cyberwar consists of militaries conducting their operations according to information based theories and principles. These terms can be broken down even further. Netwar can be broken into three main categories: Personal, Corporate, and Global.

We are constantly warned about the personal level of Netwar, we have passwords to computer accounts, never give our social security number over the telephone, and generally try to be careful about our own information. But protecting yourself from someone who genuinely wants to conduct information war against you is nearly impossible. Corporations are subject to a barrage of information security problems to an even greater extent. The stealing of company secrets is a new form of economic war that is plaguing many companies. It is also possible for one company to release false findings that indicate that a competitor has a poor or dangerous product. IBW spawned misinformation-a fertile area for denial and deception techniques-are very difficult to combat and correct. Finally, on the global level, Netwar can be waged against industries, economies, nations, or non-state groups. It ranges from intelligence and information leads, to the terrifying possibilities of terrorist groups breaking into such communications as an air traffic control system at a major US airport. The impact at the global level can be much more wide spread and all threatening than that of the personal or corporate levels of netwar.

On both sides of the war, Netwar and Cyberwar, the key to good protection and offence is good software to run the systems, encode the data, and peck holes in other's data. The vital link for the information and the technology is software, which relies heavily upon implanted logic. The newest and brightest theories and concepts of logic center around what is called 'fuzzy logic'. The name fuzzy logic makes one think of a system that is inexact, but that is not the case, instead it has an infinite exactness. Fuzzy logic expands our normal computer principle of 0 or 1, true or false, and in the place of this is infinite degrees between 0 and 1. Fuzzy logic is used every day in the development of everything from smart washers to train systems in Japan. With a smart washer, you merely press a start button and the machine figures the cycle, how much detergent, and the water use; the logic train systems are smooth as silk, quick, and always on time. The theory started with a few paradoxes one of which is The Paradox of Theseus' ship:

When Theseus returned from slaying the Minotaur, says Plutarch, the Athenians preserved his ship, and as planks rotted, replaced them with new ones. When the first plank was replaced, everyone agreed it was still the same ship. Adding a second plank made no difference either. At some point, the Athenians may have replaced every plank in the ship. Was it a different ship? At what point did it become one?

At different points in time the ship was certain degrees the original ship, for instance when half the planks were replaced, it was the original ship. This same principle of degrees can be applied to many concepts around us, and what you end up with is a very exact and reliable process for computers. When you tie this concept into ideas such as artificial intelligence, you may obtain a computer that has the capacity to learn because it can start to work with more than 0 and 1.

Because of the importance of the technical tools of IBW-and their fragility-we list below the possible contents of an IBW techno "kit-bag":

Computer Viruses - A piece of code, or code fragment, designed to begin replicating itself when a host program begins to run. It's objective is to erase data, software programs, or memory in order to interrupt the action of the computer it infests. These can be loaded unwittingly by a user off the Internet or some other disk.

Worms - Instead of being just a code fragment, a worm is an entire program in and of itself. The code begins to replicate as soon as it touches a computer system, not dependent on the start of execution of any other program. Its aim is to eat up computer resources and/or delete data to result in a crippling effect on the host computer.

Trojan Horses - As the name would suggest, a Trojan horse is a program, or code fragment inside a program, that performs a function unbeknownst to the user. It usually performs a simple task on the outside, while unleashing a virus or a worm on the inside. It can also perform information retrieval while performing a task, leaving no trace.

Logic Bombs - Similar to a Trojan horse, a logic bomb is used to release a virus, worm, or complete some other secret task. These are usually planted by a programmer or system developer. This could be useful in US military strategy, instead of open bombs, the US could plant logic bombs to retrieve specific data from foreign users. This is plausible because many of the main software development in the world occurs in the US.

Trap Doors - The use of this is similar to a logic bomb. It is a secret way back into a system left by a programmer or designer. Unlike a logic bomb that executes, a trap door is merely an unknown security flaw. Chipping - This is the term for doing any of the above to the hardware of a system instead of to the software. One can build in circuitry to a chip that performs specific functions.

Machines and Microbes - Although one thinks of Star Trek and other science fiction when the subject of nanny machines comes up, it is actually a feasible plan. machines and microbes are tiny machines, like a small insect, that "eat" electronic circuits, oil, plastics, etc. If unleashed on a computer center, the result would be total shut down.

Electronic Jamming, HERF guns, and EM bombs- These are all forms of electronic signal jamming. One can jam communications, stopping computer information flow; shoot radio signals at an electronic target to shut it down with a High Energy Radio Frequency (HERF) gun; or send out a high powered electromagnetic pulse, an EMP bomb.

Hitch-hiking- This is a group of people, a subsection of hackers, that merely sit on the net and wait. They wait for any information and interesting code to go by and then hitch a ride with it, they follow and delete it, or they simply copy and steal it. Thinking in terms of closing Pandora's Box, the following techniques will have to be considered as an IBW operational security plan is built:

Firewalls - A limited gateway to the Interment from a company or group. Only passwords and certain configurations can get in, and everything is checked for viruses, etc. Only privileged personnel, or personnel with certain system configurations can get out. If implemented correctly they can be useful.

Encryption - This growing area of interest consists on coding data so that others can not place bombs in or around it or read the data. This is growing more difficult as hackers and other groups become more efficient at breaking the codes. This is one of the areas that fuzzy logic could come into serious play. If, at first glance, the foregoing appears to be merely a "laundry list," a reading of the following paragraph will surely prove sobering to the IBW planner:

The Defense Information Security Agency (DISA) conducts vulnerability studies of military and government computer systems. Their figures are truly alarming: 88% of defense computer systems are easily penetrated. Of the successful penetrations, 96% are not detected. Even worse, 95% of the detected penetrations are not reported or responded to. Even when an intrusion is detected, it is usually impossible to determine who did it. DISA studies indicate that there were possibly 300,000 intrusions into government computer systems in 1994 alone.

THE EVOLUTION OF INFORMATION BASED WARFARE

Therefore, at times of revolution, when the normal-scientific tradition changes, the scientist's perception of his environment must be re-educated-in some familiar situations he must learn to see a new gestalt.

The Structure of Scientific Revolutions

Whereas we had available for immediate purpose one hundred and forty-nine first-class warships, we now have two, these two being the Warrior and her sister Ironside. There is not now a ship in the English navy apart from these two that it would not be madness to trust in an engagement with that little [American] Monitor.. -The Times

The most recent steps in that evolution can be found in the Military Technical Revolution (MTR) which may be attributed to Soviet Military thinkers; and, a recurrence of what is called the Revolution in Military Affairs (RMA).

In the early 1980's the Soviets noted that "the emergence of advanced non-nuclear technologies was engendering a new revolution in military affairs. They were particularly interested in the "incorporation of information sciences into the military sphere" and in the idea of a "reconnaissance-strike complex. The events in the Gulf War convinced them of their hypothesis (comparative strategies). RMAs matter principally for two reasons. First, being second best may lead to catastrophic loss in future wars. Since the only objective benchmark for determining the relative effectiveness of forces (that is, success in combat) is unavailable in long periods of peace, there is great potential for asymmetries in combat effectiveness between militaries, observable only when the next war occurs. Secondly, as equipment life cycles, especially for platforms, steadily grow to encompass decades, many of the principal weapons systems of 2025 will likely be designed and built in the next few years. Since militaries are stuck with force structures they choose for long periods, it is more crucial than ever to think about them now, in peacetime, about the revolutionary changes in the nature of war and the about what will matter in winning wars in twenty or thirty years.

Today with the United States arguably the only superpower for the foreseeable future, one might ask why this issue is especially pressing. Replicating the US force structure is clearly beyond the reach of all but a few other nations, even in the long term. This may not be relevant. Even small-to medium sized powers may be able to exploit specific technologies for significant military leverage in certain areas. The current rate of change suggests that state of the art in any technological context will be an extremely short-lived phenomenon, particularly with respect to the technologies that were key to the success of Desert Storm: space systems, telecommunication systems, computer architecture's, global information distribution networks, and navigation systems. Future revolutions will occur much more rapidly, offering far less time for adaptation to new methods of warfare. The growing imperative in the business world for rapid response to changing conditions in order to survive in an intensely competitive environment is surely instructive for military affairs.

The present RMA entails a fundamental change in who, how, and, perhaps even why wars are fought. It is driven not only by new technologies but by new operational concepts, new tactics, and new organizational structures. The impact of the current confluence of social, political, economic, and technological forces on American society and armed forces may equal-or exceed-what occurred during the 1960's and 1970's during the turmoil associated with the war in Vietnam.

The question that must be asked as we attempt to understand this RMA, is what were the results of change wrought by past Revolutions in Military Affairs? It has been suggested that accelerated interservice rivalries and over-reliance on management systems marked the last RMA, driven by the advent of atomic weapons at the end of WW II and the relatively stable and sparse defense budgets of the 1950's.

The current RMA is characterized by four types of changes:

- extremely precise;
- stand-off strikes;
- dramatically improved command, control, and intelligence;
- information warfare; and
- nonlethality

Many analysts see a number of benefits from harnessing the current revolution in military affairs and using it to build 21st century US armed forces:

- rejuvenating the political utility of military power;
- delaying the emergence of a peer competition;
- providing a blueprint for technology acquisition and force reorganization;
- and inspiring conceptual, forward-looking thinking.

Looking ahead, many believe that the current RMA will have at least two stages. The first is based on stand-off platforms, stealth, precision, information domination, improved communications, computers, global positioning systems, digitization, "smart" weapons systems, jointness, and use of ad hoc coalitions.

The second may be based on robotics, nonlethality, pyscho-technology, cyberdefense, nanotechnology, "brilliant" weapons systems, hyperflexible organizations, and "fire ant warfare."

Steven Metz and James Kievit of the Strategic Studies Institute argue that a cost /benefit analysis of the present RMA needs to be pursued. One the one hand, they argue that a case can be made that costs and risks of vigorous pursuit of the current RMA outweigh the expected benefits. These include the risk that:

- the current RMA will not generate increased combat effectiveness against the most likely or most dangerous future opponents;
- American pursuit of the RMA will encourage opponents or potential opponents to seek countermeasures;
- the current RMA might lead the United States toward over reliance on military power; and, vigorous pursuit of the current RMA might increase problems with friends and allies.

On the other hand, they argue that there are very pressing reasons for supporting the current RMA: it should bring significant increase in combat effectiveness against some mid-level opponents; a force built around stand-off, precision weapons and disruptive information warfare capabilities would be more politically usable than a traditional force-projection military; the RMA could augment deterrence; and, the United States may need to pursue the current RMA to avoid stumbling into strategic inferiority.

Lastly, they posit-and we strongly agree-that if policymakers decide to pursue the present revolution in military affairs, strategy, rather than technological capability should guide force development. The key question is: What do we want the future US military to be able to do?

Unfortunately one finds little discussion of the foregoing ideas in the DOD's recently completed "Bottom-Up" Review. Former

Secretary of Defense Aspin initiated the review with the laudable goal of rethink the basis for US defense planning. It placed emphasis in many of the right areas: readiness, keeping forces for more than one regional war, acquisition reform. This review built a substantial consensus in the Pentagon behind the new force structure. Nonetheless, the review offers a classic example of military leaders planning to fight the last war. The report's proposed force for a single regional contingency-four to five Army divisions, four to five Marine brigades, 10 Air Force fighter wings, 100 heavy bombers, and four to five carriers-mirrors almost exactly the forces deployed in Operation Desert Storm. The review offers few thoughts on new technologies or techniques that might change the nature of war in coming decades.

Clearly, the challenge is to move beyond the last war-an undertaking that is fraught with peril and promise.

An Information Based Warfare Model

We are pilgrims, Master; we shall go

Always a little further...."

-Inscription on the Clock, Bradbury Lines, Hereford, Home of the Special Air Service Regiment J. F. Flecker

We believe that it is instructive to review the Program of Analysis for FY 1996 as set forth by the Directorate for Combat Support, National Military Intelligence Production Center, Defense Intelligence Agency. Entitled, Intelligence Support to Infrastructure Warfare, the thrust of this paper is directed toward a new paradigm that is centered on the principal of attacking an adversary's infrastructure to degrade or deny mobility, support to combatants and leadership.

The paper sets forth valid arguments to support the thesis that to a large extent, recent advances in weapons and tactics were driven by the strategic objective of penetrating and rupturing the physical and psychological "centers of gravity" of the enemy warfighting capability. It is clear that new technologies have spurred an entire new generation of warfighting capabilities and, of equal importance, fundamentally altered the construct and performance of the modern nation-state.

Discrete centers of gravity are giving way to diversification and interdependence in the modern nation-state. Information is the raw material that fuels productivity and power. Critical systemic nodes in the dynamic flow of commodities-consumables, services, and information-are at the same time increasingly obscure, strategically important, and tactically vulnerable. Fine grain analysis [read Intelligence writ in large script] and precision targeting fin both the conventional and non conventional sense] of these nodes and their synergistic dependencies is the centerpiece of Infrastructure Warfare.

The primary elements of Infrastructure Warfare are:

- The nation-state as a System of Systems;
- Information as an Instrument of Power;
- Denial and Deception;
- Urban Infrastructure-The Operational Environment.

While the concept of Infrastructure Warfare is certainly a step in the right direction, we believe that this concept has several shortcomings that need to be addressed in order that it fully lead toward an answer to the strategic "bottom-line"-how do we win? We argue that the conflicts of the new world disorder will be largely fought on geography in the Third World (TW.) Driven largely by the chimera of the Gulf War, images of centers of gravity and smart weapons overshadow the tawdry back-alley settings in which actual conflict will take place in the future. In reviewing the "lessons learned" of recent wars in the Third World- where 95 percent of future conflicts will take place-a number of more accurate images appear:

First, the mix of forces facing each other has not been very different, regardless of the type of war being fought. Navies have been conspicuous by their absence or their modest role. Air forces have played a secondary role. Almost without exception, wars in the TW have been won or lost by ground troops.

Second, the type of war has not necessarily determined the tactics used; in fact, it has blurred the differences between them. Furthermore, as the frequent oscillations in tactics and strategy suggest, both irregular and regular armies in recent years have shared much in term of their ability to implement offensive doctrine.

With the exceptions of campaigns involving an industrialized power, it seems that the defense has become the most effective form of warfare in the TW. With the exception of Israel and the war in Lebanon, none of the Third World combatants that have used an offensive doctrine has been able to effect a decisive breakthrough or cause the defenders to retire in disorder or retreat.

Third, the duration of recent wars have generally been protracted and have engaged large arrays of national and subnational forces. Most of the wars fought between regular lesser developed country army's have not been shorter.

Fourth, the involvement of external nation forces has been large. Of the wars fought between 1945 and 1976, 38 percent were fought with foreign participation.

Lastly, because guerrilla wars pose particularly difficult challenges for governments, they represent a new and difficult form of conflict.

If the foregoing is correct, then we believe that the Infrastructure paradigm must address the Gray Area Phenomena (GAP). GAP is defined as threats to nation-states by non-states actors and non-governmental processes and organizations. The Gray Areas at once appear to be strikingly new and uncomfortably old. Simply put, they are the most critical issues confronting the world community as we enter into the Century. Just beyond the horizon of current events lie two possible futures-both of which look bleak. The first is the retribalization of large swaths of humankind by war and bloodshed: a Lebanonization of national states in which culture is pitted against culture, people against people, tribe against tribe-a Jihad in the name of a hundred narrowly conceived faiths against every kind of globalization and interdependence.

The second is being borne by the onrush of technical, economic, and ecological forces that demand increased integration and uniformity. The planet, it appears, is both falling apart and coming reluctantly together at the very same time.

The GAP consists of the following "arena's of conflict":

- Ethno-religious-nationalistic conflicts;
- Weapons proliferation-both conventional and nuclear, biological and chemical;

- Conflict over scarce resources;
- AIDS and other infectious diseases;
- The globalization of Organized Crime;
- Drug Trafficking;
- Economic Warfare and conflict over technology;
- Emigration; and,
- Famine.

The United States today is involved to some degree in each of the aforementioned arena's. While we strongly believe that traditional force-on-force warfare will always be with us, in the main, we sense that the present and future world situation more than makes the case for a strategy that encompasses the full-range of conflict supported by the appropriate technologies. Thus, we would add the Gray Area "arenas of conflict" to the DIA construct, and in so doing, move the ongoing debate to the new plateau of Information Based Warfare.

Tomorrow

We should be seeking tentative answers to fundamental questions, rather than definitive answers to trivial ones. —James Billington

Before framing a new definition and model for Information Based Warfare, we turn to a nonwestern look at information and warfare. Shen Weiguang, a writer who appears to be at the forefront of PRC IW theorists argues that: in a military sense alone, information warfare refers to both sides' attempt to gain the initiative of the battle through their control over information and flow of intelligence. With the support of information, both sides intend to comprehensively apply military deception, operational secrets, psychological warfare, and electronic warfare to destroy the enemy's information systems, block the flow of the enemy's information, and create false information to affect and weaken the enemies command and control capability. At the same time, they must ensure that their command and control system is not damaged in the same way by the opponent.

Further addressing the issues, Shen Weiguang illuminates a number of thoughts that cut to the heart of the concept of

Information Based Warfare. He correctly argues that IBW in one sense is the "quiet battlefield," something we attempted to portray in our opening scenario. Turning toward the concept of "centers of gravity" we feel that his descriptions of "attacks on the enemies cognitive and trust systems" perhaps better portrays the idea of attacking C2 and C4I nodes. This, he argues, is the main target of information warfare. The concepts of "hard attack" and "soft attack" with "soft damage" are noted as the two end-product manifestations of IBW; and, the concept of "war of structural damage" [read Infrastructure War] is thought to come into full play only when "it has absorbed the essence of information warfare."

Technology, he argues, does not determine superiority. It is determined by new tactics [in part this could be naval guerrilla warfare-PRC style] and "independent creations of commanders in the field. Information based warfare enables one to break with "traditional stylized engagement, " something we feel will give new impetus to the military arts.

Like a number of perceptive US thinkers, Shen Weiguang, has seized upon the Toffler' work to understand and further flesh-out the idea of "niche-warfare." And, he appears to understand that IBW will spawn special operating forces [differentiated from special forces] in the IBW setting.

His comments about command and control are perceptive:

The operational target of information warfare lies in control rather than bloodshed;

The key to victory lies in human policy decisions rather than technology [hopefully a lesson learned and re-learned in the Naval War College games]; genuine advantage does not necessary lie in the leading technology but the leading ideas. History has given evidence to the fact when some new technology brings mankind brightness, a shadow is cast simultaneously. Advanced electronic computers and information technology link society and the army to an integrated network; the result is very high efficiency and great fragility;

The input in grasping knowledge, costs far less than directly purchasing advanced weaponry [a Sun-tzuian slip, particularly in light of the fact that the PRC has taken this approach for years as it has covertly acquired primarily mid-level technology from the West, enabling them to jump the learning curve].

UTILIZE OF COMPUTERS IN UPRISING

The use of computers in revolutions highlights the importance of information control for authoritarian regimes. Without tight control of information flow, regimes cannot control the activities of dissidents. The increasing interconnection of the world provided by computers allows dissidents to "bring in "the rest of the world. They instantly broadcast atrocities and repression to a worldwide audience, with the attendant publicity often preventing a harsh crackdown by government forces.

Poland

A 1987 article in *Datamation* examined the use of computers in the Solidarity movement in Poland:

Necessity and the spread of information technology have bred a computer-savvy opposition in Poland that is capable of breaking into tv news broadcasts, producing alternative information that contradicts government data, and developing publishing and distribution systems that can spread the opposition's cause quickly and efficiently.

The Solidarity movement used information warfare tactics to get their message out to the largest possible number of Polish citizens. The actions of three astronomers and a local engineer exemplify the ability of a few individuals to influence thousands with information technology. These individuals intercepted the state-run television broadcast signal, determined the characteristics of the signal, and then used their computer equipment to time and configure their own signal. They broadcast this signal over the same frequency as the state signal, allowing 60,000 television viewers to see both signals concurrently. These viewers saw the message, "Enough price increases, lies, and repressions. It is our duty to boycott the election." The government arrested and tried the four for this action. After being held for four months, they were convicted and ordered to pay fines ranging from $80 to $120. During their trial, the prosecutor claimed that the voting turnout was ten to 20 percent lower than average in the region that viewed the pirate television broadcast.

The Solidarity movement also used computers to perform an independent prediction of the election results. This independent check ensured that the "official" government estimates were no inflated. The struggle for the Solidarity movement was not merely to show that the official count was wrong according to Konrad Bielinski, a leader of this project. "Rather, we wanted to achieve something more, namely to take away from the state its monopoly over giving us information about ourselves."

The movement also capitalized on the advantages of information technology to provide secure, reliable communication between members. Anyone can encrypt and transport a massive amount of data on disk. In addition to being easier to conceal, a computer disk is easier to destroy than a pile of paper.

Tiananmen Square

The Chinese dissidents involved in the Tiananmen Square protest in 1989 did not target computer systems, but rather utilized new technology, primarily the fax machine and the Internet, to ensure that word of what was happening in China made it out of the country. Students in the United States then took the information that was flowing out of China and sent it back into the country via fax machines. Through the use of this technology, the dissidents prevented China's leadership from controlling the flow of information. While telecommunications assets were restricted in the weeks following the massacre, telecommunications connectivity facilitated its initial reporting and continuing coverage with the rest of the world.

Zapatistas

The Zapatista uprising in southern Mexico provides another example of rebel organizations exploiting high technology. The Zapatista leadership has used the Internet to establish a worldwide organization of supporters that are beyond the control of Mexico's government. Zapatista leadership communiqués are issued via the Internet, instantly spreading their message to a worldwide audience without any interference by the Mexican authorities or news media interpretation. In the same manner as china during the Tiananmen Square uprising, Mexico lost the ability to control the flow of information both out of, and into, the country. The information received from inside Mexico fostered extensive media coverage, limiting the repressive options open to the government. While not terrorism, the ability to form transnational networks and ensure that the message of an organization is heard on a world stage is a tool that terrorists will exploiting the future. If there were no rapid communications channels out of the jungles of southern Mexico, it is likely that Mexican government would have been able to use much harsher methods to repress the rebellion.

While the actions of rebels and dissidents are not always terrorism, these incidents highlight the fact that a small number of people can have a worldwide impact and generate international publicity of their cause without government interference. These capabilities will appeal to terrorists in the information age.

THE GROW OF TECHNOTERRORISM

Electrical Distribution Networks

Electrical distribution and energy systems have been favorite targets of terrorists. The use of computers to run these networks makes them an ideal cyberterrorism target. However, as an examination of conventional terrorist and military attacks on energy systems demonstrates, these targets may be of limited value to the cyberterrorist.

Statistics show that there were 240 total attacks on "Domestic Energy-related and Military Targets" from 1970 to mid 1980. The most popular of the targets were powerlines and powerstation/ substations. This trend continued through 1988 with 283 recorded incidents of subnational attacks on energy systems in the United States. A worldwide target summary shows that power pylons and power lines remained the number one target with power substations being the third most popular target.

Thomas E. Griffith, in his thesis entitled *Strategic Attack of National Electrical Systems,* studies the military benefits accorded a state by attacking an enemy electrical system in a time of war.

The apparent lack of utility in attacking electrical systems in war may apply to terrorists as well:

Strategic attacks on national power system can be useful in fulfilling national security aims, but only under specific conditions. First, the target country's power system should be vulnerable to destruction by being very concentrated with very few interconnections. Second, the strategy behind the attacks should be focused on stopping war production over the long term. To strike electric power to affect civilian morale, increase costs to the leadership, or impact the military will waste missions and could prove counterproductive to the political aims of the war.

The "critical node" identified by Griffith is the transformer station, where power is "stepped-up" of "stepped-down" for transmission and distribution. The components at some of these sites are custom built and could take up to eighteen months to manufacture if they are destroyed in an attack.

The most recent concerted attack on energy systems in the United States was undertaken in California by a group calling itself the "Earth Night Action Group" who cut down two wooden power poles and toppled a 100-foot transmission tower in April of 1990. The result of this attack was the loss of power to 92,000 customers for up to a day. The group struck at isolated targets rather than the transformer substations, thus lessening the impact of their action. In the late 1970s, the "New World Liberation Front" bombed a Pacific Gas and Electric transformer near San Francisco that disrupted power to 75,000 homes for approximately two hours. PG&E transformers and offices were bombed 16 times between 1975 and 1978, leading Research West, a detective agency specializing in terrorism, to call PG&E the "prime victim of terrorism in the United States." As press reports have indicated, electrical lines themselves are the most accessible targets for terrorists or criminals. In the United States, up to 300 electrical insulators can be shot off by hunters and pranksters in a single day. These actions are not a concerted effort to bring down the electrical system by an organized group. Rather, they are random acts of vandalism for which the flexibility of the electrical system can compensate. Should an organized group simultaneously attack several critical nodes (step-up/step-down transformers) across he United States, the potential for disruption increases. Chuck Lane's statements before Congress indicate that the system is vulnerable, but it is robust enough to withstand nearly all attacks:

In summary, this investigation concluded that the networks [energy and telecommunication] of the United States are vulnerable to multisite terrorist attacks, that is, that targets are likely to be destroyed. However, the redundancy of built into the networks make them very dependable, and the real question is what level of service would be lost from such an attack. In many cases the consequences appear to be manageable. In a few cases, perhaps too many cases, the consequences are potentially catastrophic.

While the physical vulnerability of electrical system components to destruction is real, David Hinman states, "the flexibility of the system is its greatest security. Our security plans must be built upon this fact in order to have maximum effectiveness." Still, the capability exists, with relatively unsophisticated technology to disrupt power to a large portion of an electrical grid by targeting its critical nodes. While the weapons technology (firearms, explosives, etc.) are readily available to a terrorist group, some research is required to obtain the knowledge necessary to identify and target critical nodes in the energy system. Unfortunately, this information is publicly available. The information contained in public documents mandated by the Department of Energy, Federal Communications Commission, and Department of Transportation can be used by terrorists to plan attacks on infrastructure targets. According to a Government Accounting Office report of December 1988, a mock terrorist team utilized information obtained from a public library to plan an attack on the Strategic Petroleum Reserve in 1987.

While infrastructure systems in the United States remain vulnerable to physical attack, Dr. Robert K. Mullen, does not believe hat these incidents will increase in the future, despite a growing terrorist presence in the United States:

That being said, there are no indicators of which I am aware, insofar as trends in the U.S. are concerned, that would suggest to me the threat to energy assets here is substantially different from what the recent historical record indicates. The presence in the U.S. of terrorist support groups does no alter this view.

While the fragility and relative open nature of electrical systems has been heralded in the press, it is the secondary effects of such attacks that concern individuals like Norman Leach:

Any terrorist group with access to moderate amounts of explosives could shut down any city in the United States simply by destroying local transformer sites. Not only would vital industries and defense programs be affected but the ensuing blackouts would cause riots in the streets that would threaten the stability of the government.

While certainly a contributing factor to the civil unrest experienced in New York City's famed blackout of 1965 and 1977, the removal of electrical power from a city is neither a necessary nor a sufficient cause for "riots that would threaten the stability of the government." The riots in the streets of Los Angeles following the Rodney King verdict as well as the riots (disguised as celebrations) after major sports championships are won show that disturbances can happen with a fully functional electrical system. The labor Day 1988 Seattle blackout, in which over 1/3 of the city was without power for 4 1/2 days, proves that a blackout does not produce riots and looting. In fact, the incidence of crime in the affected area went *down*, not up, due to an intense police presence. The ability to cause a riot with a blackout alone is thus suspect. While a terrorist group may be able to exacerbate a crisis situation that it has fomented with the addition of a blackout, a blackout in isolation is not a fail-safe way to "ignite the masses."

While the above situation has focused primarily on the physical attack of energy systems to cause disruption, the increasing computer control of these and other infrastructure systems provides a potential target for a terrorist group. The California Department of Water Resources recognized the risk inherent in these systems in 1991 when they implemented strict physical security control measures to protect their central computer center. The computers contained at he center were used to control the release of water from the major dams in the state. The increased security was a result of a perceived increase in the terrorist threat during Operation

Desert Storm. The possible physical risks, such as the shutdown of power plants or release of water from behind dams, will continue to increase as computerization of control systems continues. The true "critical nodes" of any system lie in its command and control network. By striking at this link to disable or control the system, a terrorist precludes the necessity to attack elements of a distributed system physically, such as transformers or pumps.

There are many parallels between energy systems and information warfare targets. Critical nodes exist in all networks that will impair the entire system. Attacking anything but these critical nodes may result in a minor degradation of service or, if the system is correctly designed, no disruption at all. Thus, the attacks on energy distribution system components such as power lines and pylons cause limited disruption for regional customers but widespread outages are very rare. While the information on the physical layout and vulnerabilities of an energy system. exist, it has not been a particularly effective terrorist target. This may be due to the lack of organizational and manpower assets a valuable to a terrorist group. In addition, those targets that are "critical nodes" may have enough security to prevent their destruction. The pattern of terrorist attacks on electrical systems may provide an insight into information age terrorism. If systems can be engineered to be redundant in some areas (and thus able to recover from attack) and defended in others (to prevent attack), it may mitigate the risks of widespread outages.

ATTACKS ON COMPUTER SYSTEMS

While the public has perceived buildings and airplanes as the primary targets of terrorists, attacks on computers were involved in 60% of conventional terrorist acts by 1989. The pattern of criminal computer attacks, together with terrorist activity, suggest that there may be a shift toward cyberterrorism as a physically less risky means to achieve both criminal and terrorist ends.

Europe and the United States

In the 1970s the Italian Red Brigades launched 27 attacks against companies that did business in the electronics, computer and weapons sectors. In 1980, the French organization Comite

Liquidant ou Detournant les Ordinateurs (Computer Liquidation and Deterrence Committee or CLODO) undertook a series of attacks on computer companies in the Toulouse region.

The organization released a statement to the press, "We are workers in the field of dp (data processing) and consequently well place to know the current and future dangers of dp and telecommunications.

The computer is the favorite tool of the dominant. It is used to exploit, to put on file, to control, and to repress."

A Belgian Group, the Cellueles Communistes Combattants (Fighting Communist Cells) conducted a series of bombings in September 1984 directed against Honeywell Controls and Litton Industries. In November 1984, the same group attacked the Brussels office of Motorola. Computers were prime targets in each of these attacks.

Similar attacks have occurred in the United States. IBM's offices in White Plains N.Y. were bombed in March1984. The group claiming responsibility for the attack, the United Freedom Front, distributed a newsletter that stated "IBM is a death merchant... The computer is an integral part of the fascist South African government's policies of racist repression and control."

The CLODO group struck again in 1983 by firebombing a Sperry-Univac computer room in Toulouse to protest the U.S. invasion of Grenada. Upon putting out the fire, the message, "Reagan attacks Grenada- Sperry Multinational is an American accomplice." was found spray painted on an interior wall.

While the attacks on computer systems failed to cause any major political victory for CLODO, they did heighten the awareness that European computers are vulnerable to attack.

A 1979 report by the Swedish Defense Ministry recommended that the government become involved in monitoring computer security of both public and private computers.

While the proper role of the government in computer security remains open for debate, an article in the French daily *Le Figaro* states that computer attacks might be more harmful to national security than the assassination of random politicians.

Japan

In 1985 in Japan, the Middle Core Faction, a terrorist group consisting of approximately 300 individuals, attacked the commuter rail system to cause massive disruption during the height of rush hour. The group used C2W techniques to carry out its attack by first cutting strategic power and communications cables that fed the computer controls for the rail system. Secondly, the group jammed police and rescue radio frequencies in an attempt to hamper and delay response by the authorities. While no one was injured in this attack, it caused a major commuting delay affecting 6.5 million commuters and cost the Japan National Railways more than $6 million in lost ticket sales. Rather than blowing up or tampering with the physical destruction of one rail, the group focused on the critical node (control circuits) and disabled the entire system by using technoterror, attacking physical targets to cause a disruption in cyberspace. The disruption was extensive enough that the Centralized Traffic control Office of Japan National Railways (JNR) was forced to stop operation. While the attacks were successful in creating disruption, the effects were short lived, with most of the severed cables back in full service within 24 hours. This attack, while creating problems for millions of commuters, was also linked to specific objectives. The first was to show solidarity with the National Railways Locomotive Engineers' Union, which was on strike to protest the planned privatization of the JNR. The second goal may have been to influence the trial of Hiroko Nagata, the leader of the Extreme Leftist United Red Army. Her hearing was delayed because the rail shutdown prevented her defense lawyer from making it to court on time.

The combination of computer controls and energy systems raises new possibilities for terrorists. While targeting of energy systems in the past has relied primarily on the physical destruction of key assets to disrupt service, the potential vulnerability of the control systems poses an even greater risk.

Political Motivation

The rise of Information Warfare tactics may allow tomorrow's terrorists to focus their attacks on certain individuals to change their policies or courses of action. The increasing reliance on computers has opened new avenues for blackmail and political pressure. In 1984, a hacker penetrated TRW's credit report computers and obtained some incriminating information about a past small-claims court dispute involving hen incumbent Congressional candidate Tom Lantos of California. This information was passed to his opponent who further distributed the information to the press to discredit Lantos. In a second act of political computer crime, a hacker gained access to Representative Ed Zshau's computer system in Washington, D.C. and erased his data, including his correspondence and constituent database.

These events highlight the potentially selective nature of future cyberterrorism and crime. With a skilled computed operator, a terrorist group may be able to penetrate systems to manipulate a small number of people. Instead of attacking the public to affect a target audience, cyberterrorists may choose to affect the target audience to achieve their ends directly.

Environmental Groups

While "conventional" terrorist groups have targeted computer systems in the past, "eco-terror" groups, such as Earth First, have advocated attacking computer systems. In 1987, the group published a manual that advocated both physical destruction of computer equipment (conventional terrorism) and software and data manipulation/destruction (via cyberterrorism). the manual also included techniques to reduce the risk of being caught by using advance hacking techniques. The risk of cyberterrorism exists on all fronts. It is not merely limited to the "classic" conventional terrorist group. Any group with a strong interest or agenda will be able to attempt cyberterrorism.

Criminal Activity

Criminal activity directed at, or using, computers is receiving increasing attention in the press. The expansion of the Internet to include commercial ventures has sparked a debate over the correct level of security that should be afforded individuals in cyberspace. As terrorism is often crime with different intent, several criminal acts will be explored in this chapter. First, the case of a Russian hacker attempting to steal more than $10 million highlights the vast amounts of money being transferred in cyberspace. Second, the attempt to use computer viruses to hold computers hostage or attack a specific company will be examined. Finally, the possible physical risks to individuals as a result of criminal cyberspace activity are addressed in the case of a Texas professor.

Citibank. The use of computers and computer technology to perpetrate crimes has already occurred. Citibank recently "lost" $10.2 million electronically to a team of Russian hackers. A closer examination of the facts involved in this incident reveals some strengths and weaknesses of computer crime. First, the authorities can use the same technology employed by the cyberterrorist or criminal to track and capture him. Someone can, however, remain anonymous in cyberspace if they are not seeking financial gain, as virus writers have proven.

This incident, according to John Mohr, vice president of the New York Clearing House, is unique in that it utilized a personal computer. It appears that Vladimir L. Levin, a Russian computer expert employed by AO Saturn, a St. Petersburg trading company, broke into Citibank's computer system using stolen account identification numbers and passwords. With this information, he made 40 transfers from Citibank to accounts set up by accomplices in California and Israel. These transfers occurred from June to October 1994 and were tracked by Citibank to determine who was responsible for the crime. While Citibank allowed the transfers to continue, the accounts into which he was transferring the money were frozen, While Levin attempted to transfer more than $10 million in this period, Citibank has recovered all but $400,000. Amy Dates of Citibank had the following answer when questioned about the level of security at Citibank: "We move half a trillion dollars a day through the payment system. Compare hat to the $400,000 they were able to withdraw. We think we have the right level of security." Despite these statements, Citibank implemented a new computer protocol to increase transaction security.

It is still unclear how Levin obtained the account numbers and their associated passwords, but an investigation is continuing into the possibility of inside help. Citibank, has implemented a new security system for its computer accounts that entails the use of "smart cards" that will generate a new password for each transaction. This technology helps to defeat password "sniffer" programs that allow criminals to capture passwords as they are transmitted across the network for future use. This may have been how Levin obtained his passwords. He appears to have had access to the network for some time before attempting his crime as he was careful to follow the patterns of routine transactions and kept his individual transfers to below $300,000 to avoid "built-in" security programs that would have highlighted the transaction as abnormal.

While the adoption of the smart card security system and the employment of encryption technology has, Citibank hopes, corrected the security weakness exploited by Levin and his friends, the amount of money lost in this crime is relatively small. The high level of publicity afforded this incident is due to its extranormality, not its dollar value. Each year, according to the American Bankers Association, the following amounts are lost due to crime: Check fraud- $10 *Billion,* Credit Card fraud- $712 Million, ATM fraud- $18 Million, and Online fraud (as in the Citibank case)- $5 Milllion. While Citibank could use its computers to track and eventually catch Levin, computers and high technology aided in the success of a Vietnamese check fraud ring that operated undetected for seven months. The U.S. Secret Service investigated the crime under the name, "Operation Paper Dragon" and found that the ring took in $25 Million in just over half a year.These high technology money making schemes may appeal to terrorist organizations of the future who are unable to secure, or do not desire, state sponsorship. While attractive to terrorists, the security measures put in place by the banking industry to prevent criminals will likely defeat terrorists as well.

Viruses. In an apparent attempt to extort money, the computers of several universities were infected with a virus in an attempt to make them hostages. The virus demanded a ransom for the antidote to the virus.

Computer users who found the virus were told to send $2,000 to an address in Pakistan to obtain an immunity program that would rid the system of the virus. Investigation showed that the virus was written by two brothers in a computer store in Lahore, Pakistan-they had put their names, and address, and phone number in the virus! "It's like a fantasy of being a terrorist without the blood,: said Eric Corley, editor of a national hacker newsletter, 2600, whose electronic bulletin board was also infected.

The brothers' scheme did not pay well, and the virus was eradicated without their "immunity program." The "fantasy" of being a terrorist without the blood may become reality when an organization uses cyberterror weapons in an attack.

Recently, a virus was used to attack a specific business in Germany. A virus writer, known only as "The Wizard" created then released a virus that he called the "Media Market advertising virus." Media Markt is a German home-electronics group and was not involved in the virus writing or distribution. Media Markt's lawyer claims that "this is the first time that someone has distributed a virus and tied it to a company that has nothing to do with it" To stave off negative publicity, Media Markt has distributed an anti-virus program to disable the virus on affected computers.

While the true intention of the virus writer may never be known, the principle of indirect attack (attacking the general public to influence a target audience) normally utilized by terrorists was evidenced in these tactics. The virus writer, unleashed an attack on the "innocent" computer users to create negative publicity for Media Markt. In this case, Media Markt was clearly not involved in this activity. However, the anonymous and anarchic nature of cyberspace opens the possibility of creating chaos and making it appear as if someone else is responsible. While it appears that financial gain motivated the Russian hackers in the Citibank case, the possibility exists that terrorists or criminals could perpetrate electronic attacks in the future to weaken the target company, not make money. If a terrorist group could place someone "on the inside" of a software company and infect software with a virus *before* shipment, it may call the integrity of that software company into question. While there are no reported cases of terrorists staging a concerted information warfare attack on a business, the case of Citibank might be a benchmark. Despite news that it had lost more than $10 million, Citibank stock went *up* by 1/2 a point on the day that the Russian hacker story broke.

Personal Attacks. The potential exists for terrorists to single out individuals in cyberspace. In 1994, a hacker logged into a Texas A&M professor's E-mail account and used the account to send out 20,000 racist messages. To those receiving the messages, it appeared that they had come from the professor. As a result, the professor began to receive death threats.

THE THREAT FROM HACKERS TURNED TERRORIST

Penetration of computer systems is not difficult. The U.S. Defense Information Systems Agency undertook a penetration study of Department of Defense computers. In 1994, the agency attacked 8,932 servers and mainframes. They were able to gain access to 7,860 (88%) of these systems. Only 319 (4%) of these attacks were detected and only 19 (.2%) of the successful attacks were ever reported. The percentages suggest that even organizations that depend on computers to function rarely know when hackers have attacked them. Penetration of DOD systems has also been documented by other than DOD assets, such as the case of Defense computers being attacked by Dutch hackers during the Gulf War. While none of these penetrations were used for terrorist purposes, it is entirely possibly that this may occur in the future. Even if the hackers initially do not have terrorist intentions, they remain dangerous. A Government Accounting Office report on the Dutch hacker case states that, "the majority of the hackers' activities appeared to be aimed at gaining access to DOD computer system and then establishing methods for later entry. Should a computer hacker decide to work with terrorists, or be forced to work with terrorists via blackmail, these methods for later entry constitute a serious risk.

The jump from hacker to terrorist is a small one that depends entirely on the hacker's motivation and intent. While these cases prove that hackers can penetrate systems, it does not examine the motivation for the hacker. Several studies of the group dynamics and individual motivations for terrorists have been undertaken to help prevent terrorism. While similar studies on the "computer underground" have been undertaken, an analysis of how a terrorist organization might recruit a hacker would be worthwhile. As the world becomes more dependent on computers, understanding what makes hackers "tick" becomes as important as understanding what motivates terrorists.

THE INTERNET WORM

The 1988 Morris Internet worm incident highlights the incredible disruptive power of information warfare tactics for a cyberterrorist, as well as the limitations inherent in attacking computers.

On November 2, 1988, Robert Tappan Morris, a Cornell University graduate student, released a "worm" onto the Internet. While Morris maintains that it was just an experiment that went terribly wrong, the Justice Department decided to prosecute Morris, who was found guilty of a felony and sentence d to three years probation, $10,000 fine and 400 hours of community service. In March of 1991, his appeal to the U.S. Count of Appeals for the second circuit was unsuccessful. In the fall of 1991, the U.S. Supreme Court refused to hear his case.

The worm program, created as an experiment by Morris, was based on three separate security flaws that Morris had discovered in the Berkeley version of the UNIX operating system. The goals of his program were: to infect three computers per network location across the Internet, to avoid slow machines and any network that was in use (to avoid detection by operators), use infected computers to find connections to other uninfected computers, steal the password files of computers and use the passwords to gain access to even more computers.

Computers had fascinated Morris his entire life. Morris' father, Bob Morris, was a computer engineer for Bell Labs, the creators of the UNIX operating system. The area of computer security had been a hobby of Robert Morris throughout his college years. His knowledge of computer systems was so extensive that both the Naval Research laboratory and the National Security Agency, NSA (where Bob Morris was serving as director of the National

Computer Security Center) invited him to speak to the topic of UNIX operating system security. That this was a problem about which the NSA was deeply concerned became apparent during Morris's trial. The presentation to the NSA was videotaped and the prosecution intended to show part of the tape concerning "how not to get caught" to show that Morris had written his program with malicious intent to break into computers. Robert's defense lawyer, Tom Guidoboni, threatened to force Robert's father to testify about the National Security Agency's interest in computer penetration, to include divulging classified material if the tape was shown. Possibly a result of NSA pressure, the tape was not used in the trial and the NSA was able to protect its secrets.

The knowledge that Robert Morris had obtained in his study of computer security was extensive. He had been aware of two flaws in the UNIX system for over a year before his worm was released. The final flaw, in the FTP, File Transfer Protocol, program (a utility in UNIX that allows individuals on different computers to transfer files back and forth between remote systems) was corrected before Morris could finish his program, so he was forced to adjust and exploit only the remaining two weaknesses. These weaknesses were in the *sendmail* portion of the operating system and in the *finger* utility. It was a combination of these two weaknesses that allowed the worm to spread from computer to computer. The worm was originally designed to limit its growth, with each copy of the program checking to see if other copies were already running on a system before attempting to replicate. If there were other copies running, they would "negotiate" with each other to see which one would terminate. Unfortunately, the program that agreed to terminate would infect many other computers before it stopped running Additionally, one in seven of the copies of the worm would not check to see if there were other copies present before infecting a machine. In effect, it refused to dies on its own. This "one in seven" system, coupled with the fact that the portion of the program controlling worm to worm communication was improperly written, led to a massive proliferation of worms on thousands of computers on the Internet, causing delay and forcing machines to be taken off the network.

The battle to "beat" the worm was intense. The meeting of Berkeley UNIX experts was fortuitous in that several leading experts, including the creators of the operating system were in the same place and were able to collaborate on finding a solution to the problem. Within 24 hours, the Berkeley team had discovered how the program spread and had corrected the problems in the *sendmail* portion of the operating system. In less than 48 hours, all the weaknesses that the program attempted to exploit were corrected and the "fixes" were sent out to all users on the Internet. The attempt to understand the virus was hampered by its having been encrypted by Morris.

Fortunately, the encryption scheme was extremely weak and was quickly broken, allowing the experts to unscramble the code. The next step was to "reverse engineer" the code by decompiling it into source code to study its design and ensure that it did not have "malicious" (data altering/destroying) instructions hidden in the program. Fortunately for the users of the Internet, Morris did not write the worm to destroy data on infected computers, it would merely replicate out of control until the machine became overwhelmed with copies of the worm. Had the worm been written to destroy data, the recovery time would have been much longer with potentially massive data loss. Despite the rapid response of system experts, the publicity created by the incident was nearly as overwhelming in the media as the worm was to the infected computer systems. The worm caused so much disruption that the *New York Times* carried the story on page one for an entire week. Additionally, both the *Wall Street Journal* and *USA Today* gave it front-page coverage. Television news and talk shows were also filled with discussion on the worm.

This incident, while not malicious, highlights the power of information warfare techniques to cause massive disruption without physical harm to equipment or people. One man created a national computer crisis with a small program that received international attention and was addressed at the highest levels of the U.S. government. While appearing attractive for terrorists, this incident highlights both the positive and the negative aspects of information warfare for terrorism.

POSITIVE AND NEGATIVE ELEMENTS FOR THE CYBERTERRORIST

The ability of one man, in this case Robert T. Morris, to generate such an enormous amount of disruption and publicity with a small 3,000 line computer program might be very appealing to a terrorist organization attempting to achieve its aims with minimum effort and risk. Morris was eventually brought to trial for his worm, mainly because he spoke of its creation to several people. A dedicated cyberterrorist could remain anonymous in the same manner that the overwhelming majority of virus writers (such as the author of the famous Michelangelo virus - who remains unidentified) escape identification.

The personal equipment and money expenditures required for his incident were minimal as Morris had access to Cornell University's computers. While in the late 80s, Internet access was not widespread, today it is expanding at an exponential rate, with more individuals connecting to the network every day. The number of host computers connected to the Internet rose 30% from 1 July to 1 October 1994. The possible avenues of attack have expanded exponentially, as all that is required for a computer attack is a computer, a modem, and a skilled operator with the requisite information. The increasing number of host computers represent both new targets and new platforms from which to launch an attack.

As the power of computers doubles every 12-18 months, the computing power that was once reserved for major corporations and the government is now available to individuals. Since the "tools" are widely available, it is now the knowledge of how to manipulate those tools that is most important to perpetrate a computer attack. The knowledge that Morris used to attack the Internet came from extensive study of the UNIX operating system. He had known about the flaws for at least a year before writing his program to exploit their weaknesses. The correction of the FTP weakness immediately before Morris completed his worm program highlights the fragility of this information. Had that been the only weakness known to Morris, all of his work would have been for naught. An external attack on a computer system usually occurs through weaknesses in the software that are unknown to the creators of the software. Those attempting to gain unauthorized access to a system exploit these "bugs" in programs. Once a "bug" is discovered, software developers usually rapidly distribute a "patch" that will correct the error. The flaw that took a hacker several months to find can be corrected in a matter of seconds with the installations of a software patch. The hacker or cyberterrorist is then forced to search for yet another weakness in the system. That flaws in software exist, and are often unknown until exploited, is a double-edged sword for the potential cyberterrorist. If cyberterrorists learn of a weakness in a computer system, every day that they wait to exploit that weakness may allow a legitimate security professional or non-malicious hacker to discover and advertise the weakness, leading to the rapid distribution of a software or hardware fix to the problem. Additionally, if cyberterrorists wish to create massive disruption, they will be forced to "show their hands" and exploit the weakness on a large number of systems or on several high value systems. If they are clever, they may be able to throw system managers off the track for a short period of time.

Additionally, by using publicly available encryption techniques, they can scramble their program so that it will take years to decrypt and examine. This will exacerbate the fear of the unknown, as system managers will be unable to determine the true intent of the program. If malicious, it may require the systems to be completely shut down and all the software reloaded from a "known" clean source. If the rouge program could not be completely understood and then removed without damage, a complete shutdown would be required for all systems that handled critical data or were used to control systems upon which human lives depend. The disruption would be far greater than that caused by the Morris worm, as it could be controlled, decrypted and safely removed from systems without damaging any of the existing software or negatively affecting the integrity of data on the machines.

The recent controversy over Netscape Corporation's use of encryption to secure Internet transactions highlights the strength and weakness of current encryption schemes. This particular encryption program was designed to allow users to send confidential information such as credit card numbers) across the Internet securely. A French graduate student in mathematics used two supercomputers and 120 computer workstations to "brute force" decrypt (trying all possible combinations of the "key" in succession until the correct one is found) a message using this encryption program in just less than eight days. This encryption scheme used a 40 bit key (meaning its "key" length was 40 bits-a bit is a single 0 or 1 in binary code) since it was the most powerful scheme that the U.S. government would allow to be exported. The key employed by Netscape within the United States is 128 bits. This 128 bit key, utilizing the same decryption techniques, would take 10 more time to break (about 2.1918 x 10^{24} *years*).

In less than one month after the brute force decrypting of the 40 bit message, two graduate students at Berkeley discovered a software flaw that would allow them to decode a message encrypted with the 128 bit key in less than one minute. Netscape promptly fixed the problem and released an updated version of the encryption program within days to resecure the system.

The ability to create a program or send each other messages that would take law enforcement or government agencies 2.1918 x 10^{24} years to unscramble is very appealing to cyberterrorists and common criminals. If a law enforcement agency intercepts an encrypted computer message, it is useless until it can be decrypted. This may allow cyberterrorists to move away from using the slow, but relatively secure, face-to-face method communication for potentially more secure, worldwide, and nearly instantaneous communication channel offered by encrypted E-mail. The Institute for National Strategic Studies concluded that the communications signals themselves are becoming harder to intercept with the advent of "digital technology, frequency-hopping and spread-spectrum technologies, plus replacement of microwave with optical fiber for long-distance communication." The rise of public key encryption led the Institute to conclude that the capabilities of the codemakers are outpacing those of the codebreakers. The growing ubiquity of encryption, despite several setbacks, as in the Netscape case, has still made it difficult to obtain information that individuals desire to keep secure.

The value of encryption, and the ability of business to drive a response to crime, can be seen in the development of the GSM (Global System for Mobile communications) cellular phone standard, which uses encrypted digital signals to prevent eavesdropping and phone fraud. While in the United States, which uses an analog system, AMPS (Advanced Mobile Phone Service), a thief can steal the user ID to a cellular telephone (by intercepting its unencrypted signal) to perpetrate phone fraud. In GSM, this signal is randomly encrypted each time the phone is used, making it useless unless the correct "key " to decrypt the signal is in the possession of the interceptor. While the GSM system cuts down on cellular phone fraud, it also compounds the difficulty of intercepting the communications of known terrorists.

Unlike the physical world, in which a potential aggressor needs time and money to procure or manufacture its weapons, and time to train people to use these weapons, all of which can be observed and defenses readied by the target of aggression, the preparations of "weapons" in cyberspace is often the work of one (or several) individuals and occurs in the relative privacy and security of their own computers. With the explosion of processing power, the computers sitting in homes throughout the world are more powerful than the minicomputers o a decade ago. Unlike conventional terrorism, where the weapons of destruction are outlawed or restricted to use by the state, the weapons in cyberterrorism are available equally to the state and the terrorist organization. For a cyberspace WMD, the critical component becomes knowledge of computer systems, not the ability to procure fissionable material. The state and the terrorists operate on nearly equal footing in cyberspace.

The rapid recovery and complete eradication of the Internet worm, to include defenses against it ever occurring again, are not paralleled in the conventional world. A truck bomb manufactured from fertilizer and diesel fuel will cause damage and terror every time a terrorist parks it in or near a building and detonates it. Despite knowing the damage that car and truck bombs can cause through numerous attacks in the Middle East throughout the 1980s, authorities in the U.S. were unable to prevent the World Trade Center Bombing in New York City or the Murrah Federal

Building bombing in Oklahoma City. While improved technology and procedures allow authorities to respond more rapidly to these attacks and take some limited measures to prevent the attacks, they cannot ensure that a "copycat" crime will not occur. In cyberspace, once a vulnerability is noted and a software fix is distributed, a second attack of exactly the same nature will *always* meet with defeat. What was once an open door becomes an impenetrable brick wall. If cyberterrorists were planning to exploit an identified and corrected weakness, all their effort was for naught. Their cyberspace "bomb" simply will not work. They can attempt to take his bomb elsewhere, but only if computer security administrators have shirked their duties and not installed "fixes" will they succeed.

The limited and fragile nature of weaknesses in cyberspace will force cyberterrorists to choose their targets carefully. Since an attack in cyberspace is likely to be a "one shot deal," terrorists must consider the cyberspace target to be of sufficient value to use their one-shot weapon. If a target is not sufficiently valuable, a cyberterrorists may choose to risk waiting until they can penetrate a system that will carry a substantial impact if attacked. A second factor affecting the nature of a cyberterrorist target is the likelihood that the disruption created will be temporary instead of permanent, as in the case of physical destruction of a target by a conventional or technoterrorist. The temporary nature of the disruption may cause cyberterrorists to string together numerous attacks to create disrupt of increased duration.

8

Evolution of Chinese Military Doctrine and Information Warfare

IW's current cachet in both China and the United States can be partly explained by the hip, futuristic, attractively ill-defined nature of the subject, which invites the frenetic pace at which some of the nation's most forward thinkers are attempting to coin the permanent neologisms and concepts of this new type of combat. At the same time, however, I would argue that behind all the rhetoric and hype, IW presents the Chinese with a potentially potent, if circumscribed, asymmetric weapon. Defined carefully, it could give the PLA a longer-range power projection capability against

U.S. forces that its conventional forces cannot currently hope to match. In particular, I would argue that these weapons give the PLA a possible way to attack the Achilles' Heel of the advanced, informatized U.S. military: its information systems, especially those related to command and control and transportation. By attacking these targets, the Chinese could possibly degrade or delay U.S. force mobilization in a time- dependent scenario, such as Taiwan, and do so with a measure of plausible deniability.

DEFINING TERMS

Before proceeding further, it is necessary to define terms, although this exercise is fraught with terminological, political, and ideological peril. In some ways, however, the Chinese themselves have made the job a little easier. Chinese writings clearly suggest that IW is a solely military subject, and as such, they draw inspiration primarily from U.S. military writings. The net result of this "borrowing" is that many PLA authors' definitions of IW and IW concepts sound eerily familiar. For our purposes, therefore, we shall use the definition of information warfare found in Joint Pub 3-13, *Joint Doctrine for Information Operations (IO)*:

Information operations conducted during time of crisis or conflict to achieve or promote specific objectives over a specific adversary or adversaries.

"Information operations" are defined in Joint Pub 3-13.1, *Joint Doctrine for Command and Control Warfare (C2W)* as:

actions taken to achieve information superiority by affecting adversary information, information-based processes, information systems, and computer-based networks, while defending one's own information, information-based processes, information systems, and computer-based networks.

More concretely, the Army in FM-100-6 *Information Operations* defines "information operations" as continuous military operations within the military environment that enable, enhance, and protect the friendly force's ability to collect, process, and act on information to achieve an advantage across the full range of military operations; information operations include interacting with the global information environment and exploiting or denying an adversary's information and decision capabilities.

The goal of these operations is "information dominance," or The degree of information superiority that allows the possessor to use information systems and capabilities to achieve an operational advantage in a conflict or to control the situation in operations short of war, while denying those capabilities to the adversary.

By introducing these definitions, I am not precluding that the Chinese may eventually develop an indigenous IW strategy, and there is limited evidence of movement in this direction. Instead, these U.S. definitions provide a baseline by which to judge PLA writings.

IMPORTANCE OF INFORMATION WARFARE

Given the above context, one can get an insight into evolution of Chinese theories and concepts on Information Warfare (IW). As with all its military theories and strategic perspectives, Chinese traditional wisdom and strategic thought is applied to all new concepts and precepts originating from the US, Russia or elsewhere. The first wave of Chinese writings on IW appeared in the mid-1990s following the success of US information technologies in the first Gulf War of 1991. Though this war was a defining event for all militaries of the world, its impact on the PLA was greater because of the aspirations of the Chinese political and military leadership towards acquiring comprehensive national strength. The PLA was first off the block in developing theories of IW and adapting Western concepts to suit local conditions. A PLA General, writing on challenges and importance of IW, observed:

In near future, Information warfare will control the form and future of war. We recognise this developmental trend of information warfare and see it as a driving force in China's military and combat readiness. This trend will be highly critical to achieve victory in future wars.

The General further emphasised that China must use a practical combination of IW and Maoist and Marxist military thought to guide IW issues under military construction. The military must study ways of using inferior equipment to achieve victory over the enemy's superior equipment. He advocated study on how to conduct 'People's war in IW domain'. The underlying theme of Chinese concepts on IW has been emphasis on devising ways and means to attack an enemy's weaknesses and vulnerabilities, and on exploiting own strengths. The other fundamental assumption is that superior tactics can compensate for inferior technology.

People's Warfare in Information Warfare Context

According to some Chinese military analysts, because of the increasing relevance of information technology (IT) to people's lives, individuals who take part in IW are not all soldiers and that anybody who understands computers may become a fighter. IW is inexpensive as the targeted party can be delivered a paralysing blow through the net and it may be difficult for the latter to discern where the attack originated. Large amount of useless information can be created to block or stop the functioning of an adversary's information system.

Thus, a People's War in context of IW can be carried out by hundreds of millions of people, using open-type modern information systems. Even political mobilisation for war can be achieved via the internet, by sending patriotic e-mail messages and by setting up databases for education.

This finds further support from another Chinese author, who observes that "even as ... government mobilised troops, the numbers and roles of traditional warriors will be sharply less than those of technical experts...since thousand of personal computers can be linked up to perform a common operation, to perform many tasks in place of a large-scale military computer, an IW victory will very likely be determined by which country can mobilise the most computer experts and part-time fans... That will be a real People's War."

Preparing for people's war is a recurring theme in Chinese writing, as IW will be carried out by the PLA and society as a whole. This concept has found practical expression in turning some of the 1.5 million reserve forces into mini-IW regiments. The People's Armed Forces Department (PAFD) has reportedly organised militia/ reserve IW regiments at district levels in many provinces.

For instance, in Echeng district of Hubei province, the PAFD has a network warfare battalion as well as electronic warfare, intelligence and psychological warfare battalions, and also a training base for IW activities. The PAFD has also carried out 'Informaticised People's Warfare Network Simulation Exercise'. A version of this concept was also put into practice following the bombing of the Chinese embassy in Belgrade on May 8, 1999, during 'Operation Allied Force'. The Chinese hacked a number of US political, military and diplomatic web sites, and also carried out a network battle by mobilising thousands of net users for sending emails and viruses. This caused servers to crash, paralysing a large number of web sites.

Cyber Warfare

Concerns about China's net force were heightened after the aforementioned attacks on US computer systems and after the Chinese militia carried out IW exercises, which included India, the US, Taiwan and Japan as target countries. The aim of such training was to disrupt critical infrastructure like banking, power supply and telecommunication networks in the target country as part of China's strategy of asymmetric approach to warfare. In the cyber domain, the Chinese have adopted three methods for targetting such networks; the first is the use of e-mails for planting viruses; then phishing and lastly, the introduction of 'intelligent trojans' and 'vacuum trojans'. Diverse routes of planting trojans and viruses have been used to attack critical PCs, which in turn send out files or cause Chinese Concepts and Capabilities of Information Warfare 785 malfunction. Hackers' tools are becoming more robotic and simple; for instance, a vacuum trojan will extract information from a pen drive automatically when connected to a USB port. It is also believed that the next step could be planting the targeted sites with the more difficult to detect fake data or partially fake data.

In Nanjing, the PLA has developed more than 250 trojans and similar tools. Here, it needs to be remembered that foreign companies like Network Solutions, were made to hand over 300 computer viruses by the Ministry of Public Security's lab in an effort to speed up the certification of antivirus products. Further, the Chinese Academy of Sciences, which provides suggestions about national information security policy and law, has established the State Lab for Information Security. The lab has 'National Attack Project' as one of its research programmes. Also, select professionals have been inducted into militia organisations to boost combat capabilities in future wars. Thus, China has been paying much attention to offensive strategies in cyberspace even as it concentrates on defensive IW.

Definition and Goals of Information Warfare

The Chinese understanding of IW, which was initially based on western concepts, has increasingly moved towards evolving its own orientation. Chinese experts believe that IW's essence is the sum of information capabilities capable of breaking the will to resist by attacking an enemy's cognitive understanding and convictions, forcing it to give up all resistance and terminate the war. The goal is to "force enemy to regard their goal as our goal, to force the opponent to give up the will to resist and end confrontation and stop fight by attacking enemy's perceptions and belief via information energy." Xie Guang, the then Vice Minister of Science and Technology and Industry for National Defence, defined IW in December 1999 thus: "IW in military sense means overall use of various types (of) information technologies, equipment and systems, particularly his command systems, to shake determination of enemy's policy makers and at the same time, the use of all the means possible to ensure that one's own systems are not damaged or disturbed." This definition apparently includes the aspects of IW's goals at the larger national level. A further elaboration was done by two senior PLA colonels, who described IW as consisting of five major elements and two general areas. The five elements are:

- Substantive destruction, the use of hard weapons to destroy enemy headquarters, command posts, and command and control (C2) information centres
- Electronic warfare, the use of electronic means of jamming or the use of anti-radiation [electromagnetic] weapons to attack enemy information and intelligence collection systems such as communications and radar
- Military deception, the use of operations such as tactical feints [simulated attacks] to shield or deceive enemy intelligence collection systems
- Operational secrecy, the use of all means to maintain secrecy and keep the enemy from collecting intelligence on our operations.
- Psychological warfare, the use of TV, radio, and leaflets to undermine the enemy's military morale.

The two general areas are information protection (defence) and information attack (offence). Information defence means preventing the destruction of one's own information systems, ensuring that these systems can perform their normal functions.

In future wars, key information and information systems will become "combat priorities", the key targets of enemy attack. It also includes many other manifestations of IW like computer virus warfare, precision warfare and stealth warfare, all dependent in some manner on information and software programmes.

Information Operations

Information Operations (IO) are specific operations and are considered to be at the core of IW, in the same manner as IW is considered to be at the core of informationalisation. In fact, IO is a manifestation of IW on the battlefield. It can be both of the defensive and offensive types, and can be conducted at the strategic, operational, campaign and tactical levels at times of peace, wars and crises. Principles of IO have been defined by Chinese military authors to include centralised command, decentralised control (multi-level power delegation), multi-dimension inspection and testing, timely decision-making and integration of military and civil actions with focus on key links. Major General Dai Qingmin, Director of PLA's General Staff responsible for IW and IO (and also ex-Commander of PLA's IW Centre in Wuhan) observes that integrated and joint information operations give more scope and purpose to people's war. (In fact, jointness and integration is a major theme of the 2004 White Paper). He defines IO as a series of operations with an informationalised environment as the basic battlefield condition, with military information and information systems as the direct operational targets and electronic warfare (EW) and computer networks as the principal form. He has outlined various IO strategies because, as mentioned earlier, according to the traditional Chinese approach strategies can compensate for inferior equipment and technologies and, in the case of IO, it may also compensate for gaps in information or poor information about the enemy. Some of the IO strategies are:

- Jamming or sabotaging an enemy's information or information system.
- Sabotaging an enemy's overall information operational structure.
- Weakening an enemy's information fighting capacity.

- Dispersing enemy forces, arms and fires while concentrating own forces, arms and fire.
- Confusing or diverting an enemy and creating an excellent combat opportunity for on self.
- Diverting an enemy's reconnaissance attempt and making sufficient preparations for it.
- Giving the enemy a false impression and launching surprise information attack on him at the same time.
- Blinding or deafening an enemy with false impressions.
- Confusing an enemy or disrupting his thinking.
- Making an enemy believe that what is true is false and what is false is true.
- Causing an enemy to make a wrong judgement or take wrong action.

In the IW exercises conducted by PAFD, 10 methods of IO were practised and these can be viewed as tactics in the electronic battlefield. These are:

- Planting information mines
- Conducting information reconnaissance
- Changing network data
- Releasing information bombs
- Dumping information garbage
- Disseminating propaganda
- Applying information deception
- Releasing clone information
- Organising information defence
- Establishing network spy stations.

Computer Network Operations

In Chinese writings on Information Warfare, networking has also been the focus of discussions. The recent emphasis on jointness and integration apply equally to integrating various military networks. A critique by Timothy Thomas notes that the Chinese feel it necessary to prepare for a "network people's war". Computer network warfare has been included by Dai Qing as one of the six forms of IW (i.e. operational security, military deception, psychological warfare, electronic warfare, computer network warfare and physical destruction). Though there is no evidence of a formal Chinese doctrine, Chinese theorists have coined the term "Integrated Network Electronic Warfare" (INEW) and this has also been referred to by Timothy Thomas as a half cousin, given its similarities and points of divergences to the US approach.

INEW has been described as a series of combat operations that integrate electronic warfare and computer network warfare measures to disrupt the normal operation of an enemy's battlefield systems while protecting one's own with the objective of attaining information superiority. The essence of computer network warfare (CNW) is "to disrupt layers in which information is processed, by seizing and maintaining control of network space". EW is targeted at networked information systems and informationalised weapon systems in order to increase combat effectiveness. According to Dai, INEW is necessary for system to system confrontation on the informationalised battlefield, as systems are centres of gravity. Any disruption in system will lead to a disconnect between the people and weapons. Thus, INEW lays stress on coordinating and integrating all aspects of C4ISR and weapon platforms and weapon systems to produce the desired effects at the target end. The effectiveness of weapon platforms and network systems is directly proportional to its levels of integration. As in other spheres, integration produces a combat capability greater than the sum of its parts and, this is true for information operations as well.

China's computer network operations (CNO) comprise network attacks, defence, and exploitation. According to the Pentagon's Annual Report for 2005 to the Congress on China's military power, the PLA views CNO as critical to seize the initiative and "electromagnetic dominance" early in a conflict, and as a force multiplier. This concept outlines the integrated use of electronic warfare, CNO and limited physical strikes against key C4ISR nodes to disrupt an enemy's battlefield network information systems. It is believed that the PLA has established information warfare units to develop viruses to attack enemy computer systems and networks, and tactics to protect friendly computer systems and networks. The PLA has increased the role of CNO in its military exercises. Although initial training efforts focused on increasing the PLA's proficiency in defensive measures, recent exercises have incorporated offensive operations, primarily as first strikes against enemy networks.

The main area of weakness that the Chinese espy, especially with regard to US forces, is the deployment phase. US forces are largely dependent upon computer and communication systems, both military and nonmilitary, and the particularly weak links in the logistics network systems make them susceptible to computer network attacks. Logistics network systems may be relatively easy to penetrate compared to other C4 systems though it will be more useful to penetrate command and information links. However, the priority of Chinese CNW seems to be to prevent the force from deploying at the first place and thereafter breaking the linkages between decision-makers and weapon platforms. This approach rhymes with the oft-stated Chinese strategy of attacking weaknesses and avoiding strengths of the enemy. As observed by James Mulvenon, Chinese strategists theorise that:

- Computer network attack is the most effective means for a weak adversary to fight a strong one.
- It can be used as a means to deter the enemy.
- It has longer range than the conventional power projection assets, as long distance surveillance and precise powerful and long distance attacks are available to the military.

Psychological Operations and Information Warfare

Another important component of information Warfare with Chinese characteristics is psychological warfare. Chinese doctrine has traditionally focused more attention on the psychological dimensions of IW, including deception, though of late they have also been paying equal, if not more, attention to the technological dimensions. The target in psychological operations is always the people and decision-makers, so that their will and perceptions are attacked to alter their beliefs, goals and behaviour. This is aimed at both military and civil components of an adversary's populace. Psychological operations comprise of manipulation of media to support military efforts and include conventional methods of propaganda like distribution of leaflets, radio and TV broadcasts, and other means of communication. Like most of the components of IW, psychological operations are a continuum of actions in peacetime, crisis time and war time.

In August 2005, the PLA conducted a joint exercise, involving not only all its services but also troops from Russia. The exercise involved distribution of leaflets over the opponent, electronic warfare to confuse incoming missiles and adoption of electronic counter measures. These exercises involved the use of live missiles and ammunition, and showcased precision warfare capabilities as well as the latest military equipment. These exercises could also be said to have had a psychological dimension for deterring Taiwan or those aiding it in its political objectives. Here, it can be argued that the Chinese appear to have taken a leaf out of the US forces' tom-tomming of the awesome power of their arsenal and military capabilities before the start of 'Operation Iraqi Freedom', which had the effect of lowering the morale of the Iraqi military. The US forces also air dropped over 31 million leaflets for propaganda purposes besides physically attacking Iraqi forces' command and control networks based on fibre optic lines and radio and computer servers. US forces had been issued cyber-guidance as early as February 2003 for operations in Iraq. The PLA has thus been quick to absorb lessons on IW from 'Operation Iraqi Freedom'.

The Chinese also observed the power of media when CNN's broadcast of a US soldier's body being dragged through the streets of Mogadishu transformed perceptions of victory into defeat. Authors of the Chinese book titled Unrestricted Warfare reflected on the incident thus: Did CNN's broadcast of an exposed corpse of a US soldier in the streets of Mogadishu shake the determination of the Americans to act as the world's policeman, thereby altering the world's strategic situation? And should an assessment of wartime actions look at the means or the results?

PLA's IW/EW Capabilities

The 2004 White Paper shows that the Chinese military has understood that there is a large and expanding technology gap between it and modern militaries, especially that of the US. China's leaders, including President Hu Jintao, have ordered the PLA to pursue "leap ahead" technologies and "informationalised" capabilities to increase weapons' mobility, firepower and precision. This perspective applies to IW also.

The Central Military Commission's (CMC) Third or Technical Department of General Service Headquarters is responsible for strategic SIGINT and has established a number of monitoring stations to intercept signals from countries like India, Taiwan, Japan, South Korea and others. The PRC also established a Fourth Armed Forces Department in 1990 to look after offensive and defensive IW activities. It has also built "an information warfare simulation centre" for training its corps of network warriors. The centre uses high technology simulation skills and equipment to simulate information warfare and its environment. The Fourth Department has special detachments and units that manage and direct SIGINT and EW operations for the PLA at all levels and includes operations of the Air Force and the Navy.

The PRC has completed one million km of fibre optics line and communication infrastructure called "Eight Horizontal Grids and Eight Vertical Grids" supported by satellite, ground mobile receiving stations and ground to air data links. With technologies obtained from Western countries and by exploiting its booming commercial IT and telecommunications sector, it has improved the quality of its military programmes. The PLA has acquired and deployed a wide variety of air, sea and land-based intelligence, surveillance and reconnaissance (ISR) systems to enhance its ability to detect monitor and target military activities in Asia and West Pacific Ocean. Some of the latest programmes include electro-optics, synthetic aperture radar, over the horizon radars, and surveillance systems that can detect stealth aircraft.

EW is a key element in the PLA's 'Three Attacks and Three Defences' strategy (attack stealth aircraft, cruise missiles and helicopters; defend against precision strikes, electronic warfare, and enemy reconnaissance) to meet the requirements of 'local war under high tech conditions' which has now progressed to 'local war under informationalised conditions'. Both military and civil sectors are actively exploring IW concepts which could lead to developing a corps of network warriors to defend China's telecommunication, command and information networks while uncovering vulnerabilities of adversaries' networks.

At the national level, China has a C3I system based on fibre optic cables, satellite communications, micro-wave links, tropo-scatter communications and automated command and control systems. The PLA has both secured and non-secured telecommunications and has an army wide data communication network and integrated field operations communication system. Its WAN is capable of supporting peacetime operations within Chinese borders and limited pre-planned operations along China's periphery but is inadequate for large-scale joint operations.

The Chinese Army has a family of battlefield ELINT systems like DZ 9002 that detect, intercept, analyse and record an adversary's signal emissions. DZ 9001 has been developed both for defensive and offensive electronic counter measures (ECM). DZ 9300 is a man-packed radar reconnaissance system meant for special operations forces and rapid reaction forces. A bodyguard laser countermeasures system has also been developed to counter precision-guided munitions guided by laser emissions. There are also a variety of jamming systems with the ground forces.

The PLA Air Force is developing capabilities in airborne warning and control systems (AWACS), airborne early warning, and ECM aircraft and UAVs. Shaanxi Y-8 has been designed for special EW, ELINT and ECM missions. This aircraft was first observed in operation in the summer of 2004 and it is believed that some of its equipment may be from the US Navy's EP-3 ELINT aircraft that made an emergency landing in Hainan in April 2001. Another version of the Y-8 aircraft is 'Balance Beam' airborne early warning aircraft meant for tactical ISR, EW and ELINT missions. It made its maiden flight in 2001 and its finalised version Y-8 F600 flew in January 2005. The PLA Air Force is planning for 4-6 AWACS and has about 20 other dedicated ELINT aircraft like HD-5, TU-154M and HZ-6. HD-5, an older version, is being replaced by HZ-6 which has improved capabilities. UAV's configured for ELINT and EW missions are also in use. In July 2002, the PLA inducted the Israeli anti-radar hunter killer HARPY UAV.

The Chinese Navy also has over a dozen ships and several trawlers for various electronic warfare missions. Four Yuan Wang and Shiyan class ships monitor space events and are capable of collecting and monitoring missile and satellite telemetry data and communications. Chinese industry has developed three types of systems, based on Soviet-era systems, which have been further upgraded and modernised.

Space is another area where the Chinese have been making rapid advances, especially in the field of ISR and anti-satellite technologies. China considers space as a 'commanding height' and it plans to control space and win the information war after having built up an informationalised PLA. In 2003, the PLA had six dual-use dedicated satellites for military purposes. In 2004, China placed 10 satellites into orbit and has a similar schedule through 2006. It hopes to have more than 100 satellites in orbit by 2010, and launch an additional 100 satellites by 2020. In the next decade, Beijing will most likely field radar, ocean surveillance, and improved filmbased photo-reconnaissance satellites. China will eventually deploy advanced imagery, reconnaissance, and Earth resource systems with military applications. China's ZY-2 payloads have digital imagery reconnaissance capabilities and have worldwide coverage. Beijing also tested new film-based imagery satellites and small digital imagery satellites in 2003 and 2004. It is also developing its own GPS navigation system based on the Beidou series of navigational satellites. The PLA possesses anti-GPS jammers obtained from Russia, which however may not be very effective against the NAVSAT satellite system of the US.

China is also developing electronic intelligence (ELINT) and signals intelligence (SIGINT) reconnaissance satellites. These digital data systems will be able to transmit directly to ground sites, and China may be developing a system of data relay satellites to support global coverage. Furthermore, Beijing has acquired mobile data reception equipment that can support more rapid data transmission to deployed military forces and units. China is developing micro satellites for remote sensing as well as for putting into place networks of electro-optical and radar satellites. In April 2004, Beijing launched a micro satellite with a probable imagery mission. China is also conducting research to develop ground-based laser ASAT Weapons. All these capabilities will contribute to China's prowess in the field of information warfare.

Implications for India

Attaining information superiority has become one of the most important objectives to be achieved in the era of knowledge age warfare. The concept of information superiority is somewhat analogous to similar concepts of air, sea or space superiority. This is because proper use of information is as lethal as other kinds of power. Further, the concept of information superiority leads us to attainment of decision superiority. Information operations are increasingly being considered as important as sea, land and air operations. Information operations can vary from physical destruction to psychological operations to computer network defence. Wellconducted joint information operations with new RMA technologies, improved organisations and doctrine will greatly contribute to a successful and decisive outcome.

It is in this context that a Defence Information Warfare Agency (DIWA) under the Integrated Defence Staff Headquarters has been formed to coordinate efforts of the three services and certain other agencies to handle all aspects of information warfare. The Indian concepts of IW are generally based on Western concepts and according to the 2004 Army Doctrine, IW encompasses the elements of command and control warfare, intelligencebased warfare, electronic warfare, cyber warfare, psychological warfare and network centric warfare, military deception and secrecy as well as media support. Though the three Services have different set ups for IW activity, DIWA is the nodal and apex policy-making body to formulate joint and integrated responses to IW challenges. Therefore, an IW doctrine needs to be formulated, which it is believed, is under the process of being evolved by DIWA. However, it is at operational levels that weaknesses in our IW efforts exist. There is a need for joint linkages and joint planning to synchronise our response to all elements of information warfare.

The Indian armed forces have made considerable progress in establishing C4ISR networks. But given that these are service wise, there is a need for establishing a Joint Inter-Services Network. The other areas that need attention are:

- In the era of cyber warfare, information warfare and net wars, information systems, both civil and military networks, should have adequate redundancy, survivability and electronic security.

- For optimisation, the strengths of our IT infrastructure and industry and advancements in satellites and radio-based systems should be jointly exploited by the military and civil sectors.
- Joint network and individual services networks should be able to function in all environments including nuclear. For instance, they should be hardened against or be resistant to an EMP attack.
- We need to induct a wide variety of military satellites for upgrading our strategic ISR, SIGINT, ELINT, COMMINT, imagery and navigation capabilities.
- We need to reflect on the Chinese model of net force based on their militia and examine whether there is a need to adopt a similar model in our Territorial Army units. Even though Computer Emergency Response Teams (CERT) at national and lower levels have been formed to respond to cyber attacks on civilian infrastructure, the concept is more defensive in nature. A pro-active concept like that of net force may be more appropriate.

IMPORTANT CHINESE IW CONCEPTS AND TERMS: DEFINITIONS

When examining Chinese IW theories, the logical place to start is Wang Pufeng's seminal work, *Information Warfare and the RMA.* Wang defines information warfare as follows:

Information war is a product of the information age which to a great extent utilizes information technology and information ordnance in battle. It constitutes a "networkization" [*wangluohua*] of the battlefield, and a new model for a complete contest of time and space. At its center is the fight to control the information battlefield, and thereby to influence or decide victory or defeat.

Later, the author elaborates his definition:

Information war is a crucial stage of high-tech war.... At its heart are information technologies, fusing intelligence war, strategic war, electronic war, guided missile war, a war of "motorization" [*jidong zhan*], a war of firepower [*huoli*]—a total war. It is a new type of warfare.

The author distinguishes this new type of warfare from the previous paradigm:

> Information and the capacity [to employ it] together release new energy in battle; information's "networkization" opens up a new battlefield of computers. With the "informationization" [*xinxihua*] of the army, agility and speed, mobility, and depth of attack, in a battle without a front line, all create a leap ahead of the traditional methods of warfare. The area [of the battle] grows, its speed increases, the accuracy of the attack is more acute, all of which change past conceptions of space and time.

It is important to note that nothing in these definitions conflicts with American military conceptions of information warfare.

Important Chinese IW Concepts and Terms: Principles

The aim of IW in the Chinese literature is information dominance [*zhixinxiquan*], defined as the ability to defend one's own information while exploiting and assaulting an opponent's information infrastructure. This information superiority has both technological and strategic components. On the one hand, it requires the ability to interfere with an enemy's ability to obtain, process, transmit, and use information to paralyze his entire operational system. This accords with U.S. military conceptions of information dominance. On the other hand, some Chinese commentators assert that information superiority is not determined by technological superiority, but by new tactics and the independent creativity of commanders in the field, placing much more emphasis on personnel and organization-related components of the conflict.

The information battlefield itself is transformed in the PLA literature. Concepts of front and rear battlelines blur as the "multidimensional" battlefield space, integrating air, land, sea, space, and the electronic spectrum, becomes the arena of combat. Within this battlefield, military units conduct "seamless operations" [*feixianxing zuozhan*], integrating sensors with weapons systems. Operational emphasis is placed on deep strike [*zongshen zuozhan*] and over-the-horizon warfare [*yuanzhan*] against command and control facilities, which are perceived to be the "vital points" [*dianxue*] of the system. The objectives of the operation are not the seizing of territory or the killing of enemy personnel, but rather the destruction of the other side's willingness to resist.

Victory on this information battlefield will shift the focus of operations. In the words of two PLA authors, the key to gaining the upper hand on the battlefield is no longer mainly dependent on who has the stronger firepower, but instead depends on which side discovers the enemy first, responds faster than the latter, and strikes more precisely than the latter. [The two sides] vie for the advantage in intelligence and command control, i.e. to see which side holds a larger amount of and more accurate information and is faster in transmitting and processing the information. On the other hand, they have to vie for advantage in the precision of the strike, i.e., to see which side can hit the other at a longer distance and hit the other side first at the same distance.

As a consequence, detection, concealment, search and avoidance become central goals, pushing the military towards networked command and smaller, modular units.

Something Borrowed, Something Blue

One of the problems in analyzing PLA IW strategy, however, is disaggregating it from translations or outright copying of U.S. doctrinal writings, as well as Russian, German and French sources. From conversations in Beijing, it is clear that the PLA has translated both FM-100-6, *Information Operations*, and JP 3-13.1, *Joint Doctrine for Command and Control Warfare*, along with a myriad of lesser documents, journal articles, and policy papers, including more abstract research on information revolution written by the Tofflers, David Ronfeldt, John Arquilla, and Martin Libicki. PLA writings selectively steal concepts and definitions from these works, though it is rare that doctrine is adopted wholesale. As a result, the terminology, definitions, and even case studies found in most Chinese writings are similar to the debate in the United States. A sample is presented in the next three paragraphs, though one could easily add hundreds of additional examples to this list.

For example, at the highest level of abstraction, one PLA author describes the information age as the third important age in world history, following the agricultural age and the Industrial revolution. Furthermore, he characterizes the defining feature of the latter part of the information age as the exponential increase in "data production, storage, exchange, and transmission." Both of these ideas are taken without attribution directly from the Tofflers' seminal futurist books *The Third Wave* and *War and Anti-War*, respectively.

In an example of direct appropriation of U.S. military operational doctrine, one PLA author defined the aim of IW as "preserving oneself and controlling the enemy," the core distillation of the U.S. military's concept of "information dominance."

Moreover, the same author asserted that IW included "electronic warfare, tactical deception, strategic deterrence, propaganda warfare, psychological warfare, computer warfare, and command and control warfare," which is virtually identical to the U.S. Air Force's doctrinal "Six Pillars of IW."

In conceptions of the information battlefield, the similarities continue. PLA authors discuss "integration" [*yitihua*] and seamless operations [*feixianxing zuozhan*], tying together the five dimensions of warfare—air, land, sea, space, and the electromagnetic spectrum—through the integration of sensors with mobile missiles, air, and sea-based forces. These sensors are meant to facilitate "dominant battlefield awareness," which in turn permits deep strike [*zongshen zuozhan*] against enemy command and control hubs, communication networks, and supply systems, blurring previous distinctions of a clear battleline. For students of U.S. military doctrine, this conception of the battlefield is virtually identical to the core principles of Joint Vision 2010.

The question, therefore, could be posed in the following manner: Is there a *Chinese* IW strategy? There are certainly important differences between the Chinese and American IW literatures. To summarize, PLA writers universally regard IW as a strictly military subject first and foremost, while Western authors largely accept the dichotomy between information warfare waged between states or militaries (i.e., cyberwar) and information warfare waged between substate actors and states (i.e., netwar). Second, Chinese IW authors imbed their discussions within familiar ideological frameworks, such as Maoist guerrilla strategy and Sun Zi. In the Maoist vein, IW is referred to as the "New People's War," with particular attention paid to the idea of "overcoming the superior with the inferior." Both U.S. and Chinese authors are guilty of overusing Sun Zi, especially the notion of "winning the battle without fighting." While most of these references are nothing more than rhetorical flourishes, they do reflect two stark realities: (1) the extent to which Chinese (and U.S.) authors are struggling to find a framework for understanding IW and (2) the continuing pull of more traditional strategic frameworks. Third, Wang Pufeng and others emphasize the nontechnological aspects of information warfare to a much greater extent than U.S. military analysts, especially the need for new strategies and new organizational forms. Fourth, Chinese IW theorists, by virtue of the PLA's relatively backward state, are forced by circumstance to discuss IW from the perspective of a technologically inferior military, often in opposition to a technologically advanced foe.

This latter point deserves further elaboration. One of the most interesting Chinese IW concepts is the notion of "overcoming the superior with the inferior," which draws inspiration from both Sun Zi and Maoist "People's War." A basic assumption of this line of reasoning is that the PLA will most likely face an opponent capable of achieving information dominance on the battlefield. In response, the PLA has two choices. The first is to adopt nontechnological measures to overcome technological disadvantage, such as camouflage, concealment, and deception techniques. While there is some merit in this argument, the experience of the Iraqi army in DESERT STORM does not foster much optimism that this strategy would be successful against a determined opponent.

The second choice is more interesting, and I would argue, should be much more worrisome to U.S. military planners. PLA writings generally hold that IW is an unconventional warfare weapon, not a battlefield force multiplier. Indeed, many writings suggest that IW will permit China to fight and win an information campaign, *precluding the need for military action.* When this train of thought is combined with the notions of "overcoming the superior with the inferior," one can quickly see the logical conclusion of the argument: IW as a preemption weapon. According to Lu Linzhi,

In military affairs, launching a preemptive strike has always been an effective way in which the party at a disadvantage may overpower its stronger opponent.... For the weaker party, waiting for the enemy to deliver the first blow will have disastrous consequences and may even put it in a passive situation from which it will never be able to get out...

As a concrete example, he points to the Gulf War, where Iraq's failure to launch a preemptive attack resulted in their defeat:

In the Gulf War, Iraq suffered from passive strategic guidance and overlooked the importance of seizing the initiative and launching a preemptive attack. In doing so, it missed a good opportunity to turn the war around and change its outcome.

This accords with some Western military analysts, who argue that Iraq should have attacked Allied forces in Saudi Arabia at the early stage of the deployment rather than permitting the forces of the U.S. and the other members of coalition to deploy without hindrance over a six-month period.

To avert this outcome, Lu states that an effective strategy by which the weaker party can overcome its more powerful enemy is to take advantage of serious gaps in the deployment of forces by the enemy with a high tech edge by launching a preemptive strike during the early phase of the war or in the preparations leading to the offensive.

The reason for striking is that the "enemy is most vulnerable during the early phase of the war." In terms of specific targets, the author asserts that we should zero in on the hubs and other crucial links in the system that moves enemy troops as well as the war-making machine, such as harbors, airports, means of transportation, battlefield installations, and the communications, command and control and information systems.

If these targets are not attacked or the attack fails, the "high-tech equipped enemy" will amass troops and deploy hardware swiftly to the war zone, where it will carry out "large-scale airstrikes in an attempt to weaken... China's combat capability."

INFORMATION WARFARE STRATEGY: HETEROGENEITY AND INNOVATION

This chapter examines the early-stage Chinese IW literature, offering the following preliminary conclusions.

The literature:

- focuses on disrupting logistics and communications
- understands the U.S. threat and admits their own technical weaknesses, including poor reliability, survivability, and security
- reveals a surprising grasp of U.S. IW doctrine, but borrows concepts inappropriate for the PLA's technological level
- correctly identifies the important lessons of DESERT STORM, but in some cases draws the wrong conclusions
- overestimates Chinese capabilities to develop effective defensive countermeasures.

Evolution of Chinese IW Strategy

In the mythology of PLA IW study, Shen Weiguang, a soldier in a field unit, began writing about information warfare in 1985, publishing a book entitled *Information Warfare* that was later excerpted as an article in *Liberation Army Daily.* Chinese IW doctrine did not achieve an analytical focus, however, until the Gulf War in 1991. As has been documented in many other places, the Chinese military leadership was very impressed by the performance of U.S. forces in DESERT STORM, especially the ease with which they destroyed the Iraqi's largely Soviet and Chinese equipment. From their writings, it seems clear that PLA theorists believe that IW played a significant role in the U.S. victory. A commonly held belief, for example, is that the U.S. military used computer viruses to disrupt and destroy Iraqi information systems. In their descriptions of DESERT STORM, these authors point to other allied operations and technologies as examples of information war. First, Wang Pufeng singles out superior satellite reconnaissance of strategic sites and Iraqi positions, as well as attacks on Iraqi command and control systems, as key elements of the rapid allied victory against Saddam's forces.

On the lessons of DESERT STORM for the PLA, however, there is some divergence between those who believe the next war will look just like the Gulf War and those who understand that the Gulf War was a testing ground for advanced weapons and strategy to be used in a future, different war.

Most seem awed by the "perfect" [*wanshan*] execution of the attack. One writer described the new changes in information, command and control brought about by the Gulf War as a "great transformation" [*zhongda biange],* and a second suggested that strategies to defend

and attack computers and electronic systems could be as significant in determining the outcome of future wars as strategies to defend and attack citizens were in past wars. Finally, Wang Pufeng called the Gulf War the "epitome" of information war.

In addition, it has become increasingly obvious that some IW "centers of excellence" are emerging in the PLA. These researchers began to congregate at a series of high-level scholarly meetings. In December 1994, the Commission of Science, Technology, and Industry for National Defense (COSTIND) sponsored a symposium entitled "Analysis of the National Defense System and the Military Technological Revolution," which was closely followed by an October 1995 meeting that dealt with "The Issue of Military Revolution." The alleged high point of Chinese IW research was a 22 December 1995 COSTIND National Directors conference, when Liu Huaqing allegedly stated:

Information warfare and electronic warfare are of key importance, while fighting on the ground can only serve to exploit the victory. Hence, China is more convinced [than ever] that as far as the PLA is concerned, a military revolution *with information warfare as the core* has reached the stage where efforts must be made to *catch up with and overtake rivals.*

AN UNSETTLING SCENARIO INVOLVING THE UNITED STATES AND TAIWAN

In his discussion of IW as a preemption weapon, Lu Linzhi lays out a scenario in which China employs a preemptive strike to defeat a technologically superior enemy during the latter's mobilization and deployment phase. When one reads between the lines, it becomes readily apparent that the author is describing the rough parameters of a potential confrontation between China and the United States. This becomes even more clear in the following revealing passage, where he frankly discusses the technological imbalances between China and its thinly disguised "high-tech enemy":

Reconnaissance positioning satellites, AWACs, stealth bombers, aircraft carriers, long-range precision guided weapons... the enemy has all that; we don't. As for tactical guided missiles, electronic resistance equipment, communications, command and control information systems, main battlefield aircraft, main battlefield tanks, and submarines, what we have is inferior to the enemy's.

When one imagines scenarios in which the PLA would be concerned with preemptively striking U.S. forces during the deployment phase for early strategic victory, it is difficult to avoid the obvious conclusion that the author is discussing a Taiwan conflict.

For the PLA, using IW against U.S. information systems to degrade or even delay a deployment of forces to Taiwan offers an attractive asymmetric strategy. American forces *are* highly information-dependent, and rely heavily on precisely coordinated logistics networks, such as those operated by TRANSCOM.

If PLA information operators using PCs were able to hack or crash these systems, thereby delaying the arrival of a U.S. carrier battle group to the theatre, while simultaneously carrying out a coordinated campaign of short-range ballistic missile attacks, "fifth column," and IW attacks against Taiwanese critical infrastructure, then Taipei might be quickly brought to its knees and forced to capitulate to Beijing.

The advantages to this strategy are numerous: (1) it is available to the PLA in the near term; (2) it does not require the PLA to be able to attack/invade Taiwan with air/sea assets, which most analysts doubt the PLA is capable of achieving for the next ten years or more; and (3) it has a reasonable level of plausible deniability, provided that the attack is sophisticated enough to prevent tracing.

PLA'S INFORMATION WARFARE CAPABILITIES ON AN UPWARD TRAJECTORY

In end February this year, Chinese President Xi Jinping formed a new working group at the apex level on cyber security and information security. While this was seen as the political leadership's renewed efforts in underlining the threats and challenges to the national security in this arena, the military leadership has been paying particular attention to information warfare (IW) challenges since early 1990s. According to People's Liberation Army (PLA) concepts, the term information warfare encompasses cyber warfare, electronic warfare, deception warfare, psychological warfare, computer warfare, and transcends beyond the military realm.

The PLA has been adapting Western concepts to suit local conditions and considers it as a 'driving force in PLA's military combat readinesses. PLA has used the construct of People's War and devised its own precepts of 'Peoples War in IW domain' where millions of Chinese, both civilians and soldiers armed with computers, could achieve the objectives of IW. That is what has been precisely happening since over the last one decade wherein a number of cyber/information attacks are known to have originated from China with India being one among many other countries being at the receiving end. In last few years, Indian government's computers including those of National Security Council and some other important offices have been hacked with all evidence pointing towards China. PLA's information warriors and hacker groups have been actively involved in virus warfare and hacking activities in countries of their interest.

PLA has intensified its efforts in IW field since it officially pronounced its military doctrine of 'Local War under the conditions of informationalisation' in its 2004 White Paper on Defence. The objective laid down was to build an informationalised force and to win an information war and push forward the revolution in military affairs with Chinese characteristics with 'informationalisation' at its core. Since the articulation of its current military doctrine, PLA has laid solid foundations for fighting information and cyber wars. According to PLA's precepts, before any physical operations take place it would be the information and cyber domains that would be used to cripple the adversary's capabilities.

PLA's expanding capabilities in the use of space for military purposes provides it with the means to enhance its command and control, intelligence, surveillance, reconnaissance, information and cyber warfare capabilities. Space is considered as a commanding height for enabling the battlefield information operations. PLA's strategists have also stressed on the imperatives and necessity of 'destroying, damaging and interfering' with an enemy's reconnaissance and communications satellite systems. No country other than China has plans of launching almost 100 satellites till 2015. Compared to China, India's plans for launching satellites are very modest; in fact in the last 37 years, India has launched 100 missions. Such endeavours when fully realized would add to China's counter-space and IW capabilities.

PLA has also vastly expanded its optical fiber and other terrestrial networks giving it a tremendous IW capability. At the national level, China has a C3I system based on fiber optic cables, satellite communications, micro-wave links and automated command and control systems. The PLA has both secured and non-secured telecommunications and has an army wide data communication network and integrated field operations communication system which has been strengthened in the last decade. Many joint exercises carried out by PLA show that its WAN capabilities within Chinese borders have improved. PLA has been carrying out military exercises in Lanzhou and Chengdu Military Regions (which include the entire Sino-Indian border) where the PLA has practiced joint and integrated operations that include 'information operations'.

According to Pentagon's Annual Report to Congress on China's Military and Security Developments of 2013, PLA's Information Operations (IO) have matured and the top priority in peacetime is given to Computer Network Defence. As mentioned above, not only the IO/IW should be used even before the start of the campaign it would continue in all phases of war. Pre-emption also rhymes well with PLA's doctrine of active defence where counter attack can be used to gain advantage even before the commencement of hostilities. Chinese military theorists also believe that if an information campaign is won then the need for military operations may not be necessary. Such a contingency may arise possibly with nations (like the U.S.) which are information dependent.

But that is no solace for India as both military and civil arena in our country is increasingly becoming dependent on information and information networks and systems. Our critical infrastructure dependent on a wide variety of information systems remains vulnerable to information attacks. Stuxnet attack on Iranian nuclear facility did make India reflect on its vulnerabilities in the field of critical infrastructure. It has also been reported that even though the target of Stuxnet was Iran, Kaspersky Lab experts' data indicates that in fact it was India that was the epicenter of Stuxnet activity thus raising questions about its implications and motives of the originator. Some analysts aver that the largest power outage in Indian history (of July 2012) which affected more than half of India was caused by the malicious ware of Stuxnet.

One also needs to take note of the theories and concepts articulated by two senior colonels of PLA in their book 'Unrestricted Warfare' where they opine that there would be no boundaries between military and non-military areas of warfare in future.

The levels of integration between the civilian and military efforts of PRC in all the fields of information and cyber warfare have been on the rise. The top political and military leadership of China is thoroughly seized with the significance of acquiring information and cyber warfare capabilities. The concept of Computer Network Operations (CNO) and Integrated Network Electronic Warfare is germane to their doctrine of IW. PLA's Third and Fourth Departments of General Staff have been made responsible for executing CNO. While the Third Department has been tasked to collect intelligence and carry out defensive operations, the Fourth Department has the responsibility for network attacks and other offensive IW operations.

China's defence budget (as also the internal security budget) has witnessed a double digit growth (in percentage terms) every year for over a decade. According to one study, the Chinese government actively funds IW related research in commercial IT companies and civil and military universities. The number of universities conducting such research is put around 50 which indicates the importance and priority given to security related aspects of information technologies. Further, China's commercial IT companies involved in R & D actively seek collaboration with foreign firms to obtain cutting edge technologies which have dual use and therefore, in the end, benefit the PLA also. In certain cases, the civil use is only nominal and routing the research and development through the civil entities is undertaken as a matter of expediency. Such a subterfuge also helps in lowering the costs for the PLA. As is well known, China's official defence budget is said to be much less than the actual one.

In fact, in January this year, Chinese telecom equipment companies Huwaei was accused of hacking into Bharat Sanchar Nigam Limited (BSNL)'s network and sabotaging its expansion plans in Rajahmundry in coastal Andhra Pradesh. A five-member team comprising senior officials from the National Security Council Secretariat, Intelligence Bureau, Ministry of Home Affairs and BSNL was formed to investigate the issue. Even a US Congressional report highlights the security threat posed by the Chinese companies like Huwaei and ZTE.

In conclusion, security threats and challenges to India in information warfare domain that includes cyberspace cannot be overemphasized. The Indian armed forces have promulgated a joint Information warfare doctrine and a tri-service Cyber Command is in the process of being established. Some efforts by the government have also been made in the shape of establishing a Computer Emergency Response Team and formulation of a National Cyber Security Policy-2013. However, what is needed of integrating the efforts of a number of ministries and stakeholders in this field. Allotment of additional funds for R & D and supporting such activities in educational institutions and universities is an imperative. Creating of space assets that support the information and cyber warfare efforts is also an imperative.

Bibliography

Ahuja, Vijay: *Network and Internet Security*. Academic Press, Inc.: Boston, 1996.

Allison, Graham: *Nuclear Terrorism: The Ultimate Preventable Catastrophe*, New York: Times Books, 2004.

Atkinson, Rick: *An Army at Dawn: The War in North Africa 1942–1943*, Henry Holt, New York, 2002.

Bernauer, Thomas: *Genes, Trade, and Regulation: The Seeds of Conflict in Food Biotechnology*, Princeton, Princeton University. 2003.

Bradley, John. *Learning to Glow: A Nuclear Reader*. Tucson: University of Arizona Press, 2000.

Buzan, Barry & Eric Herring: *The Arms Dynamic in World Politics*, London: Lynne Rienner Publishers, 1998.

Chandler, David G: *The Campaigns of Napoleon*, Macmillan, New York, 1966.

Citino, Robert M: *Blitzkrieg to Desert Storm: The Evolution of Operational Art*, University Press of Kansas, Lawrence, 2004.

Clausewitz, Carl: *On War*, Michael Howard and Peter Paret (trans and ed), Princeton University Press, Princeton, 1989.

Cordell, Bruce and David T Zabecki : *On the German Art of War: Truppenfuhrung*, Lynne Reimer, Boulder, 2001.

David S: *Understanding Information Age Warfare*, CCRP Publications, Washington DC, 2001.

Duffy, Christopher: *The Military Life of Frederick the Great, Atheneum*, New York, 1986.

Garrelick, Renee. M.I.T. Beginnings: The Legacy of Nuclear Metals. Concord, MA: Nuclear Metals, Inc., 1995.

Garstka, J J and F P Stein: *Network Centric Warfare: Developing and Leveraging Information Superiority*, CCRP Publications, Washington DC, 1999.

Gast, A. P. : *The impact of Restricting Information Access on Science and Technology* Retrieved October 1, 2008.

Gibson, James N. *Nuclear Weapons of the United States: An Illustrated History*. Atglen, PA: Schiffer Publishing Ltd., 1996.

Hasan-Askari Rizvi, *Chemical Terrorism and South Asia,* Albuquerque, NM: Sandia National Laboratories, February 2003.

Hittle, James D: *The Military Staff: Its History and Development,* The Stackpole Company, Harrisburg, 1961.

Janowitz, M.: *The Professional Soldier: A Social and Political Portrait,* N.Y., The Free Press, 1960.

Joel Moses: *The Computer Age, A Twenty-Year View.*Cambridge, MA, The MIT Press, 1979.

Laquer, Walter, *The New Terrorism: Fanaticism and the Arms of Mass Destruction*, Oxford: Oxford University Press, 1999.

Miller, Richard L. *The U.S. Atlas of Nuclear Fallout, 1951-1962*, Woodlands, TX: Legis Books, 2001.

Montgomery, Bernard Law: *A History of Warfare,* World Publishing Company, New York, 1968.

Norris, James A.: *The First Afghan War 1838-1842*, Cambridge, University Press, 1967.

Posen, B.R.: *The Sources of Cyber Crime,* Ithaca, 1984, Cornell Univ. Press.

Rhodes, Richard, *The Making of the Atomic Bomb*, New York: Simon and Schuster, 1988.

Rothenberg, Gunther Eric: *The Art of Warfare in the Age of Napoleon,* Indiana University Press, Bloomington, 1978.

Schroeer, Dietrich: *Science, Technology, and the Cyber Crimes,* Ontario: John Wiley & Sons, 1984.

Sidney Fox: *Klaus Dose, Molecular Evolution and The Origin of Life,* New York: Marcel Dekker, 1977.

Stern, Philip M. The Oppenheimer Case: Security on Trial. New York: Harper & Row Publishers, 1969.

Van Creveld, Martin: *The Art of War: War and Military Thought,* Smithsonian Books/Collins, Washington DC, 2005.

William Aspray: *Computer, A History of the Information Machine,* New York, Basic Books, 1996.

Winkler, Allan M. *Life Under A Cloud: American Anxiety About the Atom.* New York: Oxford University Press, 1993.

Index

❑❑❑